THE COMPLETE HANDBOOK FOR RECOVERY MINISTRY IN THE CHURCH

THE COMPLETE HANDBOOK FOR RECOVERY MINISTRY IN THE CHURCH

A practical guide to establishing recovery support groups within your church

Bill Morris, M. Ed.

OLIVER NELSON

THOMAS NELSON PUBLISHERS
Nashville

128767

Published in Nashville, Tennessee, by Oliver-Nelson Books, a division of Thomas Nelson, Inc., Publishers, and distributed in Canada by Lawson Falle, Ltd., Cambridge, Ontario.

The Bible version used in this publication is THE NEW KING JAMES VERSION. Copyright © 1979, 1980, 1982, Thomas Nelson, Inc., Publishers.

Library of Congress Cataloging-in-Publication Data

Morris, Bill, 1953–
    The complete handbook for recovery ministry in the church / Bill Morris.
        p. cm.
    Includes bibliographical references.
    ISBN 0-8407-9649-8
    1. Mental health—Religious aspects—Christianity.
2. Church group work.   3. Twelve-step programs—Religious aspects—Christianity.   I. Title.
BT732.4.M65   1993
259'.4—dc20   92–41596
                                                            CIP

Printed in the United States of America.
1 2 3 4 5 6 — 98 97 96 95 94 93

This book is dedicated to three very special people in my life, who are very much a part of who I am and why I have come to write this book.

To my father, also Bill Morris,

who taught me to love and value the truth. He showed me that words could be used to express the truth, but more important, that a life could be lived according to the truth. He is my model and my hero.

To my wife, Valerie,

who has loved me in spite of myself and given me the courage and the strength to accept and believe in myself. She sacrificed her time, including our tenth-anniversary plans, so that I could have the time to write this book. She is my treasure.

And in loving memory of a precious friend, Mo Mills,

who shared her warmth and her smile with me and brightened up a time in my life that was dark, confusing, and lonely. I regret only that I did not get to share this moment with her. She was a gift and a blessing.

CONTENTS

FOREWORD

I first met Bill Morris in the fall of 1989 when I did a conference on addiction with Frances and Judith McNutt and Father Jack McGinnis. I had the opportunity to get to know him and his ministry in January of 1990 when my husband, Len, and I spoke at Mount Paran Church of God in Atlanta. My husband held a conference on intercessory prayer. I spoke to some five hundred women about compulsive-addictive behavior, then shared my healing story and testimony the next day at the Sunday night service.

I wasn't surprised by Bill Morris's caring heart—you expect that of a pastor. What impressed me most about Bill were his warmth and joyousness as a person. Then I learned where the intensity of his concern for hurting people came from as he shared his experiences with me and the things that he had struggled with in his life.

No wonder Bill Morris is writing a book on recovery ministry. He is a survivor, an overcomer. He has been through the fire.

I am enthusiastic about this book—*The Complete Handbook for Recovery Ministry in the Church*—because support groups have greatly helped me. I was in and out of psychiatric wards in the 1970s because of alcoholism and a prescription drug addiction, ending up in the Montana State Mental Hospital in 1978. Thanks to a group of intercessors back in Billings, Montana, who prayed many years for me, plus the Lord's intervention in a miraculous way, my life was turned around, and I was released.

But I still needed months of treatment and help from support groups. I needed a place to go where I could vent my pent-up feelings and risk letting others help me in my recovery journey. Only as I worked my program of recovery was I able to reach out to other addicted people.

In my travels across the United States ministering in churches, I have been horrified and saddened at the brokenness, turmoil, and debilitating addictions that I see controlling the lives of people. We have the healing power of Jesus Christ. Why is the church stumbling in the darkness in these areas? Why aren't Christians walking in freedom and newness of life?

Generational bondages handicap us. Fear paralyzes us and keeps us from seeking help. Ignorance and innuendo veil us from the truth. But these self-destructive life-styles can end! "My people perish from lack of knowledge," said the Lord.

I've often said that Twelve-Step programs are like little boats that take us across the sea of the horrors of our addictions, compulsions, and bondage to the rock of Jesus Christ. Jesus steps into the boat with us and takes us out into the healing stream of His life and love for us.

The greatest support group was formed two thousand years ago. Jesus gathered together twelve hurting, flawed men who would hardly have been called leadership types. They fellowshipped together, had disagreements, shared their hurts, and grew stronger together. Their Master taught them and brought out their gifts. As they were helped, they were able to help others. What they learned in their group situation gave them the strength to go boldly into the world and make an impact that is still being felt today.

Bill Morris has done a herculean task of assembling years of experience and wisdom and offering them to the church. He has learned what works and what doesn't work. This recovery handbook will be a life-saving tool for those who have the passion to minister healing and freedom to God's people.

Sandra Simpson LeSourd

ACKNOWLEDGMENTS

How do I acknowledge and thank the people who have been a part of my life and my ministry, whose lives have made mine what it is today so that this book is even possible?

I have to start with my family: my mom and dad, and my sisters, Polly and Susan. Despite everything, we made it as a family, and I have much to be grateful for. Special thanks go to my wife, Valerie, who gave me the time and space needed to write this book. I love you all. You have blessed my life. I hope I have made you proud.

God brought into my life people who encouraged me in the direction that I eventually followed. I may not have stopped to thank them: Ted Cochran, Ansel Owen, Chuck Finley, the people who grew me up at Saint Matthew Methodist Church in Greenville, South Carolina, Joe Alley, Will Willimon, Archie Morgan, Patti Fowler, Cathy Garrett Dellinger, Kathy Garrison, Alan and Tricia Weeks, and especially Preston Reid. And Sandy LeSourd, who adopted me as her little brother, with all of its inherent rights and responsibilities! To all of you, wherever you may be now, thanks for being there and for offering your care and encouragement.

The staff and people of Mount Paran Church of God in Atlanta, Georgia, have been my family and church home for the past fifteen years; they allowed me to struggle and grow, and they kept believing in me. To Dr. Paul Walker, Dr. Mac, Bob Laughlin, Jeff Bendert, Mike Atkins, Mylon LeFevre, Arvel Burell, Steve McBrayer, Marie Brannon, Mel Holmes, Geri Ward, Paulette McGeorge, Jim Chambers, the old Thursday Night Group, those who have been a part of the lay ministry at Mount Paran with me, and the many others who have shared, worshiped, and prayed with me and for me, words cannot express my gratitude for all of the nurture and support that you have given me. I'm particularly thankful for Jay Lee, our staff computer whiz. If not for his assistance with the word processor and printer, I would have had to start a new support group for people like me who are powerless over computers!

To those who have shared the vision of recovery ministry with me, and helped to start the different support groups by sharing their lives with others: I cannot adequately express appreciation for what each of you has shown me through your life and given to me as we have taken this journey of recovery together. To those who have worked with me as part of the counseling ministry staff—Deanna Poff, Sandy O'Bannon, Peggy Jordan, Susan Holcombe, Paula Douglas, and Beth Donaldson—and to those in the support groups who have lived this book and taught it to me—L. D., T. P., G. R., M. N., T. S., S. P., C. F., A. A., S. N., P. A., D. S., W. C., L. W., C. B., D. D., J. M., G. C., B. S., R. B., K. H., W. B., S. Y., F. T., B. A., J. B., L. S., J. C., D. B., P. W., A. W., J. P., V. D., P. S., J. M., R. H., S. F., K. H., S. S., J. D., P. B., G. S., M. B., K. T., and many, many others—well done, good and faithful trusted servants! The Lord has blessed others and me through your lives of faith, hope, and love.

Last, but certainly not least, I wish to acknowledge the greatest trusted servant, who is the source of the vision, of recovery, and of life itself—Jesus Christ, Lord of my life and Lord of all. To Him, be all honor and glory and praises for the great things that He has done with me, through me, and in spite of me!

INTRODUCTION
Divine Inspiration or Human Desperation?

I wish that someone had written this book years ago. I didn't have the foggiest notion of what I was about to get myself into when I began to pursue the idea of a recovery ministry at my church. I had no way to anticipate the problems and pitfalls I would encounter. I had no idea how many mistakes it was possible to make or how discouraged I was going to feel one minute and how elated the next.

I wish I had known that others were going through the same thing, and that I wasn't alone in what I was trying to do. I didn't know or couldn't find anyone who could share the experience with me. I had no one to guide or encourage me. There was no map charting the course, no trail blazed that I could follow. There were no resources to draw from. Yet I had a sense of purpose about a recovery ministry.

The writer of the book of Ecclesiastes had a lot of wisdom about that sense of purpose. He knew that there was an appointed time for everything, and "a time for every purpose under heaven" (3:1); he had seen the task God had given "the sons of men" with which they were to occupy themselves (3:10); and he understood that God made everything appropriate in its time (3:11).

Although I had no knowledge or understanding of what was to be involved in a recovery ministry, I believed that it was God's appointed timing. Perhaps a more honest feeling at the time was that I *hoped* it was God's timing. I felt that I had been given a task to do, and that God was going to have to make everything appropriate in its time.

I wish I could claim that the idea came out of divine inspiration. Actually, it came more out of human desperation. Often, that is what it takes for God to be able to get my full attention so that He can do what He needs to do in my life. When I am completely overwhelmed with my sense of utter powerlessness, then I let go and let God. Before I became involved with recovery ministry and Step One of the Twelve-Step process, I had never understood what Jesus meant when He said, "For whoever desires [tries, attempts] to save [control] his life will lose it, but whoever loses his life [gives up, gives in, acknowledges powerlessness] for My sake [My way, My will, My plan] will find it" (Matt. 16:25). Now, I know.

I was at a point of desperation on two different levels of my life. Professionally, as a pastor, I was struggling with my responsibility as director of counseling ministry at my church. Personally, as a human being, I was at a point of crisis.

In the spring of 1986 our senior pastor offered me a position in our church's counseling ministry. Prior to that, I had been director of middle school ministry for almost eight years, and I had spent a year and a half in an administrative position as director of church operations. Although a part of the administrative position was a challenge that I enjoyed, I have always been oriented to working with people and being directly involved with ministering to their lives. I had a master's degree in counseling that I had really never used, and it seemed like the perfect opportunity to move in a new, more satisfying direction personally and professionally.

At the time that I moved into the counseling ministry, I was a staff counselor working with a part-time counselor, a full-time counselor, an assistant director of counseling, and a director of counseling ministry. I provided pastoral counseling to my caseload of church members—individuals, couples, and families—about twenty-five people in all.

Things went along fairly well for the first six months or so. I was enjoying what I was doing. I was knocking the rust off my counseling skills and beginning to feel a sense of competency in what I was doing. But then a string of events occurred, and each of the other persons in the counseling ministry left; no one was replaced. So, in less than a year, I became the director of counseling ministry.

As director, I was basically directing myself and my secretary. And I was being called on to minister to a congregation of more than ten thousand members who were presenting several thousand requests for counseling support a year. Before long, I experienced a growing sense of panic. How was I going to meet all of those needs? What was I going to do to keep from getting buried under the pressing weight of the responsibility?

That was my moment of professional desperation. Out of my sense of desperation and a deep survival need came the idea of a recovery ministry.

I observed that a number of persons and families were dealing with the impact of a chemical dependency on their lives. I knew little about the nature of addiction, but I was aware of a group meeting at our church called Alcoholics Victorious. Some church members and other Christians who had been a part of local Alcoholics Anonymous fellowships desired to get together with other Christians and share in the process of recovery from their addictions. They wanted to name Jesus Christ as their higher power and confess their powerlessness over their addictions to one another. They prayed for and encouraged one another that they could do all things through Christ, overcoming the addiction and becoming new creations in Christ. At that time they were considered to be an outreach of the church and were placed under the umbrella of the special ministries office.

I turned to the Alcoholics Victorious group for help and information. I discovered an exciting and growing fellowship of men and women depending on the power of Jesus Christ to help them overcome and remain victorious over the addictive power of alcohol and drugs in their lives. I watched them minister to one another and provide a safe, supportive community in which people were being healed and made whole. And the idea began to develop. Why not other groups like this one? What if there was a group for all the persons who were going through the death of a loved one or the loss of a relationship due to divorce? I was seeing individually so many persons confronting those issues. Wouldn't it be more healing to have a whole family who understood what was being experienced because they were going through or had gone through the same thing? Wouldn't it be good to have them available to call on one another for encouragement and support whenever it was needed, not simply at an appointed time? Wouldn't that also help people dealing with sexual abuse issues, eating disorders, phobias, dysfunctional family backgrounds, problems with lust, and so on and so on?

At the same time I was responding to my sense of professional desperation, I was experiencing a sense of personal desperation. I don't think that the two things happened at the same time by accident. Together, they provided me with a powerful motivation and a strong sense of purpose to meet not only the needs of others but also some of my own needs by providing a safe, supportive place to confront and deal with personal issues.

When I joined the counseling ministry in 1986, the director sent me to a conference on adult children of alcoholics. I went to find out about the impact of chemical dependency on family members, and I did do that. But along the way I came to some very personal realizations—realizations that brought a tremendous feeling of sadness and yet an overwhelming feeling of relief. As I sat there in that conference, I heard speaker after speaker talk about my family and describe the way I felt and acted. What I learned was exciting but also confusing because there was no alcoholism in my family. Later, a speaker in the conference, Rokelle Lerner, cleared up the confusion for me. She shared that a person didn't have to come from an alcoholic family to experience the things being talked about. The key issue was that a family filled with confusion, chaos, conflict, and crisis affected a child's need for love, security, and a sense of belonging. The damage was done whenever a parent (or parents) wasn't there physically or emotionally for the child, and the child wasn't able to get enough of whatever was needed for whatever reasons.

For me, it all made sense. I had grown up in a family with mental illness. My mother is a manic-depressive who was not treated with lithium until I was in college. I grew up watching her endure numerous hospitalizations and electroshock treatments, and my family felt like it was on an emotional roller coaster. Good moments of happiness, calmness, and order would be followed by terrifying plunges into out-of-control emotions, rage, and despair. I lived in it, I survived it, but I didn't realize how much it affected me until later.

By the time I was sent to that conference, it was all beginning to catch up with me. I have always been a driven person, and I was beginning to wear out or burn out, maybe both. I was really struggling in my relationships with others. I had so much stuff bottled up inside that I sometimes felt like I was going to explode, but I really didn't know what I was feeling and I couldn't express it. I had a terrible sense of being unworthy and undeserving of anyone's love and respect, including God's. My self-esteem plummeted. I knew *what* was going on. I just didn't know *why,* and I didn't know what to do about it. The conference that weekend helped me understand.

I came away with a sense of what I needed, and I realized that others needed it, too. My life had become ruled by my experiences, my beliefs about myself, and the behaviors that I had learned to get what I needed or to protect myself. Claudia Black in her book *It Will Never Happen to Me* identifies the three key survival rules in families of dysfunction: don't talk, don't feel, and don't trust. I learned them well, and my life was being controlled by those rules rather than by God's Holy Spirit. I realized that to overcome, recover, and regain control of my life so that I could be who God created me to be rather than who I had learned to be, I was going to have to break the rules! I had to quit doing what I was not doing, as Robert Ackerman puts it.

But to do that, I realized I needed a safe, supportive place where I could be honest, where I could be me. A place where I could set aside the expectations of others, and of myself, and be loved and accepted for who I was while being encouraged to become all that I could be and all that God desired me to be. My personal survival, then, as well as my professional survival depended on support groups.

The summer of 1987, I advertised in our church publications for anyone who would be interested in helping to form and lead support groups in whatever area of need they had experienced. I spoke to the leaders of the Alcoholics Victorious group about their experiences and my need and vision. That group would become the cornerstone on which the recovery ministry would be built; the members had been meeting together as a support group since the early 1980s. About two dozen persons showed up for that first meeting, representing needs that were met by the formation of our first support groups. In addition to the Alcoholics Victorious group (which also accepted group members with any drug dependency), we organized groups for family members of those who were chemically dependent, persons with eating disorders, persons who grew up in dysfunctional families, persons grieving the loss of a loved one, and persons going through divorce recovery.

This book is about their experiences and the experiences of the other groups that have formed since that initial meeting. It is an honest book. I am not out to impress you with any false sense that ours is a perfect ministry and that it is a perfect model. It is simply what we understand about recovery ministry to this point.

We have made many mistakes, and I will share what we learned from them so that you don't have to repeat them unnecessarily. You may need to make them for yourself to find out what works and doesn't work in your unique situation, but at least you will have some idea of what to expect.

Some groups failed from the very beginning; other groups struggled and eventually died away. Some were successful for a season and then passed away. Others continue to flourish and will do so as long as needs are met. I want to share our failures as well as our successes because both are opportunities to seek God's wisdom and learn, trusting that He will make all things beautiful in His time.

We are still in a growth process in our understanding of recovery ministry. *Growth*, by definition, is "an orderly process toward a mature state." Sometimes, it would have been hard for anyone to convince me that what we were experiencing was orderly! But all that has happened to us has a meaning that ultimately is becoming clearer as we trust God with the process.

You will go through this same growth process with your support groups and your recovery ministry. Don't become discouraged or impatient. It is the process of God making everything appropriate in His time. What I have to share with you comes from our experience with that process. I believe that we are on the verge of maturity as a ministry. We have not arrived, although a lot of good, exciting things have happened in the groups and in the lives of people. There have been many miracles of new life and new life-styles in Christ.

Several years ago I heard someone share some thoughts concerning the Alcoholics Anonymous (AA) group movement that were attributed to Bill Wilson, one of the cofounders of AA. He believed that it took five years for an AA group to mature so that it would have members with enough recovery to teach others how to pass recovery along. Paul, in his epistles, encourages believers to pass along what he has taught them to those who can teach others (2 Tim. 2:2). Mature growth brings with it the ability to reproduce itself. This process is necessary in the lives of groups and individuals. This is discipleship. It takes time. It must be nurtured. Be patient with the process. Be excited about the possibilities.

You may be a pastor or a layperson reading this and wondering if you are qualified to begin a recovery ministry in your church or facilitate a support group. Let me assure you that you don't need a background in counseling or special qualifications. Availability, compassion, and commitment are the key characteristics needed to establish a successful support group ministry. A recovery ministry is a lay ministry. Although I do have a professional degree and am a counselor, laypeople started and continue to facilitate our groups.

This book is divided into five sections. In the first section, we will develop a philosophy: Why should the church consider being involved in the recovery movement? In the second section, we will define the purpose: What does it mean to be a Christ-centered support group? In the third section, we will determine a strategy: How do you go about organizing and starting support groups? In the fourth section, we will decide on a structure: How do you nurture and maintain a recovery ministry? Finally, in the fifth section, we will listen to others as they tell their stories of the impact of Christ-centered support groups on their lives. Ultimately, this book is not about structure and organization; it is about people and their lives and the new life in Christ that they have found through the recovery ministry.

I believe that I am supposed to write this book now for those who have the same sense of desperation that I had, professionally or personally or maybe both! Meeting the needs of people overwhelmed by losses, addictions, dependencies, phobias, and more calls for a new vision. A recovery movement that began within our society has become a growing force within the church. I saw a magazine on the newsstand recently whose cover identified the 1990s as "the Compulsive Age." As our world grows increasingly complex and stressful, people will be increasingly tempted by those substances and experiences that seem to offer some relief and a way to fill the hole in the soul that only God was meant to fill. What was intended for relief and comfort soon becomes the thing that controls our lives and separates us from ourselves, others, and God.

In such times and circumstances, Christ and His church should be the most relevant. Jesus told the religious leaders and His disciples that He had come to bring healing not to those who were well but to those who were sick. He came to minister not to the righteous but to sinners. He came not to rescue those who were already free but to bring release to the captive. He made it clear that He desired compassion rather than sacrifice (Matt. 9:10–13).

Then Jesus taught His disciples a parable. No one would think of putting a patch of new cloth on an old garment. It wouldn't do the job. Also, no one would think of putting new wine in old wineskins. The old wineskins would break, and the new wine would be spilled and lost (Matt. 9:16–17). He was referring to Himself as the new wine, but He indicated that the new wine was not going to be put in the old wineskins that people, especially the religious leaders, had become accustomed to. Instead, it was to be put in new wineskins.

The present age doesn't require that the wine be replaced. Christ is the new wine poured out to cleanse, heal, and meet the needs of people to the end of the ages! But we need new wineskins to hold the new wine. The recovery movement and support groups are bringing the new wine to the church as well as the world in new wineskins. They are bringing life to those who are dying—physically, emotionally, and spiritually—from addictive-compulsive behavior and from dependencies and codependencies.

I had a wonderful experience as I sat down to begin this book. It was on the first day of October. As I searched through my files for material that I wanted to include in the various sections, I came across the original minutes from that first meeting of people interested in starting a recovery ministry. The minutes recorded the groups that we determined to start and the date that we targeted to have the first meetings, the birthday of our recovery ministry. The date was October 1, 1987.

In 1987, it seemed time to start a recovery ministry at our church. Today, it seems time to write this book to the church and for those of you who feel now as I felt then. My prayer is that God will use this book and our experiences to open your eyes to this possibility in your church, and that you will join with all who are catching the vision for this recovery ministry that God is establishing in His church.

Bill Morris

Section 1

DEVELOPING A PHILOSOPHY:

 Why the Church Needs a Recovery Ministry

Many years ago when I was in the stage of deciding what I wanted to do with the rest of my life, I shared my dilemma with a friend. I knew that I had been called to ministry, but I wasn't sure exactly what direction to go. He gave me a piece of advice that has stuck with me.

"Bill, your ministry should always follow where your heart already is. Where is your heart right now?"

I thought about that. *Where was my heart? What had God given me compassion for?*

The word *compassion* simply means "with passion for." A passion is more than just a feeling. It is a deep, burning desire for. So the question was, For whom did I have compassion, and about what did I have a strong desire to minister to?

Initially, that passion was for young people. I worked in Anderson, South Carolina, with Archie Morgan in a crisis ministry and shared his passion to see a halfway house for young people established. I spent two summers of my life following my junior and senior years at Davidson College setting up a crisis ministry to young people called Helping Hand in the North Myrtle Beach, South Carolina, area. Both ministries continue to this day because of the passion involved in their birth.

I followed that passion to Atlanta, Georgia, to pursue a master's degree in counseling at Georgia State University and soon found myself director of middle school ministry at Mount Paran Church of God. I have always had that sense of passion, and even when I moved into the counseling ministry, I regularly was involved with the youth ministry. I think that passion for kids is reflected in some of the support groups that we have started for young people.

I have watched my wife, Valerie, go through the process of finding her passion. It is not easy being the wife of a minister. She is almost automatically expected to have her husband's passion and calling, and while I believe that she should share in them and encourage them, I also believe that God has a calling and a passion for each person. Valerie found hers at Shepherd Spinal Clinic here in Atlanta. She discovered a gift and a passion for persons who had suffered spinal cord injuries and were quadriplegics and paraplegics. She became involved in working with them and ministering to them, and she now travels with them to all of their activities.

I say all of this to make a point. If you are going to set up and run a recovery ministry, you must have a passion for it. Deep in your heart, you must have compassion and a desire for this ministry. Otherwise, you may be overwhelmed by the intensity of the experience and discouraged by the naturally slow, imperfect process of growth and change.

In this section I am going to share with you three things that I hope will put passion in your heart for this ministry.

First, I am going to share the statistical reality of our world. Tremendous populations of hurting people desperately need the support required for healing to take place. Either the church will begin to show them the relevancy of the gospel and the power of Jesus Christ to meet those needs, or the church will lose them by default to the New Age and humanistic movements.

Second, I am going to present the biblical mandate for the church's involvement in the recovery movement as a ministry. We should not attempt to follow or copy the world simply for the sake of relevancy. We do what we do as a recovery ministry because it is the way that Jesus Himself indicated that God works in our lives, demonstrates His presence and power, and reveals His truth, which ultimately sets us free.

Finally, I am going to detail the specifics of the Mount Paran Church of God recovery ministry. I want you to get a sense of what you can do and the impact you can make on your church and your community.

When you finish this section, I hope that you will have a passion for this ministry and consider what's involved in setting up such a ministry. My prayer is that you will understand, support, and encourage persons in the body of Christ who are called to such ministry, even if you are unable to join us in this new way that God is bringing healing to His church and to His world.

Chapter
1

The Statistical
Reality

When I was in college and graduate school, I hated my statistics courses. Even to this day, whenever I entertain the notion of going back to work on a doctorate, the thought of the statistical research very quickly dispels the idea. But I appreciate what statistics can tell us. I hope that the church will face the statistical reality and respond appropriately. If the gospel is anything, it is about the realities of life and the reality of Jesus Christ to make lives new and whole.

Later, I will share with you the needs that our support groups have attempted to address and how they have done, but for now, I want you to examine the statistical reality and consider its implications for the church. We will look at the following areas, and you can draw your own conclusions about the importance of recovery ministry to these needs: grief, divorce, chemical dependency, eating disorders, sex addiction, abortion, homosexuality, spending/gambling, and abuse (sexual and physical). We will also look at some general trends.

Grief

I will start with a simple statistic: 100 percent of all people die. And all of us, unless we die tragically young, will be affected at some time or another by the death of someone we are very close to. And where there is loss, there is grief.

Grief is the God-given process that carries us to accepting the loss and to healing. It takes us through the valley of the shadow of death and back into life again on the other side. The book of Ecclesiastes declares it to be part of the normal seasons of life (3:1–8). In the Sermon on the Mount, Jesus declared that it is blessed to mourn, in order to experience the comfort of God (Matt. 5:4).

Is it possible or healthy to grieve alone? I don't believe so. In the past, elaborate and prolonged rituals of grieving would identify a person's loss to the community so that others could recognize and respond to it. This process validated the loss and allowed the person to grieve. The person was expected to go through a period of mourning.

That time and those rituals have been lost to the complexity, alienation, and pace of our contemporary society. Following the death of a loved one, we are expected to go back to work after a few days or a week at the most and to resume our normal functioning. The church provides food, and an elder or a minister visits for a few weeks. Family members and friends may be there or continue to call for the first month or so. But then a person is often left alone with the loss just as the denial wears off, and just as all of the first anniversaries of the significant moments with the lost loved one occur.

People need community to grieve. Unsupported, unresolved grief, in my experience, leaves them with the sadness bottled up inside where it can settle into a depression that prevents them from fully rejoining life. A support group provides that sense of community so desperately needed but often unavailable. The need for community is especially great when the loss involves suicide (which is rising at an alarming rate!), miscarriage, stillbirth, or SIDS (sudden infant death syndrome).

Divorce

About one in every two marriages will end in divorce. Divorce is another form of loss, but with a distinct difference. When a relationship is lost due to death, there is no sense of the person's choosing or desiring to die, except possibly with suicide. But when a relationship is lost due to divorce, there is the element of the person's choosing to leave. The sense of abandonment and rejection and the damage to a person's self-worth and the ability to trust accompany the grief.

A person needs a safe, supportive place to go through divorce recovery. This is not the time to debate the question of the sin of divorce. Christ came to heal us and free us from the impact of sin on our lives. This is the time to heal. A person must grieve the loss and have the opportunity to patiently and gently rebuild self-esteem and the ability to trust others.

Divorce doesn't affect just the adults involved. At least 60 percent of all children will experience divorce in their families *at least once* before they reach the age of eighteen. That statistic is frightening! Most of our children carry with them damage to their self-esteem (since children tend to assume the responsibility for what happens in their families unless they are told and helped to understand otherwise), insecurity and difficulty in trusting, and poor models for building and maintaining a healthy relationship. A tremendous population of children needs support.

Divorce creates another population of need: single parents. In addition to the loss, the person now has the stress of being a single parent. Even after the loss issues are resolved, single parents will continue to need a support group. Needs of single parents are much different from those of the general single population and must be more specifically addressed.

Chemical Dependency

General estimates are that one out of every ten Americans is a problem drinker, and that one out of every ten drivers on the road on any given weekend night is driving under the influence of alcohol. Those figures do not include the millions more who are dependent on illegal drugs or who have become chemically dependent inadvertently on prescription medications. They also do not include the millions who are chemically dependent on nicotine and are unable to quit smoking despite the desire to do so.

Chemical dependency is a problem that can only get bigger as the complexity, stress, and alienation of our society increase. Unfortunately, many Christians' lives are controlled by a substance rather than by God's Holy Spirit. They are reluctant to admit that they are powerless over a substance and that their lives have become unmanageable, and yet they must do that to overcome something so destructive to them and their loved ones. Support groups permit Christians to confess their powerlessness over their chemical dependency and experience the encouragement and accountability to deal with addictive substances.

For every chemically dependent person, probably ten more persons are directly affected by the dependency. They include spouses, children, other family members, friends, employers, and even strangers who are at risk when a person is driving under the influence. But usually the immediate family feels the greatest impact. When thoughts and feelings are distorted by mood-altering chemicals, a person can't deal with life and relationships honestly and directly. Communication and interaction break down. When a person loses control to a substance, often innocent others are hurt; most violent and abusive incidents involve alcohol or other chemicals.

Chemical dependency is not just an individual problem; it is also a family problem. Family members, especially the children who are the most vulnerable and the most at risk, will need as much help and support to deal with the chemical dependency as the addicted person.

And what of the adults who grew up in chemically dependent families, or other dysfunctional families for that matter? What impact has that experience had on them? Damage was done to self-esteem, the ability to feel and express feelings honestly and appropriately, and the ability to trust and enter into healthy, intimate relationships. Between twenty-eight and thirty-four million adults grew up in alcoholic families. Millions more grew up in families of confusion, chaos, and conflict. They need the safe, supportive atmosphere of a Christ-centered group to experience the healing touch of

Jesus Christ on the invisible wounds and the emotional dis-ease they carry inside them. Unless there is a place for them to heal, the sins of the fathers will indeed be visited to the third and fourth generations as they pass the pain that they have inherited along to their children.

Eating Disorders

At this very moment 50 percent of all women and 25 percent of all men are on a diet trying to control their use of food. By the time they are eighteen, almost 50 percent of all teenage girls will have already gone on some form of diet. The proliferation of weight-loss centers, books, and programs has resulted in a multibillion-dollar industry, and our obsession with approval and appearance, coupled with the use of food to comfort, nurture, and ease the stress in our lives, has resulted in the escalation in the cases of bulimia and anorexia.

Eating disorders—compulsive overeating, bulimia, and anorexia—point to people's abuse of food in an attempt to nurture their spirits, not just nourish their bodies. People use food to fill empty hearts instead of empty stomachs. The food becomes a best friend who will help them deal with situations or feelings that are uncomfortable. The statistical reality points to the need for a place for people to focus on feelings and the internal self-image rather than food and the external body image.

Sex Addiction

Pornography has become a major industry. More and more marriages are affected and destroyed by infidelity. Increasing numbers of men and women are indicating that they have had at least one affair while in a marriage relationship, not to mention all the people involved in compulsive promiscuity outside marriage. Many adults are in bondage to compulsive masturbation, and sex offenses—ranging from voyeurism and exhibitionism to sexual abuse and rape—occur at alarming rates.

The Bible defines the core problem as one of lust: using sex inappropriately to meet other deep, unmet needs. The need for sex or the pursuit of the sexual thrill becomes compulsive and obsessive. It becomes an addiction with the power to determine what a person thinks, feels, and needs. A person becomes powerless over the damage that sex or the need for sex may be doing physically, emotionally, relationally, and spiritually. Some Christians find themselves caught up in this law of their flesh resulting in death.

To overcome, a person needs a higher power than the power of the lust and the addiction. A law of the spirit in Christ Jesus can overcome this law of the flesh, but according to 1 John, it requires an absolute honesty that brings everything out into the light. A person must take total responsibility and be accountable to others. But encouragement and support without condemnation must enter in if a person is going to be able to take such a risk in our society and in most church settings. The support group provides a safe place for healing.

Again, as with chemically dependent persons, spouses and family members are affected by sex addicts. Their lives can become as out of control as those of the sex addicts. They, too, are robbed of their serenity and bear a tremendous load of guilt, shame, and depression. Whenever one person's life is out of control, others may lose control of their well-being as they try to deal with and control the addiction and its impact. They, too, desperately need a safe, supportive place to come out of their isolation, secrecy, and shame, and into the freedom that Christ offers.

Abortion

Approximately 1.5 million abortions are performed annually in the United States. But at a conference on postabortion syndrome that I recently attended, Anne Speckhard put that figure into a different perspective. The statistical reality of that figure translates into the fact that one in every five women has experienced an abortion at some point. Of all women who experience abortion, at least half later exhibit symptoms of postabortion syndrome, which is a traumatic emotional reaction related to the posttraumatic stress disorder widely publicized in Vietnam veterans.

Immediately after the abortion, many women feel that what they did was terribly wrong. They begin to think they were not given all of the facts. They experience the immediate emotional pain of guilt and the sadness over the loss of a child.

Christians are not necessarily exempt from experiencing the same pressures and fears that lead non-Christians to consider abortion. But some women who had abortions before they became Christians and had been able to deny the reality of their experience now face the overwhelming realization and grief over what they have done. All these women need a safe, supportive place for the healing process of grieving the loss of a child, but there must be a place where the burden of self-condemnation can be lifted through the cleansing process of forgiveness. They may cognitively understand that God forgives them, but they must go through the emotional process of learning to forgive themselves. For that, they desperately need a support group.

Homosexuality

Practicing homosexuals make up 1 to 5 percent of the population, with some gay organizations claiming the figure is closer to 10 percent. From my experiences in working with those coming out of the life-style, as well as in talking with others who are a part of homosexual recovery ministries, I found that chemical dependency and depression are commonplace in this population. Many homosexuals feel pain and shame, especially those who try to reconcile their behavior with their Christian beliefs.

I have come to view homosexuality as any other controlling addictive process that separates people from God, themselves, and others. All that we can do for persons who steadfastly maintain they are not powerless, their lives are not unmanageable, and they do not need to be restored is to love them, pray for them, and continue to speak the truth to them *in love*. Persons who feel that they are caught up in a self-defeating life-style but feel trapped in the bondage of their thoughts, feelings, and behavior, need a Christ-centered support group. Their group must also address gender, relational, and trust issues.

This issue deeply affects persons close to the homosexual, from parents and siblings to spouses and children. The AIDS epidemic has drastically altered this issue from one of caring concern to one that may be a matter of life and death for male homosexuals. I have seen many families in our church and the Christian community in tremendous need of a safe, supportive place to seek God for wisdom and help within a community of love and concern.

Spending and Gambling

Although two distinctly separate issues, spending and gambling involve money or the pursuit of money, so I have grouped them together. Both involve the compulsive-obsessive pursuit of obtaining or spending money as a way to manage internal feelings of insecurity and inadequacy. They can become just as destructive to lives as chemical substances.

The gambling industry feeds off the compulsive gambler. Gamblers Anonymous is one of the fastest growing segments of the Twelve-Step movement. Spenders Anonymous is a new group. The amount of consumer debt that we as a nation have accumulated is staggering. Madison Avenue campaigns encourage us to pursue money, material things, and external trappings as a way to feel good about ourselves and be attractive and desirable to others. Credit is easy to get and even easier to abuse. Bankruptcies and foreclosures are skyrocketing toward unprecedented levels, and consumer credit bureaus are swamped by persons desperately trying to manage the unmanageable consequences of their out-of-control spending behavior. In the counseling ministry at our church is a waiting list of six to eight weeks' worth of persons wanting to work with our financial counselors. For some, their compulsive spending habits have created their serious financial difficulties.

As with all persons whose lives are out of control, whether it is due to a substance or an experience, others are directly affected and harmed by their behavior. Family members need practical as well as emotional help and support. And the persons in bondage to their pursuit of money or the spending of it need the same help in dealing with their dependency on spending or gambling as addicts do with their dependency on chemical substances. They need a safe, supportive place that provides acceptance and encouragement while offering the discipline of structure and accountability that is part of the Twelve-Step process for overcoming addictive-compulsive behavior.

Abuse

To me, this statistical reality is the most disturbing one for the church to confront. Estimates indicate that from one-quarter to one-third of all girls will have been sexually abused in some way by the time they are eighteen, and that from one-seventh to one-sixth of all boys will have been abused by that same age. Even the most conservative figures are shocking. I happen to believe that the number of men reporting childhood abuse is so much less because of extreme denial and difficulty in admitting to it.

The impact of sexual abuse is devastating. The sense of shame destroys self-worth. People lose innocence and the ability to trust and feel safe. They have overwhelming feelings of anger and depression that must be controlled through addictive-compulsive behavior. They desperately seek love and acceptance through promiscuous relationships. They are vulnerable to helplessness that often results in revictimization. Their difficulty with intimacy manifests itself emotionally in under- or overreaction, and physically in sexual dysfunction or compulsive sexual acting out.

Three major populations require healing. In the first group are the adults who were sexually abused as children. They are frequently the walking wounded; their lives and relationships are just not working very well. In the second group are the children who have just experienced the trauma of abuse. And in the third group are the support persons who are involved in the lives of the sexual abuse victims. They are the parents, the siblings, the spouses, or the boyfriends or girlfriends. All of these lives are tremendously affected by the sexual abuse, and they may feel victimized by what happened to their loved ones.

The healing process is slow and requires the special grace of all aspects of the fruit of the Holy Spirit. There must be a safe, supportive place to go through the long-term process of feeling and healing, where Christ Himself can wash away all tears and cleanse the unrighteousness that has been done to His Father's precious children. A support group for this population becomes a true refuge and shelter under the wings of the Almighty.

I realize as I am writing about those who have been sexually abused that everything I have said also applies to those who were physically abused. Frequently, sexual abuse and physical abuse happen in the same households. Often, physical abuse accompanies chemical dependency in a family. Physically abused persons need a safe, supportive place to heal the internal wounds that are so much deeper than whatever external wounds were created.

Other Groups

Other major statistical populations that are a part of our society are represented in every church. They are sitting out in the pews of your church every Sunday. People may need the support and experience of those who are going through the same circumstances and can understand without judging or offering quick, easy answers to problems.

With the increase in the number of divorced persons comes the increase in the number of persons experiencing remarriage reality. For them, having a place to learn from past mistakes so that things can be different the second time around may be very helpful.

Remarriage reality may often bring with it the blending of families. Merging two family units into one always requires adjustments and the ability to adapt to unique situations and pressures. Having the support of others who are going through the same adjustments and learning from one another's successes and failures may prevent a lot of problems and help to handle the ones that occur.

Another group includes parents in pain. For whatever reasons, their children are struggling with life, discipline, and authority. They are making the wrong choices and reaping the consequences with school authorities, work authorities, and often legal authorities. They may be going to, in, or coming out of prison. Parents need help in dealing with their guilt and sense of failure as Christian parents in raising their children, and they need a place to learn to practice love that sets limits and allows children to have free will and be responsible for bad choices.

Infertility is another major problem affecting about one in ten couples temporarily or permanently. In a support group they can share information and encouragement as well as frustration and pain with others who know what to say and what not to say.

Finally, some situations temporarily create populations that need support during a crisis. One of our most successful support groups was formed for family members of those who were a part of Operation Desert Storm. Other situations may be unique to your church or community.

This chapter by no means exhausts all of the populations or possibilities for support groups to minister to. But it presents the statistical reality of what people are experiencing in our society, and Christians are not isolated from or immune to it. If we are to minister to the needs of those within the body of Christ, we must understand and address these issues. And that is equally true if we desire to minister to a lost world, bringing light to a dark place and replacing powerlessness with the good news of Christ's resurrection power.

Once we accept the statistical reality, we must decide whether support groups are part of God's plan and purpose for carrying out His will in the lives of people. Is there a biblical mandate for a recovery ministry in the church? I steadfastly believe that there is such a mandate. Turn to the next chapter to see why.

Chapter
2

The Biblical Mandate

The statistical reality may determine that there is a need, but the manner in which God typically meets that need must be biblically mandated. Otherwise, we are depending on our self-will to understand and our efforts to change. Jesus was very clear about where that would lead. He warned that people who tried to save their lives would ultimately fail, but those who lost their lives for His sake would certainly gain them. I never fully understood what Christ meant until I became involved with Twelve-Step recovery ministry. When I learned the first three steps, I began to understand the meaning of surrender; the process of denying my self-will daily allows God the opportunity to do whatever work in my life needs to be done.

So, what is God's way to work in the lives of people? Certainly, God works directly and individually with each of us. But God also has given us a powerful resource for change and growth—the power of community. God knows our natures. He knows that it is not good for us to be alone (Gen. 2:18). He understands that we may be able to survive in isolation, but we can never thrive and be who we were created to be apart from relationship with others.

The Bible reserves a special word for the power of caring community. The word *koinonia* indicates the special fellowship of the body of Christ. I believe support groups in general imitate koinonia. But unless the group is Christ-centered, the key ingredient in the power of that fellowship is missing. For the power of koinonia lies not just in our fellowship with one another but in the very presence of Jesus Christ in the midst of that fellowship.

Christ knew the power of koinonia. He used it to bring together a group with diverse backgrounds and temperaments and unify them into a force that would change the world. He took His disciples through the process of building koinonia with one another, with Himself as the center of their fellowship. He taught them the principles of community that would ultimately make them much stronger as a unit than any of them had the power or ability to be individually. It was a process that took place over the three years of their fellowship together.

When it was time for Christ to physically leave and end His earthly fellowship with His disciples, He again used the community to give them the power to influence their world. He instructed them to wait together in an upper room. The size of the community had increased from twelve to seventy. For forty days they waited for the power that Christ promised them. The community was bound together by common experience and belief. The seventy persons must have encouraged one another, exhorted one another, prayed for one another, and built up one another by reminding one another of all that Christ had done and promised to do. But as powerful as that experience of community must have been, it still did not give them the power they needed to leave that upper room and change their world.

It wasn't until the presence of God again became the center of their fellowship that they experienced the power they needed. God, who had represented Himself to them through Christ when He was on earth, now represented Himself through the presence of His Holy Spirit. That presence, in the center of their fellowship, gave them the power as a group to burst from that room and affect their world. Their lives and testimonies were so compelling and convincing that hundreds and thousands were daily added to their fellowship.

The early church continued the process of koinonia. As a group, they daily gathered together to build community and experience communion with God. They shared their lives together, they prayed together, and they ministered together. They acted as one body, reflecting the unity that Christ had prayed to God to give them in His final prayer at Gethsemane (John 17). Paul was very much aware of the presence and power of koinonia. He likened the experience to that of one body with many parts, each part valuable in and of itself but needing the other parts to do much more together than they could do individually. And always with one head, that of Jesus Christ Himself, present in their lives and fellowship through the power of the Holy Spirit (1 Cor. 12:12–27).

This same process of koinonia takes place in support groups. The process of experiencing community is in and of itself very powerful, and secular support groups experience its power. But Scripture indicates that God chooses to be present and reveal Himself when He is made the center of this process through the invited presence of His Holy Spirit and the acknowledgment of His Son, Jesus Christ, as Lord of the proceedings. Jesus told His disciples, "Where two or three are gathered together in My name, I am there in the midst of them" (Matt. 18:20).

In the midst of Christ-centered support group koinonia, God promises to act on their behalf. Jesus promised that "if two of you agree on earth concerning anything that they ask, it will be done for them by My Father in heaven" (Matt. 18:19).

In the midst of Christ-centered support group koinonia, God's perfect law is fulfilled as we "bear one another's burdens" (Gal. 6:2). And what is God's perfect law? The teachers of the law asked Jesus that question, and He replied, "'You shall love the LORD your God with all your heart, with all your soul, and with all your mind.' This is the first and great commandment. And the second is like it: 'You shall love your neighbor as yourself.' On these two commandments hang all the Law and the Prophets" (Matt. 22:37–40). God's perfect law is a law of love. Love covers and allows us to overcome a multitude of sins, and we are instructed above anything else to fervently love one another (1 Pet. 4:8). There is no fear in love, but perfect love casts out fear because fear involves punishment (the fear of shame) and the one who fears is not perfected (mature) in love (1 John 4:18).

In the midst of Christ-centered support group koinonia, God makes His healing power available. James 5:16 instructs us to confess our sins to one another and pray for one another to be healed. I believe that healing is not just physical healing but also involves the healing of the whole person and the restoring of balance to lives that are out of control or are being overwhelmed by circumstances.

I think Jesus understood that when He sent His disciples out two by two to experience for themselves the process of koinonia and the power available to them when God was present in the midst of their fellowship (Luke 10:1–24). This process takes place in support groups. This power is available in the groups to deal with the statistical reality of the age. The power comes from experiencing koinonia with Jesus Christ as the acknowledged head and source of the group.

According to the Bible, many qualities are to be present in the fellowship of the body of Christ. As these qualities are present and Christ is made the center of the fellowship, koinonia will be experienced, and power will be available to overcome any reality of life. But do support groups reflect those biblical qualities? More crucial still, how do support groups make Jesus Christ the center of their fellowship? We must answer these two questions if we are to be confident that we have a biblical mandate for a recovery ministry.

I have identified in Scripture six qualities that are to be a part of the koinonia fellowship that Christ desires the church to experience and offer to others. They appear in Scripture in the form of commandments, instructions, admonishments, and expectations. These qualities include (1) honesty, (2) acceptance, (3) respect, (4) openness, (5) encouragement, and (6) responsibility. All of them must be present if the healing power of koinonia group fellowship is to be fully experienced in the hearts and lives of people.

1. Honesty

Koinonia fellowship has to begin with honesty. It can't take place where we are hiding behind our denial and our need to maintain an image in front of others. What a waste of time and energy! God knows our hearts before we consciously face ourselves. Why pretend? One of the most powerful, freeing, healing passages in all of Scripture is 1 John 1:5–10:

> This is the message which we have heard from Him [Christ] and declare to you, that God is light and in Him is no darkness at all. If we say that we have fellowship with Him, and walk in darkness, we lie and do not practice the truth. But if we walk in the light as He is in the light, we have fellowship [koinonia] with one another, and the blood of Jesus Christ His Son *cleanses us from all sin*. If we say that we have no sin, we deceive ourselves, and the truth is not in us. If we confess our sins [honestly], He is faithful and just to forgive us our sins and to *cleanse us from all unrighteousness*. If we say that we have not sinned, we make Him a liar, and His word is not in us (emphasis added).

The Bible says, " 'Fess up!" and experience the power of koinonia fellowship that is capable of overcoming and cleansing the effect of any sin. James 5:16 directs us to confess our sins to one another so that we may be healed. There is healing in honesty and confession. As long as we remain secretive and dishonest, His Word can't work in us and be the powerful resource that it is, living and active in our lives, sharper than any two-edged sword, piercing as far as the division of soul and spirit, joints and marrow, able to discern the thoughts and intentions of the heart (Heb. 4:12). As long as we remain in the darkness, we can continue to do only the works of darkness and be bound by guilt and condemnation.

Koinonia fellowship begins with and is built on honesty. But the second quality of koinonia fellowship involves the response to that honesty, and that is the quality of acceptance.

2. Acceptance

Acceptance is the state of unconditional regard that allows us to look beyond what people do and see who they are and can be. Acceptance removes any sense of shame that would disqualify us from experiencing God's grace and allows us to know that "there is therefore now no condemnation to those who are in Christ Jesus" (Rom. 8:1). Acceptance removes the barriers and obstacles that keep us from feeling worthy and deserving of God's love and able to act on that belief.

Paul questioned the Romans about their need to judge and their inability to accept one another:

Why do you judge your brother? Or why do you show contempt for your brother? For we shall all stand before the judgment seat of Christ. . . . So then each of us shall give account of himself to God. Therefore let us not judge one another anymore, but rather resolve this, not to put a stumbling block or a cause to fall in our brother's way (Rom. 14:10–13).

In that same chapter, Paul warned that if our brother is hurt by our lack of acceptance, we are no longer walking according to love, and we are not to destroy with our lack of acceptance a person Christ died for (v. 15). Who are we to judge the servant of another? To his own master he stands or falls; and stand he will, for the Lord is able to make him stand (v. 4).

Paul went on to indicate that those who are strong should bear with those who are weak and not become impatient, demanding, or critical. We are to accept one another, just as Christ accepted us for God's sake (Rom. 15:1, 7).

The fear of judgment and the lack of acceptance damage relationships and prevent the experience of koinonia. Jesus issued a stern command:

Judge not, that you be not judged. For with what judgment you judge, you will be judged; and with the measure you use, it will be measured back to you. And why do you look at the speck in your brother's eye, but do not consider the plank in your own eye? . . . Hypocrite! First remove the plank from your own eye, and then you will see clearly to remove the speck from your brother's eye (Matt. 7:1–5).

Jesus demonstrated what our attitude of acceptance is to be in His encounter with the woman caught in the act of adultery (John 8). It is a picture of God's acceptance despite the sinful state that we may be caught in, and Christ's ability to set us free from the bondage of guilt and shame. No one was allowed to judge the woman caught in adultery, and Christ assured her that she was accepted and not condemned. Because of that acceptance, He was able to encourage her to "go and sin no more" (v. 11).

It is not recorded in Scripture, but do you ever wonder what happened to that woman and whether she was able to change her behavior after that experience? I would imagine that she did. That is the power of acceptance in the fellowship of koinonia.

All of this takes place in an atmosphere of respect, which is the third quality of koinonia fellowship. While acceptance refuses to judge worth according to actions, respect communicates the high admiration and esteem that belong to a person inherently as a child of God.

3. Respect

Paul knew how important the attitude of respect was to the fellowship of koinonia. You can almost hear him pleading with the Philippians,

If there is any consolation in Christ, if any comfort of love, if any fellowship of the Spirit, if any affection and mercy, fulfill my joy by being like-minded, having the same love, being of one accord, of one mind. Let nothing be done through selfish ambition or conceit, but in lowliness of mind let each esteem others better than himself. Let each of you look out not only for his own interests, but also for the interests of others (Phil. 2:1–4).

Paul also indicated the source of the attitude from which the actions of respect will arise:

Let this mind be in you which was also in Christ Jesus, who, being in the form of God, did not consider it robbery to be equal with God, but made Himself of no reputation, taking the form of a bondservant, and coming in the likeness of men. And being found in appearance as a man, He humbled Himself and became obedient to the point of death, even the death of the cross (vv. 5–8).

Again and again Jesus demonstrated this attitude of respect through His actions. Some of His closest friends were fishermen. He dined with tax collectors. He talked with a Samaritan woman. He ministered to the soldiers of an occupying force. He spent time with children. He paid attention to people with disabilities. He did not avoid lepers.

People were drawn to Christ because He showed them respect. He did not hold on to His equality with God but humbled Himself and esteemed them as equal in His sight. People are drawn to koinonia fellowship when they are shown respect through the attitudes and actions of the group, which is reflected in the openness of members toward one another.

4. Openness

The fourth quality of koinonia fellowship is that of openness. To be open is to not limit accessibility or receptivity. It is to be available mentally and emotionally so that others can have access to what we have to offer and they can offer things to us.

People opened up to Jesus because of His openness and willingness to listen and understand. He was always asking questions and listening to the thoughts and feelings of others. He never became impatient or critical with those who were earnestly seeking. He reacted in anger only to people who were dishonest and closed others off from being able to approach His Father. He was appreciative when people shared their true fears and struggles with faith.

Perhaps the greatest example of Christ's openness to the feelings and needs of others took place at Jacob's well with the Samaritan woman (John 4). Jesus was tired, thirsty, and hungry (vv. 6–8), and yet He took the time to be concerned about her situation and to answer her questions. She was surprised that He was willing to speak to her since she was a Samaritan woman, for Jews typically had no dealings with Samaritans (v. 9). When they returned, the disciples were amazed that He had been speaking with her (v. 27). Jesus knew that was part of the will of God for Him and essential to accomplishing His work (v. 34).

This same openness is essential if koinonia fellowship is to be experienced and accomplish the work for which it is intended. James warned against interfering with this process when he advised that we should be quick (open) to hear, slow to speak, and slow to anger (react), for our anger does not achieve the righteousness of God (James 1:19–20). Anger, overreaction, and defensiveness close people down and drive them away, but openness allows for God to work in our lives and bring us to a place of righteousness, just like it did in the life of the woman at the well. Openness can take place only in an atmosphere of encouragement, which is the fifth quality of koinonia fellowship.

5. Encouragement

To encourage means to put courage into a person. On the other hand, to discourage means to take courage out of a person. Our word *courage* is derived from the root word *coer,* which literally means "heart." We use the word *coronary* to refer to matters related to the care of the heart. So, to encourage others actually means to put heart into them, while to discourage them is to take the heart out of them. I believe that this is the heart, or courage, needed to overcome or change the circumstances in our lives.

Acceptance and approval stimulate courage. Conversely, disapproval, criticism, judgment, and shame stimulate discouragement, which often makes it impossible for a person to change. Experiencing acceptance in koinonia fellowship stimulates encouragement.

Paul knew that there was no room in the body of Christ for discouragement. He warned,

> You are inexcusable, O man, whoever you are who judge, for in whatever you judge another you condemn yourself; for you who judge practice the same things. But we know that the judgment of God is according to truth against those who practice such things. And do you think this, O man, you who judge [discourage] those practicing such things, and doing the same, that you will escape the judgment of God? Or do you despise the riches of His goodness, forbearance, and longsuffering [qualities of encouragement], not knowing that the goodness [encouragement] of God leads you to repentance [change]? (Rom. 2:1–4).

The writer of the book of Hebrews talks about the courage we have been given in Christ that should result in the encouragement we give to one another:

> Therefore, brethren, having *boldness* to enter the Holiest by the blood of Jesus, by a new and living way which He consecrated for us, through the veil, that is, His flesh, and having a High Priest over the house of God, let us draw near with a true heart in *full assurance* of faith, having our hearts sprinkled from an evil conscience and our bodies washed with pure water. Let us hold fast the confession of our *hope* without wavering, for He who promised is faithful. And let us consider one another in order to *stir up love and good works*, not forsaking the assembling of ourselves together, as is the manner of some, but *exhorting one another,* and so much the more as you see the Day approaching (Heb. 10:19–25, emphasis added).

These qualities of encouragement—goodness, forbearance, and longsuffering—lead us to repent, change, and choose a new direction in our lives. Christ knew that we had to be set free from the bondage of discouragement if we were to become all that God intended for us to be. He knew that His ministry was to be one of encouragement to the discouraged and downtrodden. As He stood up in the synagogue in Nazareth that day and the book of the prophet Isaiah was handed to Him, He opened it to the place where it was written,

> The Spirit of the LORD is upon Me,
> Because He has anointed Me
> To preach the gospel to the poor;
> He has sent Me to heal the brokenhearted,
> To proclaim liberty to the captives
> And recovery of sight to the blind,
> To set at liberty those who are oppressed [discouraged];
> To proclaim the acceptable year of the LORD.

And He declared to them, "Today this Scripture is fulfilled in your hearing" (Luke 4:16–21).

We, too, have been called to the same ministry of encouragement. It is the essence of koinonia fellowship. When we feel encouraged, we can then courageously face ourselves and begin to take full responsibility for our lives, which is the sixth quality of koinonia fellowship.

6. Responsibility

The final quality that is a part of koinonia fellowship is responsibility. Responsibility is the ability to be answerable or accountable for the things within our power and control. We are aware of personal limitations, and we acknowledge there are things over which we have no control and for which we are not responsible. We must leave them to God and to others to be responsible for. We are willing to take complete responsibility for the things that God gives us the wisdom to understand and the courage to change. We take responsibility for ourselves; we give responsibility to others. Responsibility is, literally, the ability to respond. If we do not have that, we are powerless and helpless, and we will become either victims or martyrs.

Paul was well aware of the significance of responsibility within the body. He pointed out the balance between our responsibility and God's: "Therefore, my beloved, as you have always obeyed, not as in my presence only, but now much more in my absence, work out [be responsible for] your own salvation with fear and trembling; for it is God who works in you both to will and to do for [be responsible for] His good pleasure" (Phil. 2:12–13).

Paul also pointed out the balance between our responsibility toward one another and our responsibility for ourselves:

> Brethren, if a man is overtaken in any trespass, you who are spiritual restore such a one in a spirit of gentleness, considering yourself lest you also be tempted. Bear one another's burdens, and so fulfill the law of Christ. For if anyone thinks himself to be something, when he is nothing, he deceives himself. But let each one examine his own work, and then he will have rejoicing in himself alone, and not in another. For each one shall bear his own load (Gal. 6:1–5).

Paul understood the healthy balance in a koinonia fellowship between helping and taking responsibility for another person's problem or trespass. We are to bear (help) and encourage one another in a spirit of gentleness, but we must examine ourselves and be responsible for our own lives (bear our own load).

In the ministry of Christ there was always the balance between doing for others what they could not do for themselves and making them responsible for doing what they were able to do. What Christ was responsible for (His will and power) often depended on what people were responsible for (their faith and actions). When there is that balance of what I am responsible for and what God or others are responsible for, koinonia fellowship works together with God to produce change and growth.

I believe that all six of these qualities of koinonia fellowship are present in a healthy support group. They are the essential qualities that the guidelines of a group must nurture and protect. Later, when we discuss group guidelines, you will discover that all of these qualities have been established by our recovery ministry as absolutely essential to our fellowship.

Jesus' Place in the Fellowship

If there is to be a biblical mandate for support groups, not only must the qualities of koinonia fellowship be present, but Christ must be the center of the fellowship. Jesus made that relationship very clear. It is the only way to experience His power working in our lives to enable us to grow and live fully and productively, but it depends on making Him Lord and doing things according to His way and will, not our own. He said,

> I am the true vine, and My Father is the vinedresser. Every branch in Me that does not bear fruit He takes away; and every branch that bears fruit He prunes, that it may bear more fruit. You are already clean because of the word which I have spoken to you. Abide in Me, and I in you. As the branch cannot bear fruit of itself, unless it abides in the vine, neither can you, unless you abide in Me. I am the vine, you are the branches. He who abides in Me, and I in him, bears much fruit; for *without Me you can do nothing*. If anyone does not abide in Me, he is cast out as a branch and is withered; and they gather them and throw them into the fire, and they are burned. If you abide in Me, and My words abide in you, you will ask what you desire, and it shall be done for you. By this My Father is glorified, that you bear much fruit; so *you will be My disciples*. As the Father loved Me, I also have loved you; abide in My love. *If you keep My commandments*, you will abide in My love, just as I have kept My Father's commandments and abide in His love. These things I have spoken to you, that *My joy may remain in you*, and that *your joy may be full* (John 15:1–11, emphasis added).

In that same passage, Jesus commanded His disciples to maintain the same relationship of love that He had with them with one another. In other words, we must also be a part of koinonia fellowship for Christ to produce the work (fruit) that He desires to do in our lives, and that we desire Him to do.

In our ministry, most of the support groups are based on a Twelve-Step model. We will talk more about the Twelve-Step process later, but for now, it is enough to know that the first three steps in Christ-centered recovery require that Jesus Christ be made the Lord of our lives and the source of our healing. Step One calls on us to admit that we are powerless and our lives are unmanageable. Step Two establishes that we must believe that a power greater than ourselves is necessary to restore us to sanity. Step Three requires that we choose to turn our will and lives over to God as we know and understand Him through Jesus Christ. Even our groups that are not based on a Twelve-Step model follow the first three steps (and, actually, most of the rest of the steps) in acknowledging that Jesus Christ is Lord of all that we are, all that we do, and all that we are becoming.

A group never begins its meeting without opening in prayer and acknowledging God as our perfect heavenly Father who loves us with an everlasting love and desires our healing, Jesus Christ as the source of the grace, truth, and power that we need to change and grow, and the Holy Spirit as the comforting presence that unites our hearts and minds into koinonia fellowship. The group then invites them to be present in its midst. A group never ends without praying the Lord's Prayer.

As we develop, nurture, and protect the qualities of koinonia fellowship, and as we make Christ the head of our fellowship by following the first three steps of the Twelve Steps and opening and closing in prayer, I believe that support groups fulfill the biblical mandate for Christ-centered fellowship, and that His presence is with us and His power is made available to us to deliver and heal.

One woman in a support group expressed it this way: "I felt lonely and depressed when I came to church. No one knew what was going on in my life, or if I tried to tell them, it either overwhelmed them or they were critical and offered no support, only quick, easy answers to a difficult and painful problem. I needed a refuge where I could feel safe and heal. The very first evening I attended the support group I knew I was accepted and understood. I was finally able to open up and get all of the junk that I had been carrying around out. I felt connected to my church family. At this point in my life if I had to choose between attending the church service and going to my support group, I would have to go where I have been able to feel the love of God. Right now, that is the most important thing in my life. It is what is keeping me going."

I believe that we experience in support groups what Paul described in 1 Corinthians 12 when he likened koinonia fellowship to one body consisting of many members working together with Jesus Christ as the head of the body. To me, that is reason enough to consider the need for recovery ministry in the church. It was what I turned to when I saw the reality of the needs in our congregation. Next, I would like to share with you the Mount Paran experience of recovery ministry to illustrate why the church needs recovery ministry.

Chapter
3

The Mount Paran Experience

The statistical reality indicates that large populations of people would benefit from Christ-centered support groups. Those persons are not only outside the church waiting to be ministered to but are also found every Sunday sitting in the pews of our churches. The biblical mandate indicates that Christ-centered support groups based on koinonia fellowship are a part of God's plan and can be a powerful healing force in the lives of people. I would like to share the Mount Paran experience of recovery ministry, the needs that it has been able to address, and the impact that it has had on our congregation and the community.

Original Groups

In the early 1980s some church members who were in recovery from alcoholism began to meet together. They had attended Alcoholics Anonymous meetings, but they wanted to supplement their AA experiences with a recovery meeting where they could make Christ the center of their Twelve-Step recovery process. Thus was born the Alcoholics Victorious (AV) group. By 1987, when we began to consider expanding into a recovery ministry, this group had outgrown two rooms, and fifty to sixty persons regularly attended weekly meetings. The group ministered to all chemical addictions in addition to alcohol. It eventually reflected that fact by changing its name to Alcoholics and Addicts Victorious. It is our "mother group" and remains in existence today. It has even expanded to two meetings a week.

When we started the recovery ministry in 1987, two other groups of people, who had joined the AV group, were split off to become two new entities. One group became Eating Disorders Victorious to help persons deal with any compulsive and out-of-control use of food, whether it involved overeating, anorexia, or bulimia. That group still meets weekly. The other group was Families Victorious, which helps family members and loved ones of chemically dependent persons. This group has expanded to a second meeting each week.

Three other new groups that year focused on dealing with losses. The Heartmending Grief Group ministered to those who had lost a relationship with a loved one through death. This group has tended to remain a small fellowship, and only this year has begun meeting periodically after regularly meeting every other week.

The two other groups involving loss were Divorce Recovery and Children of Divorce. Divorce Recovery was for adults who lost a relationship and a loved one due to divorce, regardless of who filed for the divorce. Initially, the group consisted solely of women, but in the last year men have begun to participate. The group fluctuates in size but continues to meet every other week and is considering meeting weekly.

Children of Divorce is actually a program with five groups to minister to families and children who have been through the experience of divorce. Four groups are for children: kindergarten and first grade; second and third grades; fourth and fifth grades; and sixth through eighth grades. In addition, there is a parents' group for the custodial parent as well as the noncustodial parent. This program is based on Rainbows for All God's Children (a Christian support program developed by Suzy Yehl to help children deal with issues of loss due to divorce or death within their families) and is held in the fall. Every year it meets the needs of thirty to forty children and their families.

The last group originally formed was Adult Children of Confusion. It was for adults who grew up in dysfunctional families and continued to manifest that dysfunction in some way as adults. I started this group out of my own experiences of growing up in a family that experienced mental illness. We chose the name Adult Children of Confusion because we didn't want to label or judge our families, and because we didn't want to exclude anyone who needed our support. The confusion could have come from any addictive or compulsive behavior. It could have been the result of physical, sexual, or emotional abuse. It could have been the result of mental illness or chronic physical illness. The rigidity and perfectionism of a military or religious family background could have created it. This group meets weekly and has grown to be our largest group (sixty to eighty persons) at present.

Other Groups

In the next several years other groups were formed. Couples Victorious gives couples a chance to share together and learn how to develop healthy relationship skills. This group meets twice a month.

Another group spun out of Families Victorious. Several group members realized that they were dealing with problems of chemical dependency and with out-of-control sexual acting-out behavior by their spouses. They began to meet on another night during the week and became Families Victorious—SAFE, which stands for Families Victorious Over Sexual Addiction Through Fellowship and Encouragement. This group continues to grow and meets weekly. At present, the group is only for women, but the need is certainly there for men as well.

After the success of the Children of Divorce program, we realized that there was a need for a Children of Addiction program. We patterned the groups after the Children of Divorce program and used the Children Are People curriculum. (The Children Are People curriculum is a secular program to help children deal with chemical dependency within their families. We adapted it to fit within a Christ-centered setting.) Initially, we held the Children of Addiction program in the spring after holding the Children of Divorce program in the fall, but as this program grew, we made some changes. Children of Addiction became Kids Victorious, which includes children from any kind of dysfunctional family system. Students in middle school and high school formed Teens Victorious. They meet every week during the school year, except for brief breaks. The group now uses the Confident Kids program, which is biblically based, and ministers to thirty to forty families each year. (Confident Kids is a Christ-centered support program developed by Linda Kondracki for children from families where addiction is present and from other dysfunctional families.) A parents' group meets while the children meet.

We started Phobics Victorious to give support to persons struggling to overcome panic attacks, phobias, and anxiety disorders. This group has tended to run in cycles and will occasionally take a break from meetings for a few months. As phobics get better, they seem to want to get into the mainstream of life again, and they are reluctant to remain in the group and be reminded of the old fears.

Another group that began several years ago is Sexual Abuse Survivors Victorious. It is presently for women who were sexually abused as children. The group meets every week and is now one of our fastest growing groups. A men's group has just begun and is meeting a great need already.

Recently, several more groups have gotten started. Living Stones is a fellowship of men *and* women desiring recovery from homosexual thoughts, feelings, and behavior. This group meets weekly. Some men began to meet together as Sex Addicts Victorious. This group is for men only and deals with problems with pornography, compulsive masturbation, affairs, and any other forms of sexual acting out. The group meets weekly and is growing slowly but steadily. Eventually, we hope to provide a similar group for women dealing with compulsive promiscuity, sexual acting out, and addiction to unhealthy and abusive relationships.

Codependents Victorious has started as strongly as any support group we have ever offered. The emphasis is on becoming more dependent on God to determine worth and value and less dependent on other people, circumstances, and things. This group meets weekly.

Partners of Survivors Victorious is for the spouse, friend, or family member who is in a relationship with someone who is a sexual abuse survivor, whether male or female. Relationships can be severely affected by past sexual abuse experiences and can even fail if both partners are not working together to understand and heal. This group is starting slowly, but we expect it to meet a great need as it continues to grow. It meets twice a month at the same time as Sexual Abuse Survivors Victorious.

In addition to all these groups, other groups have met needs for a season that has now passed. These groups are no longer active, but each was successful for a period of time. We will talk later about the various reasons why some groups become established and other groups struggle or eventually fail.

Remarriage Reality helped couples deal with the reality of experiencing marriage the next time around as well as blending two families into one. Caring Couples provided support for couples struggling with the discouragement of infertility. Although the couples no longer meet as a group, some couples continue to minister to others. We have also had a cancer support group.

Parents in Pain was for parents whose children were out of control, were experiencing difficulty with authority, or were in trouble legally. Learning Disabled Victorious was for adults dealing with their own learning disabilities or those of their children.

One last group deserves a mention because it was very successful. Thankfully, it had a short season. Persons with loved ones in the Persian Gulf crisis met weekly.

I am sure that other new support groups will be started in the future. At present, we are in the planning stages to begin groups offering support to those struggling with depression and manic depression, a group for women who are in or have been in abusive relationships, a veterans group, a group for ex-offenders, and a group for friends and family members of persons with HIV/AIDS. I imagine some of our current support groups may run their course. But what is important is the impact of these support groups, not what kind or how many we have.

Impact of Groups

Some of that impact can be measured in numbers. Although we do not monitor attendance or attempt to accumulate detailed statistics, some general numbers are meaningful.

Our two children's support group programs have ministered to over two hundred families and more than five hundred children. We know that because the families register for these programs at the beginning of each fall. About one-third of the families participating are from outside our church membership. Some of our referrals come from the courts and lawyers who recommend the program as a place for families to heal together. That tells me we are reaching out to the community and affecting it for Christ. But the greatest thing about these statistics is that at least five hundred children will have a better opportunity to have a happier childhood. They can look forward to healthier relationships in the future and be part of families with a little less pain in them.

Our support groups range in size from six to seventy-five persons. The average attendance is generally about fifteen to twenty in each group. People are constantly coming into and going out of support groups as their needs are met.

One group was able to provide some statistics because it gave out a newcomer's packet to each new person. Last year alone, an average of ten new persons visited the group each week! About one-fifth of them were still actively involved in the group three months later. This is our largest group and not all groups will make quite as big an impact, but it does point to the need for support groups.

One of our group members did a project to satisfy a class requirement for his undergraduate degree. He wanted to determine the effectiveness, statistically, of the Twelve-Step recovery ministry at Mount Paran. I was relieved when the conclusions from his data indicated that the groups were effective! Several statistics from his study were especially revealing to me as a pastor and a counselor.

The fellow surveyed all of our Twelve-Step groups. He learned that of all the persons involved in the support groups at Mount Paran, 45 percent were church members when they began attending the groups. That meant 55 percent had come into the groups from outside the membership of the church. If your church is interested in outreach, that is a significant statistic. Since we do not advertise our groups other than in church publications, group members must be sharing (witnessing) a lot to create that kind of word-of-mouth effect.

I think I know the next question that some of you may be asking. How many of that 55 percent eventually found their way into the church fellowship? Of those persons who were not church members when they came into the groups, 47 percent considered Mount Paran their church home even though they were not members, and almost 17 percent at some point became members of the church.

Several other statistics intrigued me, especially in light of what we have already talked about in regard to the biblical mandate for koinonia fellowship. Ninety percent felt that everyone in the group was given a chance to share. Ninety percent felt accepted by the group. Eighty-six percent felt that people listened when they shared, and that people in the group did not try to "fix" them. Eighty-six percent also felt that they were learning to trust God through prayer. Eighty-three percent did not feel judged in any way by the group, and they felt forgiven in spite of their wrongs. Eighty-three percent knew that others were there for them when they needed help or support. Eighty percent felt that they understood themselves and their feelings better. Seventy-nine percent were learning to praise God as part of their relationship with Him. Seventy-six percent of all group members felt that they were affirmed for being honest and encouraged when they shared.

One final statistic. Although I cannot (and would not even if I could) put a sign up outside our support group rooms and indicate how many persons have been served here, I do know that it has been thousands. Hiring pastors or counselors to lead all the groups or minister to all the persons and families who have been helped by the support groups would be cost prohibitive, I would think, to almost any church. And yet, because the groups are self-led and self-supporting (which we will talk about later), the recovery ministry at Mount Paran has cost the church only room space and the price of a cabinet for each group's literature and materials. How many of you have rooms in your church that are unused on most evenings during the week? For a total investment of less than a thousand dollars a year, our church has received the benefits of the recovery ministry described here. Your cost would obviously depend on the number of groups.

But what about my time and the cost of having a staff person to implement and run this ministry? For all the time that I spend on the recovery ministry, there is ultimately an exponential lessening of my time load as the groups do more effectively and efficiently the things that would drain me if I had to do them alone. And that doesn't take into consideration what support groups give financially to the church. Those persons who are now coming to church as a result of recovery ministry are often giving tithes and offerings to the church. Our support groups generate more than ten thousand dollars each year in the offerings they collect, and a portion of that goes back into direct benefits to the church or saves the church from spending that money to offer services to people who are being helped by the groups. As persons are helped by support groups, they will want to help others in return. One support group member refurnished the church's counseling rooms. Others have given large and small gifts to help other people and other ministries. To me, the conclusion is obvious; recovery ministry is ultimately cost-effective.

However, statistics don't tell the whole story of the Mount Paran experience with recovery ministry. That is found in the lives of the people who have been affected by it. That is why I have included a whole section of some of their stories at the end of the book. They speak better to the Mount Paran experience than I can.

I have seen people, Jews and Gentiles, accept Christ in our support groups without altar calls being given or anyone preaching. I have seen spouses who were separated and divorced reconciled. Numerous people have related how hopeless and depressed they felt before they joined their group, and they recognized that God used their group to save their lives. One woman said that even as she sat in her parked car intending to take her life, she looked over and saw a church publication with the support groups listed. She decided to see if any help was there. There was, and she found a reason to go on living.

I have witnessed addicts delivered from all manner of chemical dependency and those with eating disorders lose and maintain a weight loss of almost two hundred pounds. I have seen homosexuals turn to a heterosexual life-style and sex addicts learn to overcome lust. I can see people sitting in our congregation who have had the wounds of severe childhood trauma healed and resolved. I have seen an abuser ask for forgiveness, and I have seen a recovering sexually abused person offer it; then I watched as the two embraced.

I have watched as a van load of people drove almost one hundred miles one way every week for months to participate in a group until they were able to go back to their community with what they had learned and start their own group. I have seen a person commute weekly from another state to come to a group, finally moving to Atlanta to more regularly attend.

I have met with or talked with people in over sixty churches in the past few years and helped them to consider or set up recovery ministries. Part of my reason for writing this book is that I cannot talk fast enough on the phone or over lunch and I do not have enough time in a day or weekend to share all of our experiences and what we have learned.

But if I am partial to any experiences in our years of recovery ministry, they would be the experiences in the lives of children. I weep when I see parents and children able to grieve together and learn to comfort one another as God heals the pain in their families. I rejoice when I see parents learning how to be parents and be there for their children. I thrill when a parent shares with me that her daughter, who was so angry with God for what she thought He had done to their family, is now praying to her heavenly Father again. And I laugh when a mother shares with me the experience of her child, who came into the group afraid to fail because of her dad's temper.

One day, when her mom blew her cool over an insignificant mistake, the girl said, "Mom, chill out! I'm just a child, and I'm not supposed to be perfect!"

A lot of God's children are hurting and need to hear their Father say to them, "Hey, chill out! You're My child, and you're not supposed to be perfect." I don't think He would use those exact words, but you know what I mean. The Mount Paran experience with recovery ministry has taught me that God desires to work in the lives of His children of all ages, helping them to face whatever reality they are struggling with, and overcoming it through the power of koinonia fellowship in support groups.

But the church must face one major obstacle as it develops a philosophy of recovery ministry. It is a legitimate question that must be asked and answered, and I will share my perspective on it in the next chapter.

Chapter
4

New Life
or New Age?

I do not profess to be a theological scholar, nor do I pretend to know everything about the New Age Movement. I do know that it has generated much concern in the church, which it should rightfully do, as should anything that would make Jesus Christ less than Lord of all. I also am aware that it has created much controversy and confusion in the church. And in some cases it has brought about a skeptical response to any new work that God may be doing in the lives of His people today.

When I talk about recovery ministry, especially Twelve-Step recovery ministry, I often run into two opposing points of view. One group looks at Twelve-Step recovery ministry as a biblically based, relevant way to minister to contemporary society. The other group questions the true intent of the Twelve Steps and believes that the recovery movement is another subtle way that the church is conforming to the age, or the New Age, rather than transforming it. So, is it new life, or is it New Age?

Basic Understanding

At the risk of sounding simplistic, I will be, for I am basically a simple person who desires to see God work in my life and in the lives of others. I want to know enough about the New Age to be able to recognize that it is faulty and dangerous, but I don't want to spend so much of my time wrapped up in it that I miss knowing God's true, perfect, and pleasing will for my life. Others have written whole books on the subject to help Christians understand the New Age, and I recommend them to you. As for me, I have come to the following basic understanding about the difference between new life and New Age.

First of all, I don't think that the New Age Movement is really new. It has always existed as a philosophy diametrically opposed to God's perspective of humankind. It is being presented and marketed in a more polished form by more eloquent proponents in an age of high-tech communication.

As I understand the New Age Movement, the core of its philosophy is the belief that human beings can find within themselves their own true meaning and value and tune in to the power(s) of the universe to enable them to become who they determine themselves to be. They acknowledge the concept of a higher power, but it is for them to use and control in their self-actualization. People who seek wisdom and healing through the New Age Movement do so by refusing to acknowledge the reality of Jesus Christ, who He declared Himself to be, and His requirements to be His disciples and know His truth and resurrection power.

So, on the one extreme, are those in the New Age Movement who would leave the lordship of Jesus Christ out of the recovery process. On the other extreme, however, are those who would leave the truths of the recovery movement out of God's plan for healing grace to the church and to the world. Jesus alone is all the world needs. The recovery movement is a lie, a manifestation of the New Age, and a trick of Satan. Christians, and the church, should steer clear of the recovery movement, according to proponents of this view.

Is there a position between the two extremes? Is there a point balanced between the two where Jesus Christ is Lord and the truths of the recovery movement are part of His will for the church and can be used for His glory? Obviously, I believe that there is, and that it is necessary to find that balance and maintain it if God is going to use Christ-centered recovery ministry for His glory.

In Scripture the beginning of that balance comes in the acceptance of the futility and powerlessness of our self-will to accomplish anything good in and of ourselves. The prophet Isaiah recognized that when he observed,

> All we like sheep have gone astray;
> We have turned, every one, to his own way;
> And the LORD [God] has laid on Him [Jesus]
>   the iniquity of us all (Isa. 53:6).

Our way and our efforts lead us in ways that are counterproductive and even destructive to our own well-being. Only Christ is capable of removing from us the terrible consequences of our shortcomings.

We have already seen how Jesus warned His disciples that in and of themselves they could not produce good fruit in their lives. He used the analogy of the vine and the branches to illustrate that instead of trusting in their own efforts and resources, they must learn to abide in Him—His way, His word, and His will—if they were to grow. Apart from that relationship with Christ, they would be able to do nothing. Their best efforts would ultimately wither and die and would be useful only if they were gathered up and burned. But if they acknowledged Christ as Lord and abided in Him and His word, He would do what they could not do for themselves. They would bear much fruit, and their lives and joy would be made full and complete (John 15:1–11).

Paul clearly understood his limitations and inability to do for himself what he wished to do. He knew that ultimately his efforts were futile and even self-destructive, and that only the power of Jesus Christ could overcome what he was powerless over: his own flesh, his own self-will. He wrote to the Romans and shared that understanding with them:

For I know that in me (that is, in my flesh) [my efforts, my self-will] nothing good dwells; for to will is present with me, but how to perform what is good I do not find. For the good that I will to do, I do not do; but the evil I will not to do, that I [continue to] practice. Now if I do what I will not to do, it is no longer I who do it, but sin that dwells in me. I find then a law, that evil is present with me, the one who wills to do good. For I delight in the law of God according to the inward man. But I see another law in my members, warring against the law of my mind, and bringing me into captivity to the law of sin which is in my members. O wretched man that I am! Who will deliver me from this body of death? I thank God—through Jesus Christ our Lord! So then, with the mind I myself serve the law of God, but with the flesh the law of sin (Rom. 7:18–25).

That is the powerlessness, the law of the flesh and sin, that only Jesus Christ can overcome.

Our Christ-centered recovery groups differ from New Age recovery groups in our acceptance of personal powerlessness and our affirmation of Jesus Christ as the only power able to do what we are unable to do for ourselves. In this way, we are not truly a self-help group. We understand and accept that all power and authority has been given to Jesus Christ (Matt. 28:18). We recognize that God has given Jesus the power and authority over all humankind (John 17:2). We acknowledge that "we have this treasure in earthen vessels, that the excellence of the power may be of God and not of us" (2 Cor. 4:7). We have discovered, like Paul, that God's grace is sufficient in us, for His power is perfected in weakness. We now boast about (confess openly and honestly) our weaknesses so that the power of Christ may dwell in us (2 Cor. 12:9). Numerous other Scriptures remind us that the power of Christ working in our lives saves and heals.

How, then, do we understand the place of human insight in the process of recovery if Christ must be the center of recovery? Why do we use the recovery concepts that people have discovered and identified? Why do we follow the Twelve-Step process established and set forth by Alcoholics Anonymous more than fifty years ago? Because Christ *is* the ultimate source, we can use recovery principles and processes as part of the way that God supplies all of our needs according to His riches (resources) that are in Christ Jesus (Phil. 4:19). They may be part of His gifts of healing to His children, and we know that every good thing bestowed and every perfect gift is from above, that it comes down from "the Father of lights, with whom there is no variation" or shifting shadow (James 1:17).

Please note that I said those principles and processes *may* be part of God's good and perfect gift. Scripture teaches that there is a way to discern whether Christians can utilize those things discovered and established by people as part of God's gift to us. We can use a biblical test to determine whether something is new life or New Age.

The Test

Paul wrote to his young disciple Timothy some excellent advice to eliminate his confusion about what is of God or what is of the world: "For every creature of God is good, and nothing is to be refused if it is received with thanksgiving; for it is sanctified by the word of God and prayer" (1 Tim. 4:4-5). We can use that test to determine whether something is new life or New Age.

Three elements in this passage are key to whether something has been created by God and can be accepted as one of His good and perfect gifts for us or whether it should be rejected. When we evaluate an idea, such as the Twelve Steps, or a concept, such as that of recovery ministry, we look for the presence or absence of these three elements to determine whether we, as individuals or as a church, are receiving a gift that is part of God's good, perfect, and pleasing will for our lives.

The Word of God

Verse 5 points to the first two considerations. If something is to be received as one of God's perfect gifts for us, it must be sanctified by the Word of God and prayer. To sanctify something is to remove any impurities so that what is left is holy and acceptable to God, able to be used for His glory.

To sanctify something through the Word of God means to first examine it in light of Scripture. Is the truth being presented consistent with the truth of God's Word? If it is consistent with God's truth, it will set people free, whether they credit God or humankind as the source. If it is God's truth, Christians will properly credit the source of that truth, while non-Christians will tend to give humankind the credit. Some ideas will be completely consistent with God's truth and can be fully incorporated into the church's ministry as another manifestation of God's healing grace available to us. Other ideas will contain elements of the truth while also presenting people's opinions, which may distort the truth or be contrary to it.

If something contains elements of the truth but also has "impurities," does that mean we must totally reject it? I don't believe so. I believe that is why God has given us the gift of discernment and He desires that we have the mind of Christ in us. We are to grow in the wisdom and knowledge of Christ and the things of God so that we can readily discern the difference. Or if we are unable to discern the difference, we are to find safety in the counsel of others who are spiritually wise and discerning. We then remove the impurities and use the truth. I believe that is how everything is to be sanctified by means of the Word of God as instructed in verse 5.

In that regard, I can find the biblical basis for each of the Twelve Steps. For me, they are totally sanctified and can be used as a tool and instrument for God's healing truth to be known and His power to be revealed. In light of Scripture, I can understand various concepts, such as codependency, as being true, and I can use them as part of my ministry. I can use certain techniques because their ultimate validity and effectiveness come not out of the wisdom and skill of human beings but out of God's principles of wholeness and holiness for our lives. I don't completely agree with some secular authors; nevertheless, they have identified and shared some of God's truth without being able to properly credit it to Him. I can use those books and that truth if I am careful to discern those things that are of human beings and not of God.

Prayer

But those things must also be sanctified through prayer.

Has the person offering this truth come by it through prayer? In other words, does the author or presenter of this truth follow Jesus Christ and seek God with all the heart, soul, mind, and strength as Christ instructed? Has that person sought the Lord for this truth, and does that person listen to and hear from God? If the person has pursued the truth through prayer, it is *likely* to be sanctified. If it is not, the next element of the process of sanctifying through prayer always comes into play.

Has the person receiving this truth come by it through prayer? In the book of James, we are advised that if we lack wisdom (God's truth), we are to ask God (the source) for it, and it will be given generously and without any disappointment or disapproval (James 1:5). Proverbs, the book of wisdom, makes over fifty references to the value of seeking wisdom. We are to seek wisdom in the same manner that the miner seeks silver and gold (Prov. 2:1–5). We are to always seek wisdom, which is God's truth, from the source of that truth, which is God Himself. Have we sought God for the truth in prayer? Has He given that wisdom and confirmed it to our hearts? The wisdom of God will always be confirmed through three sources: His spirit, His Word, and His people.

An Attitude of Gratitude

The process of sanctification, the removal of impurities, takes place by means of the Word of God and prayer. But the third element that determines whether something has been created by God for us and is not to be rejected involves the attitude with which it is received.

First Timothy 4:4 indicates that nothing is to be refused or rejected if it is received with an attitude of thanksgiving, or gratitude. That is a favorite saying in Twelve-Step groups. An attitude of gratitude acknowledges that the belief developed in God's ability to restore our lives to sanity expressed in Step Two is true. Whether something is sanctified to God's use or not depends on this attitude. If something causes us to look to God and appreciate His doing for us what we can't do for ourselves, that attitude, along with the Word of God and prayer, can purify and sanctify anything that God has created, and we are not to reject it. If, on the other hand, a philosophy or technique or movement encourages us to depend on our efforts or those of others on our behalf, that attitude does not appreciate God, and we are to reject the source of that attitude.

God has placed many things in the body of Christ in this age as food to nurture and heal His people. New ideas and concepts, such as the Twelve Steps, are sanctified by the process Paul shared with Timothy. A new movement, the recovery movement, is calling people to a whole new level of honesty and accountability to be healed and overcome those things separating them from themselves, others, and God. I believe that the recovery movement can be sanctified to God rather than left in the hands of others who do not acknowledge the ultimate source of the truth that is setting them free. It can be a gift to those who appreciate the powerlessness of their efforts and gratefully draw near to God for the strength and grace to do what they can't do for themselves. The results then become new life in Christ.

Our support groups always open with prayer that acknowledges God to be our perfect heavenly Father, who has shown His everlasting love to us through His Son; confesses Jesus Christ to be the Lord of our lives and circumstances, who offers us the grace that is the source of, and is sufficient for, our healing; and invites the Holy Spirit to be present and unify us as a fellowship to encourage and support one another. The meetings traditionally end with the Lord's Prayer: God is to be honored by His name being hallowed; His kingdom is to be established; His will is to be done; His authority (kingdom), His power, and His glory provide us with all that we need, cleanse us and make us whole, and allow us to overcome any evil controlling our lives.

With an attitude of gratitude, and as all things are sanctified through the Word of God and prayer, we are able to share in everything and not reject anything that God has created for our good. We believe and know the ultimate source of truth, and that truth sets us free and allows us to experience new life in Christ. In the next three sections I will share with you our experiences in setting up and maintaining a recovery ministry that enables people to come together and experience that new life and develop new life-styles.

Section 2

DEFINING THE PURPOSE:

What It Means to Be a Christ-Centered Support Group

As you begin to establish and implement a recovery ministry, you must understand what a support group is and what it does, the differences between a secular support group and a Christ-centered support group, and the goals and expectations for participants in the groups. The next three chapters will address these issues in detail.

People participate in various group experiences, especially in a church setting. As they do, they develop certain understandings and expectations about what should happen in groups. If those expectations are brought into a recovery ministry and you are not clear about what a support group is and does, confusion and frustration can very quickly sabotage a group. That is why you must establish your definition from the very beginning so that people know what they will experience and what is expected of them.

We didn't do this when we started out in 1987. We didn't realize it would be a struggle to keep support groups focused on their purpose. Some groups began successfully, only to fall apart as they lost the understanding of what gave them their unique place in the ministry of the church. Some groups that were effective in meeting needs became ineffective as group members lost sight of the crucial differences between their Christ-centered group and a secular group. Some groups became unsupportive because group members didn't understand and pursue the goals that all support group members are expected to strive for.

Eventually, we learned what to do and what not to do. We established our definition, identified what made our groups distinctive, and developed our expectations that now guide our ministry. Group leaders are trained to understand them, and group members are made aware of them from the moment they attend a group. People are taught, through words and actions, the goals that they are expected to strive for as members of a support group.

You may agree or disagree with our definition. You may choose a different set of distinctive characteristics for your Christ-centered groups. You may have different goals and expectations for your group members. My purpose here is to stimulate your thinking so that you can develop what will best reflect your church situation. The important thing is that *you* are clear in your understanding so that your support groups will be clear in theirs. According to the Bible, people and groups flounder in confusion and ultimately may perish for lack of clear understanding and vision (Prov. 29:18).

Chapter
5

Definition
and Purpose

As I mentioned in the introduction to this section, people may participate in many groups, especially within the church setting. They develop expectations about what they should do and should not do in a group. They must understand the differences between the groups that they have experienced and the support groups that they are now joining; otherwise those expectations may come into play and frustrate the persons and the groups.

Many church members have been in a *prayer group*. Although prayer definitely plays a big part in a Christ-centered support group, it may not take place in the ways or forms that people associated with the prayer meeting. If they expect that group members are going to come together and pray for one another for an hour and a half once a week, they will be very disappointed and frustrated. They may even question whether or not the group is really Christ-centered if there is no emphasis on prayer.

I believe that prayer has a place whenever there is any fellowship with other Christians, but I do not believe that the primary purpose of a support group is prayer. The group's primary purpose is to pursue a rigorously honest examination and sharing of members' true selves.

Having said that, let me say that every group meeting should begin with prayer. Here is a simple opening prayer that we use:

Father God, we seek to understand and know You as our perfect heavenly Father who loves us with an unfailing, everlasting love that nothing can separate us from;

Lord Jesus, we desire You to be Lord of all and the power greater than ourselves and our situations, and we ask You to restore our lives to sanity and balance through Your grace;

Holy Spirit, we invite You to be present and unify us as one family of love and acceptance so that we may encourage and support one another in the process of growth and change. Amen.

Many of our groups use the opening three lines of Reinhold Niebuhr's Serenity Prayer, a prayer often used at Twelve-Step meetings, before they begin their sharing time: "God, give us grace to accept with serenity the things that cannot be changed, courage to change the things which should be changed, and the wisdom to distinguish the one from the other."

All of our groups close with the Lord's Prayer as we follow the example of the disciples who recognized the power of prayer in the life of Christ and asked Him to teach them how to pray.

In addition to these times of prayer, people may minister to one another immediately following a group meeting. This ministry of prayer takes place individually as it is desired and sought after. Prayer is often a major aspect of a relationship with a sponsor (discussed in a later chapter).

A second experience that can create confusing expectations for a support group is a *Bible study group*. Although the Bible is the source of all truth concerning who we are in Christ for persons in recovery, talking about it and studying it can often be used to avoid doing what it calls us to do. We avoid examining ourselves, confessing our sins, and walking in the light because we talk about the Bible and what it says rather than talk about ourselves and what the Bible has revealed to us about our struggles and what we need to do to overcome them. A support group is a place to share truth—and God's

Word is truth and the source of life—but it is not a place to study the Bible. It is a place to live the Bible by practicing the fearless honesty and humility required before God can lift us up by His power in His time.

A third experience that often causes confusion within a support group is a *sharing group*. This group is similar to a support group in the emphasis on sharing, but a support group provides a specialized function. In a support group all of the sharing takes place with other persons who have had common experiences, whether relating to addiction, divorce, sexual abuse, or something else. We become aware and accept that we have experienced temptations common to others, and that God is faithful to provide us with a way to deal with those temptations as Paul points out in 1 Corinthians 10:13. That awareness and acceptance, that sense of understanding and support, give people greater permission and opportunity to explore deeper levels of honest examination and sharing than would normally be experienced in a general sharing group.

The level of honesty in a support group may be difficult and even threatening for people who expect a less-intense sharing experience. The group may drift toward becoming more generalized and superficial to feel safe. The emotional honesty and the vulnerability at the core of the support group healing process are watered down as a result.

One last group bears mentioning, even though it may not be a part of a church's experience, and that is a *counseling or therapy group*. Often people will enter a support group when they really desire and need a more intense directed counseling group. Or they will become a part of a support group and expect it to operate according to the same dynamics as a therapy group. A support group is not a therapy group. No one directs anyone. No one confronts anyone directly. No one does therapy on anyone. Yet, in a support group, therapeutic things—honesty, openness, trust, risk, acceptance, vulnerability, and affirmation—happen. They just happen naturally as a result of koinonia group process, not as a result of directed experiences created and led by a counselor or professional.

There is a big temptation for support groups to become therapy groups and group members to become therapists for one another. That is not the purpose or meaning of support groups. This expectation must be resisted, or the group may do serious damage to people by opening up things that they are not equipped to handle and by getting ahead of God's plan and timing for individuals. Support feels very accepting and safe. People often perceive therapy as confrontive and threatening if they are not ready and prepared for it.

So, if support groups aren't prayer groups, although they pray; if they aren't Bible study groups, although they seek God's truth; if they aren't just sharing groups, although they share; and if they aren't therapy groups, although therapeutic things happen, what are they?

A Support Group Is . . .

About a year ago I met with several dozen people who had been a part of our recovery ministry from its earliest beginnings and asked them that same question. We considered all that we had experienced in our support groups, what we had learned about them, and we developed our definition of what a support group is and does: *As a support group, we are a fellowship of people who come together to share our common experience, strength, and hope with one another so that we can identify in our struggles, learn about life and relationships, and grow in the ability to trust God and become all that He created us to be.* Each aspect of that definition carries implications about what takes place in support groups and makes them different from other group experiences that Christians may be a part of, so we will examine our definition in greater detail.

Fellowship

A support group is first and foremost a *fellowship* of people in recovery. According to the dictionary, *to recover* means "to get back or regain one's health (from a state of dis-ease), strength, and control of one's self (and life)." Each group has its own recovery purpose. Support group meetings should never feel like just meetings. There is to be a sense of fellowship that reflects the six qualities of koinonia fellowship previously discussed. The atmosphere of a support group is vital to the group's effectiveness. Meetings, in and of themselves, do not heal. They simply allow the opportunity for healing to take place. The power of God, present in the koinonia fellowship of His people, heals.

After a support group meeting one night, a couple thanked me for the recovery ministry of the church. They were not members of Mount Paran. They had been separated, and plans were being made for divorce. The wife was so distraught that she was considering suicide, but she decided to first attend a secular support group that she had read about in the paper in one last desperate attempt to find an answer or any kind of hope. She never got there. She got lost and somehow ended up at the church. When she asked for help, she was directed to the only support group meeting that night. It turned out to be the group that she needed to be in. She began to attend the group. She was able to persuade her husband to attend, too, and give their marriage one last chance. As a result of what they learned in the group and the fellowship they experienced, they recommitted their lives to the Lord, the depression lifted, and they reconciled their marriage and were back together. That is the power of koinonia fellowship to heal.

This sense of fellowship must be established, nurtured, and maintained from the very beginning. Any other environment will be toxic to individuals who will be bringing their sense of failure and shame to the group and to God for healing. Instead of being able to breathe deeply the cleansing atmosphere of koinonia fellowship, they find themselves choking on the toxic atmosphere of judgment and condemnation often experienced in the world and, sad to say, in some church groups.

Sharing

A support group is a fellowship of people who come together to *share*. A support group is not meant to be a spectator sport. Everyone present must be able to participate in and feel a part of it. Everyone must have the opportunity to regularly share and know that others will listen. People must understand that it is their responsibility to get what they need from the group, and that the only way to accomplish that is through sharing what is going on in their lives.

It is very easy to sit back in support groups, just as we can do in other group situations, and play it safe. We may try to maintain the illusion that we have everything under control and do not need others and God to do for us what we cannot do for ourselves. That attitude of denial will certainly prevent others from really knowing us and protect us from their disappointment and disapproval, but it will also keep our true selves hidden away in darkness and secrecy where the light of God's healing grace cannot penetrate. We must share. We must bring things out into the light if we are to be healed and experience freedom from the bondage that we all too often find ourselves in, even as Christians.

Groups must remain small enough so that everyone can share and can personally know other group members. (We will talk more about this in the sections on beginning and maintaining support groups.) People often gain a vital sense of belonging in support groups. Within a month after I started one support group, I received four phone calls from people to thank me for providing the group and to say how much it meant to them. They all expressed the same sentiment; they were in the process of transferring to another church because they felt our church was too large to meet their needs. When the support group provided the experience of belonging that met their needs, they decided to remain.

So, support groups are a fellowship of people who come together to share, but what exactly should they share? People can talk about any number of subjects in a group setting. A support group can get off track, and meaningful conversations can disintegrate into futile debates, pity parties, blame games, or gossip sessions. The focus on people sharing *common* experience, strength, and hope with one another can keep them on track.

The sharing must be pertinent to those things that each person has in *common* with other group members. Each group defines its common purpose from the very beginning. It is the experience that every member has in common with every other group member. For example, if you are in an addicts support group, it is your addiction. Or if you are in a phobics group, it is your fear. You do not focus on food issues in a divorce recovery group; you do not focus on adult children issues in an addicts group.

That does not mean all other issues are insignificant. It means there are other times and places to deal with those issues.

Several of our groups have struggled and failed because they lost their common purpose and focus. Our first support group, the addicts group, had always been one of our largest and strongest fellowships. We had to move them three different times into bigger rooms to accommodate their growth. But they began to get off track and focus on other issues, such as codependency and adult children issues, for which we already had groups. As a result, people who were coming to get help in getting and staying clean, sober, and straight were not getting the support they needed. In less than a year that group went from fifty to sixty per meeting to less than ten. All of the leaders got discouraged and stepped down, and we had to temporarily disband the group to reorganize and reestablish the group's purpose. Within three months the group began to meet again, and it is slowly rebuilding its fellowship as it remains faithful to its purpose.

Experience, Strength, and Hope

As a support group, we are a fellowship of people who come together to share our common *experience, strength, and hope* with one another. These, then, are the three key elements involved in sharing that are going to lead to koinonia fellowship and result in group members finding the resources for recovery and healing.

Sharing experience in a support group means telling our stories of what has happened and what is happening in our lives. We honestly admit the thoughts, feelings, and behaviors that we are struggling with and are powerless over. We must step out from behind the wall of denial and take off the mask that we may be wearing and accept ourselves and our lives the way they truly are. We must choose to take a risk and trust that others and God will not leave or forsake us, and that nothing we can say or do can separate us from His love and from the acceptance and support of others in the group who share our common experience.

I remember a person who told his story and shared what he was experiencing in his life for the first time after he had been in the group for several weeks. As he shared, he began to weep. When gently asked about the tears, he said that they were tears of relief and joy, not sadness. For most of his life, he felt as if he had committed the unpardonable sin and could never be loved and accepted by God or by others because of what he struggled with. The greatest relief to him was to find out that "I am not alone."

Storytelling is not something that is done all at once. It is shared over a period of time as trust is developed and experienced by each person. To me, it is similar to peeling the layers of an onion. I begin by sharing the surface things in my life. That may be all I am willing to share initially. Perhaps that is all I am able to be aware of and accept about myself in the beginning. But as my level of trust grows in the group and in myself, I am able to share more. As I am listened to and accepted without judgment and condemnation, I am able to look for and see the things that I have so long denied and avoided facing in my life. I begin to slowly peel back the layers of the onion and let myself, others, and God get down to the very core of my being where healing needs to take place.

Some people may need to feel accepted and safe before they find the courage to take the risk of telling their stories and revealing themselves. That is why the right to pass is such an important part of the guidelines, as we will see later. Others have been carrying their burden alone for so long that it is a relief to share it and have others help to lift it from them and turn it over to God. Just remember that *God* must be in control of the timing.

Experiencing koinonia fellowship also requires sharing our common strength. Paul instructed the fellowship of the church in Rome that "we then who are strong ought to bear with the scruples of the weak, and not to please ourselves. Let each of us please his neighbor for his good, leading to edification [encouragement]" (Rom. 15:1–2).

We should constantly share the things that God is doing in our lives or showing us to strengthen one another. We should consistently encourage one another as we share successes, urging one another to try, to not grow weary, and to keep pressing on. As we share common strength, all receive the affirmation and encouragement to overcome and to recover.

A sexual abuse survivor shared her story with me after a group meeting. It was one of violent abuse. The hurt and the pain were so great that deep resentment and bitterness had taken control of her life. She had determined that what had happened to her was unforgivable; she would never trust and be vulnerable again. The inner vow destroyed any relationship that she desperately looked to for love and acceptance and resulted in self-destructive addictive-compulsive behavior. In the group she experienced support and gentle encouragement; she was able to see the damage she was doing to herself by holding on to her bitterness. Over a period of time she moved from understanding to acceptance. Her compulsive acting out ceased, and she was developing some healthy, trusting relationships. She told me, "I have finally begun to understand the purpose and the power of forgiveness."

Encouragement is one of my favorite words. I think it is the most powerful force for healing that God provides to the body of Christ next to love. To encourage means to put courage into people. To encourage is to put heart into them. Encouragement comes as group members share their common strengths and affirm one another's efforts. There is a saying in Twelve-Step support group circles: it is the effort that counts, not the results. Support groups should focus on efforts and build on the common strengths. By doing so, people will get the nurture that they need to continue to try and to trust God with the results.

Support group members need to share common hope. Hope is the belief that things will turn out for the best. For me, hope is the ability to visualize what can be. The faith referred to in Hebrews 11:1 provides "the substance of things hoped for, the evidence of things not seen." The love mentioned in 1 Corinthians 13:7 "bears all things, believes all things, hopes all things, endures all things." That does not mean we deny or ignore the reality of our experiences. On the contrary, we have already become aware of and accepted our reality through sharing our common experiences and the strengths that we have gained through our struggles. But a support group must not allow its members to wallow in the past or remain so focused on the present that the group becomes a gathering of martyrs and fellow sufferers.

I once talked with two family members in our groups about what they had experienced in their lives. Both had the same background, but they were at two entirely different places in their lives. One was pessimistic, always blaming others and circumstances for problems. The other was optimistic, always finding ways to learn from every situation and using the things that happened as opportunities to grow. In separate conversations when I asked them why they thought they were the way they were, I was surprised to get almost identical answers: "When you've been through what I've been through, you can't help becoming what I've become." The difference was that one used the experiences as an excuse not to try because of them, while the other used the same experiences to understand and grow in spite of them.

Modeling and Mirroring. The atmosphere created within the group must encourage members to expect that things can change and that they will change. I think that this is best accomplished through the modeling and mirroring that group members do for one another.

Modeling takes place when group members lay claim to small successes and call on the group to celebrate. I must see people change if I am going to believe that change is possible. The reality of changed lives is the most powerful witness to the power of the gospel of Jesus Christ, and that same reality is the most powerful motivator for people to see themselves the way they could be rather than the way they are. It is up to group members to share that reality with one another to create hope for change. There must be plenty of good models available to follow.

What makes a good model? The first quality of a good model is availability. We must cultivate an expectation in support groups that the way to keep what we are getting is to give it away to others. This is the process of discipleship, and it requires that we remain in the group as a model for others.

Some people have gone into support groups, received what they needed, and then gone on their way. They leave the support group with no models. An attitude of gratitude for what God has done in our lives keeps us available to others who can then follow after us.

A second aspect of good modeling requires that the model be identifiable and accessible to others. If we do not readily and willingly share our experiences with others, they will not be able to identify with us and feel a personal sense of hope that God will do the same thing in their lives. We must be accessible to others and communicate that accessibility so that other group members feel free to approach us about our experiences.

Finally, a good model must be honest and realistic. Change, usually, does not take place instantly or easily. Constant effort, perseverance, and discipline are required. We must daily deny self. We must take many small steps over and over again until the footing becomes sure. We must learn and practice new behaviors until they become automatic. We must be willing to do whatever is necessary and pay whatever price is required to change. Nothing is worse than false hope. It raises expectations unrealistically and sets us up for disappointment and discouragement that may leave us believing we are not capable or deserving of having our lives change. According to Proverbs 13:12, hope deferred (due to unrealistic expectations) makes the heart sick, but desire fulfilled is like a tree of life. The ability to hope and see those desires fulfilled nurtures and sustains us.

One person who joined our groups had been discouraged and depressed for years about his life. He had made several suicide attempts. He later told me that the one thing giving him enough hope to go on until he developed his faith that things could change was listening to and watching others in the group. He said, "I saw that other people's lives were different, and I began to believe that mine could be, too."

A second element to develop hope is that of mirroring. Mirroring means having the group reflect to me a view of myself and my ability to change that I may not have or be able to see. I must experience positive, encouraging mirroring if I am going to experience the hope necessary to change.

When I was growing up in Greenville, South Carolina, my family used to go to the county fair each year. I loved going through the tent of mirrors. Inside the tent was a maze that led to mirror after mirror. Each mirror distorted my shape in some way. In one mirror I looked stretched out like a rubber band. In another I looked short and round like a bowling ball. In still another I saw myself in the shape of an hourglass.

I knew I didn't really look the way I appeared in the mirrors. But in real life we often have had such distorted, discouraging views of ourselves mirrored to us by circumstances that we have come to accept as reality a view of ourselves as hopeless, helpless, defective, and undeserving. The Bible clearly exposes that view as faulty, and it is up to the members of a support group to accurately mirror to one another a view that is consistent with the way God sees us. Second Corinthians 5:17 declares, "If anyone is in Christ, he is [capable of and responsible for becoming] a new creation; old things have passed away; behold, all things have become new." Philippians 4:13, which has always been a treasured verse for me, affirms that I can do all things through the strength that Christ will give me. I am made worthy, adequate, and capable through what He has done and will do in my life.

One of our group members had been so angry that she acted out in destructive ways to herself and to others. It was very difficult for her to trust the group because she didn't feel that anyone, especially God, could love her. Initially, she was so angry that other group members were afraid to get close to her. She has been in the group over two years, and the group has become a mirror to her that has changed the way she views herself. She still has a long way to go, but I watched in amazement last week as she went around after the meeting laughing with and hugging other group members.

When we mirror that view to one another in meetings, we will inevitably have the hope necessary to change. But another aspect of sharing our common hope has to do with the individual's responsibility to change. Second Corinthians 5:17 tells me not only that I am capable and will have the opportunity to become a new creation, but that I have the responsibility to seek to become that new creation. That responsibility involves setting concrete behavioral goals for my life. It means that I clearly state what I no longer want to do, but what I now hope to do differently. It is visualizing who I know God wants me to be and I now desire to become with His help and the support of the group. A major part of sharing our common hope involves setting those goals that we desire to pursue, allowing others to mirror and affirm us as we pursue their accomplishment, and remaining accountable to the group to attain them.

In the sharing of common experience, strength, and hope, several important things do *not* happen. The group does not attempt to solve anyone's problems. People simply share the insights and strength that they have received. No one tries to counsel with or do therapy on any other member. People share their hope for change and their goals for their lives. And yet, somehow, individuals get what they need from God, and the whole group is built up.

It's like a buffet dinner. Instead of taking individual orders and trying to serve each individual need, a support group asks each person to put experience, strength, and hope on the table. From the buffet created, group members can take whatever they need that looks nourishing and appealing to them and leave the rest for someone else. Somehow, God takes the loaves and fish offered up to Him in the support group's sharing, blesses them, and multiplies them to meet each person's need according to His riches in Christ.

Identifying, Learning, and Growing

Three primary needs are met through this buffet of common experience, strength, and hope. A support group is a fellowship of people who come together to share our common experience, strength, and hope with one another so that we can *identify in our struggles, learn about life and relationships, and grow in the ability to trust God and become all that He created us to be.*

A powerful healing experience in recovery ministry occurs the moment we walk through the door and into a group for the first time. Isolation comes to an end. We may have an immediate sense of relief at finding others who can understand what we are going through. We are no longer alone in feeling what we are feeling and experiencing what we are experiencing. We may be imperfect and sinful, and our lives may be affected and presently controlled by that condition in ourselves or in others, but God has provided a Savior to save us from that condition. Now that we have the acceptance and support of others who are going through the same thing, we can face and deal with that condition.

Identification allows support group members to empathize. Identification makes us quick to listen and slow to speak. Identification ensures that no one is likely to cast the first stone of condemnation. Christ knew the importance of identifying in our struggles. Hebrews 4:14–15 declares that Jesus is our high priest who can identify with our struggles and our imperfections, although He was without sin. When there is identification, trust can be developed. When there is identification, risks can be taken. When there is identification, it is much easier to be honest, knowing that understanding and acceptance are available.

Identification takes place automatically as we share. We introduce ourselves briefly to the group at the beginning of each meeting. That way all can realize that we are in the same boat and need the healing power of Jesus Christ to work in our lives if we are to overcome. Identifying in our struggles creates the atmosphere of safety so essential to healing. That identification is also encouraged by our responding to what someone shares in the group if we have had a similar experience or similar feelings. That validation of who we are and what we have experienced or may be experiencing affirms us. Then we can face ourselves honestly and openly, ready for God to work in our lives and in the lives of others in the group.

By sharing our common experience, strength, and hope, we learn about life and relationships. If we are to be set free, John 8:32 tells us, we need the truth. If we are to no longer be conformed to the world and our old ways, we can be transformed only through the renewing of our minds (Rom. 12:2). We need new information. We have to challenge faulty and distorted beliefs. We must learn new skills and behaviors if we are to experience different results in our lives.

In a support group we pool the truth that God reveals to each of us. Through the mistakes that are being made and shared without fear of failure or condemnation, we learn from one another about how to respond to and live life more effectively. We bring to the group all of our experiences and what God is teaching us and the new skills we are learning. Others may then learn these same skills and apply them to their lives.

Here we can develop and practice relationship skills in a safe environment with acceptance and encouragement. Here we can learn how to express feelings moderately and appropriately. Here we can practice being assertive and setting healthy limits. Here we can learn to own our feelings and respectfully listen and accept the feelings and thoughts of others. Here we can learn how to ask others for what we may need and how to meet the needs of others in a healthy, balanced manner. A support group is a laboratory of relationships. It is a place to learn how to be honest, to risk, and to trust.

As we share our common experience, strength, and hope with one another, we grow in the ability to trust God to do the work in us that we cannot do in ourselves. The accountability in the group keeps us from falling back into dangerous patterns of self-will. As we see ourselves mirrored by other group members as worthwhile and valuable, we gain hope and believe ourselves deserving of God's work in our lives. We take the risk of trusting.

I have observed that people may have difficulty in turning their will and lives over to God and really trusting Him to work in them because of experiences of mistrust in their previous human relationships. Some may have a recent history of betrayal or abandonment in relationships with spouses, friends, coworkers, or even other church members. Some may be carrying the hurt and fear of neglect or abuse in childhood by parents, teachers, or other family members. Support groups give wounded persons a new family, a place to rebuild trust and restore a damaged spirit. Until that happens on a human level, they will be unable to trust God on a spiritual level.

When they can experience a true sense of the family of God as there for them and trustworthy, they will then be able to approach God as their heavenly Father with childlike faith and trust.

Several years ago a man walked into our church office needing to see a pastor for help. He was concerned because whenever he tried to go to a church service, he had a severe panic attack and had to leave. As we worked in individual counseling for a few sessions, I found a pattern of severe parental abuse that had distorted his ability to relate to a loving heavenly Father. God was so fearful to him that he had to run away from God in the same way that he had learned to flee from the abuse of his earthly parents. Part of what I recommended to him was to become involved in Adult Children of Confusion. The group became a very healing place for him, and as he developed trusting relationships in the group, he was able to develop a trusting relationship with God. I received a call from him the day after he was able to sit through a church service for the first time in months. I remember his excitement as he told me, "God is my Father, and the support group is my new family!"

When I was in graduate school, I read a story as part of my course work in group counseling about the meaning and power of support groups. For me, it is the best picture of how and why support groups work.

The story took place in two scenes. One scene was set in hell. People were seated around a long table. In the center of the table was a large bowl of delicious beef stew. Its incredible aroma filled the room. All of the people sitting at the table were emaciated. Each had a long wooden spoon attached to one hand so that the person could not put it down or remove it. The spoons were long enough to reach the bowl, but when the people tried to bring a bite of stew to their mouths, the spoons were too long. They remained constantly frustrated.

The second scene was set in heaven. There, too, was a table with a large bowl of stew in the middle. People sat around the table with the same long wooden spoons attached to their hands. But these persons looked entirely different. They were content and well-fed. They always had enough to eat because each person would dip the spoon into the bowl of stew and then reach over and feed the person on the other side of the table. In doing so, they were all able to eat.

To me, this picture represents the meaning and purpose of support groups. When people come together and share with one another their common experience, strength, and hope, they offer support and nurture to everyone, and all get their needs met. I believe the power of a support group lies in its simplicity. It is not supposed to be anything other than what it says, a group that provides support. There are plenty of other groups, each with its own purpose and its vital place in the body of Christ, but there is also a place and a need for a support group. Resist the temptation to make it more, or less, than it is. Do not allow it to become another Bible study, prayer meeting, or sharing group. Do not let others try to make it into a therapy group. Let it accomplish its purpose and be the ministry of healing that it can be in the church.

A recovery movement is sweeping across the country. Approximately 500,000 support groups meet weekly to address numerous life circumstances. In the Atlanta area, groups address almost 150 different issues. By the end of this century, estimates are that there will be one million groups, and that sixty million Americans will be participants. The church must either provide a relevant place to minister to those needs or watch as proponents of the New Age and the secular humanists take over and influence the lives of people with their message rather than the gospel of Jesus Christ. But we are not to provide just another support group. The church must know and clearly present the distinctive characteristics of what it means to be a part of a Christ-centered support group. A recovery ministry has something to offer that secular support groups do not have. We'll take a look at these vital characteristics in the next chapter.

Chapter
6

Distinctive
Characteristics

We have already discussed the power of koinonia fellowship as the basis for the effectiveness of support groups in helping people to change. Secular support groups appropriate and use that truth to be successful and are able to do so to a great degree. God's truth is God's truth, and it benefits all of His creation, whether He is acknowledged as its source or not. But several distinctive characteristics of the Christ-centered support group should and do differentiate it from the secular support group. These characteristics are the essential reason why I believe that the Christ-centered support group can be even more effective than the secular support group, and why it is vital that the church become active in providing support groups to its members as a ministry and to the community as an outreach.

Support groups, whether secular or Christian, work because they are based on the principle that as people experience a new relationship with others who are going through a similar experience or struggle, they will change in the way they relate to themselves. But more is needed if people are to change not just their understanding about themselves but their actions that have become a pervasive and controlling force in their lives.

Alcoholics Anonymous certainly knew that change was not based on understanding and willpower, although it always begins with awareness and decisions based on that awareness. Change depends on a relationship with a power greater than myself that is able to do for me what I am unable to do for myself. That is the foundation of the Twelve Steps. It is the acknowledgment that I am powerless, my life is unmanageable, and I must turn myself completely over to the power greater than myself that can restore my life.

Stated in biblical terms, what I have just described is the process of conversion. Out of my awareness of my true state comes the need for faith. That faith leads to repentance; I turn from my way to God's way. This relationship is crucial to recovery from anything. My relationship with myself, no matter how much insight and determination I may have, will not be sufficient in the long run because I am imperfect and limited. My relationship with others, no matter how much support and encouragement they may give me, is not capable of changing my life ultimately because they, too, are imperfect and limited. That is why I cannot allow others to become my higher power, although for a time I may depend on them to show me the way. Another essential relationship is involved in recovery, and that relationship must be with a power greater than myself and others that is perfect and unlimited.

Alcoholics Anonymous has understood and accepted this premise for more than fifty years now. Only within the last decade has the proliferation of Twelve-Step groups patterned after AA sprung up and embraced this understanding. (One new Twelve-Step movement leaves out the concept of God as a higher power and relies on self and others, with their limitations and imperfections, to be the higher power. I believe that it will be limited in its ability to help people change for that very reason.) But most Twelve-Step groups acknowledge what has been basic Christian theology for two thousand years, even though our actions may not necessarily be consistent with those beliefs. We still try to go our own way and control our lives, asking God for help as we go along but struggling to be totally honest and walk completely in the light. The apostle Paul was completely honest about his limitations, the ultimate failure of human effort and willpower, and the absolute need for a power greater than himself:

> For I know that in me (that is, in my flesh) nothing good dwells; for to will is present with me, but how to perform what is good I do not find. For the good that I will to do, I do not do; but the evil I will not to do, that I practice. Now if I do what I will not to do, it is no longer I who do it, but sin that dwells in me. I find then a law, that evil is present with me, the one who wills to do good. For I delight in the law of God according to the inward man. But I see another law in my members, warring against the law of my mind, and bringing me into captivity to the law of sin which is in my members. O wretched man that I am! Who will deliver me from this body of death? (Rom. 7:18–24).

Paul understood what he desired to do. He certainly had the love, support, and encouragement of the Christian community of his time. But he knew that he needed a higher power than himself or others to set him free from his body of death. He named the higher power that he learned to depend on:

> I thank God—through Jesus Christ our Lord! So then, with the mind I myself serve the law of God, but with the flesh the law of sin. There is therefore now no condemnation to those who are in Christ Jesus. . . . For the law of the Spirit of life in Christ Jesus has made me free from the law of sin and death. For what the law could not do in that it was weak through the flesh, God did by sending His own Son in the likeness of sinful flesh, on account of sin: He condemned sin in the flesh, that the righteous requirement of the law might be fulfilled in us who do not walk according to the flesh but according to the Spirit (Rom. 7:25—8:4).

Paul recognized that the law, which to me represents our best human efforts to make ourselves good and acceptable to God and to others, was weak and inadequate. Only God through His Son Jesus Christ can do for us what we are incapable of doing for ourselves, no matter how hard we try to follow the law and do what we know we need to do. Paul then described how that changes the focus of our concentration. We no longer depend on our efforts; we depend on the work of the Holy Spirit. We must pray for and seek the knowledge of God's will for us and the courage to carry it out and put it into action in our lives, but the power to do so comes from the presence of the Holy Spirit working in us:

> For those who live according to the flesh set their minds on the things of the flesh, but those who live according to the Spirit, the things of the Spirit. For to be carnally minded [our own efforts and way] is death, but to be spiritually minded is life and peace. Because the carnal mind is enmity against God [and His way]; for it is not subject to the law of God, nor indeed can be. So then, those who are in the flesh cannot please God. But you are not in the flesh but in the Spirit, if indeed the Spirit of God dwells in you. Now if anyone does not have the Spirit of Christ, he is not His. And if Christ is in you, the body is dead because of sin, but the Spirit is life because of righteousness. But if the Spirit of Him who raised Jesus from the dead dwells in you, He who raised Christ from the dead will also give life to your mortal bodies through His Spirit who dwells in you (Rom. 8:5–11).

Paul said that the spirit we receive is not one of slavery to God leading us to fear Him but one of adoption by Him, which lets us know that we are children of God. We can approach Him confidently and eagerly as Abba, Father! We have an inheritance of life as His beloved children (Rom. 8:14–17). Twelve-Step research indicates that people who ultimately recover do so as a result of a belief in a higher power who is personal and knowable and cares for them. Christ-centered support groups have a power available to them that cannot be experienced in a secular support group.

Four Distinctive Characteristics

The distinctive characteristics of a Christ-centered support group have to do with knowing the *person* of God as the higher power and understanding the *process* He desires for us to experience. Knowing the person of God involves how we comprehend and relate to Him, Jesus Christ, and the Holy Spirit. Understanding the process He desires to accomplish in our lives through the group means accepting His call to the ministry of reconciliation. These factors uniquely define a Christ-centered support group and must be clearly stated within the group's purpose.

Let's consider how we are to comprehend and relate to the triune aspect of God first. In a Christ-centered support group,

1. God is understood and known to be our perfect heavenly Father who loves us with an unconditional, unfailing, and everlasting love that has been revealed to us in Christ Jesus.

2. Jesus Christ is acknowledged to be Lord, with all power greater than ourselves and our situations, who through His grace restores us to sanity and balance as we yield our lives and will to Him.

3. And the Holy Spirit represents Christ Jesus in our midst and unifies us as one family to encourage and support one another in the process of growth and change.

These three aspects give a Christ-centered support group its distinctive difference and make it much more effective in the lives of people than a secular support group. God can and does work in the lives of His people even through secular means, but we are instructed not to forsake the opportunity to fellowship with other Christians and stimulate one another to love and good deeds (Heb. 10:24–25).

1. God Is Understood to Be Our Perfect Heavenly Father

I have already mentioned the finding that people in a support group are more able to find and maintain recovery if they relate to a higher power who is knowable, personal, and caring. In a Christ-centered support group, people can find that higher power in a relationship with God through Jesus Christ. When the disciples wanted to know how to get to the Father, Jesus said,

> I am the way, the truth, and the life [the ultimate source of recovery]. No one comes to the Father except through Me. If you had known Me, you would have known My Father also; and from now on you know Him and have seen Him. . . . He who has seen Me has seen the Father. . . . Do you not believe that I am in the Father, and the Father in Me? The words that I speak to you I do not speak on My own authority; but the Father who dwells in Me does the works. Believe Me that I am in the Father and the Father in Me, or else believe Me for the sake of the works themselves (John 14:6–11).

God can be seen and known. He has a name and a face. His name is Jesus. Only Christ-centered support groups can offer that access to the Father. Only Christ-centered support groups offer a true understanding of the nature of God because He has been revealed in the words and actions of Jesus.

Because of Jesus, we know God to be our perfect heavenly Father. This fact is crucial, especially to persons who have experienced imperfect earthly parents. One of our support group members countered every passage I used to point out the love of God with another passage to find fault with herself. She lived with constant criticism from parents who picked out every flaw and imperfection and verbally and physically abused her. She had located these verses in the Bible and could quote them from memory. Another support group member could not bring himself to pray because he was so sure that God would not keep His promises and he would be disappointed or his prayers would be ignored. As a child, he had asked his father for a bike for Christmas and instead had been given another toy while an older, favored sibling received the bicycle.

Jesus contrasted the nature of God as our perfect heavenly Father with that of our imperfect earthly parents to show that God is attentive and responsive to our feelings and needs and to illustrate His unfailing love for His children (Luke 11:9–13). In the book of John, Jesus called God Father over one hundred times. Paul referred to the spirit of adoption that we have received from God that allows us to approach Him without fear and cry, "Abba, Father" (Rom. 8:14–16); the word *Abba* is a term of endearment and familiarity similar to calling a parent Daddy today. James noted the trustworthiness and the unfailing consistency of God as our Father (James 1:17). Every good thing given to us and every perfect gift is from our heavenly Father, with whom there is no variation or changing of nature.

Christ commented on the unconditional love of God: "For God so loved the world that He gave His only begotten Son, that whoever believes in Him should not perish" (John 3:16). It is agape love, an absolutely unconditional love. It depends not on the worth of the receiver but on the nature of the Giver. Paul reflected that same understanding in Romans 5:8: "But God demonstrates His own love [agape] toward us, in that while we were still sinners, Christ died for us." God's love does not depend on our merits and efforts, which are imperfect and fail miserably due to sin and its various manifestations in our lives; it depends on His unconditional love for His children.

Finally, Jesus spoke of God's everlasting love. We are Jesus' flock, and He is our shepherd who, because of His love, lays down His life for His sheep so that we will not perish. Jesus declared that by doing so, He has given us eternal life, and no one can snatch us out of His hand. God, His Father, is greater than all, and no one is able to take us out of the Father's hands (John 10:25–30). Paul was convinced that "neither death nor life, nor angels nor principalities nor powers, nor things present nor things to come, nor height nor depth, nor any other created thing, shall be able to separate us from the love of God which is in Christ Jesus" (Rom. 8:38–39). That is the essence of everlasting love.

2. *Jesus Christ Is Acknowledged to Be Lord*

The second vital aspect of a Christ-centered support group that makes it different from what the secular world can offer to people is that Jesus Christ is acknowledged to be Lord, with all power greater than ourselves and our situations, who through His grace restores us to sanity and balance as we yield our lives and will to Him.

While secular support groups may look to many higher powers to enable them to do what they cannot do for themselves, the Christ-centered support group looks only to one power. Jesus Christ is acknowledged to be Lord, including Lord of our recovery. That is clearly acknowledged in Steps Six and Seven of the Twelve Steps. We believe what Christ said about Himself to His disciples when He declared, "I am the way, the truth, and the life. No one comes to the Father except through Me" (John 14:6). We affirm what Paul reminded the Philippians: "God also has highly exalted Him [Jesus] and given Him the name which is above every name, that at the name of Jesus every knee should bow, of those in heaven, and of those on earth, and of those under the earth, and that every tongue should confess that Jesus Christ is Lord, to the glory of God the Father" (Phil. 2:9–11).

Jesus is Lord not just because He is a higher power but because He is the highest power. His teaching amazed people with its power (Luke 4:32). He had the power to heal (Luke 5:17). He had the power to forgive sins (Matt. 9:6). He had the power (authority) over all humankind (John 17:2). He had the power (resurrection power) to lay down His life and to take it up again (John 10:18). He was able to give us the power, since He possessed it, to become the children of God (John 1:12). In the same way He was able to give to His disciples the power to cast out demons and heal the sick (Luke 9:1). After His resurrection, He declared that He had all power, including power over death, in heaven and on earth (Matt. 28:18); that when He returned, it would be with great power (Mark 13:26); and that He is now sitting at the right hand (the place of authority) of the power of God (Luke 22:69).

For all of His power to do wondrous works and mighty miracles, His resurrection power establishes Him as the highest power. No other person or source can claim that power. Paul reminded the Romans of that when he observed, "[Christ was] declared to be the Son of God with power according to the Spirit of holiness, by the resurrection from the dead" (Rom. 1:4). Later on, as he established the power necessary to deliver us from the bondage of the law of sin and death, Paul went straight to the heart of the matter: "But if the Spirit of Him who raised Jesus from the dead dwells in you, He who raised Christ from the dead will also give life to your mortal bodies through His Spirit who dwells in you" (Rom. 8:11).

There can be no greater power available in support groups to help people overcome in any area of their lives than that of Jesus Christ. Anyone who calls on the name of the Lord Jesus Christ, and the power that is associated with that name above all names, will be saved (Rom. 10:13). We need to be saved from many things in our lives by a power greater than ourselves. Jesus came to save us not just from judgment but from the works of our flesh, the world, and Satan in whatever ways we are being deceived or destroyed by them. His desire is to restore our lives fully to the balance that is God's will for us. Jesus stated His purpose for being: "I have come that they may have life, and that they may have it more abundantly" (John 10:10).

But to experience this highest power working in our lives, we must realize it can be accomplished only through the grace of Christ, and it requires that we yield our will and our lives to Him.

Paul reminded the Ephesians of the power of God's grace that is in Christ and also of how undeserving we are to receive it and how incapable we are of earning it through our efforts. It is truly a gift of unmerited favor. Paul counted himself as one who needed and experienced the grace of God to overcome the desires of his flesh and mind:

> And you He made alive, who were dead in trespasses and sins, in which you once walked according to the course of this world, according to the prince of the power of the air, the spirit who now works in the sons of disobedience, among whom also we all once conducted ourselves in the lusts of our flesh, fulfilling the desires of the flesh and of the mind, and were by nature children of wrath, just as the others. But God, who is rich in mercy, because of His great love with which He loved us, even when we were dead in trespasses, made us alive together with Christ (by grace you have been

saved), and raised us up together, and made us sit together in the heavenly places in Christ Jesus, that in the ages to come He might show the exceeding riches of His grace in His kindness toward us in Christ Jesus. *For by grace you have been saved through faith, and that not of yourselves; it is the gift of God, not of works [our best efforts], lest anyone should boast.* For we are His workmanship, created in Christ Jesus for good works, which God prepared beforehand that we should walk in them (Eph. 2:1–10, emphasis added).

Paul understood the power of the grace of Jesus Christ. He accepted his limitations and weaknesses as an opportunity to experience the sufficiency of the grace of Christ. He realized that his weaknesses offered to Christ resulted in Christ's giving him the strength and power to overcome (2 Cor. 12:7–10). This awareness of the limitation of self-will and effort is key to the power available for healing in Christ-centered support groups.

I knew a very talented young woman who struggled with a personal sense of dis-grace. She became driven to make things happen in her life through her own efforts. She never could fully turn her will and the control of her life over to Christ and rest in His grace. Her life was extremely compulsive and out of control, and yet she never would admit that she needed the help of others and seek support. Eventually, when circumstances that she could no longer control overwhelmed her, she committed suicide.

As we will discover later, the first three steps of the Twelve Steps lay a foundation for recovery. Step Three calls on us to turn our will and our lives over to the care of God. This is the only action that we are capable of taking and are called to take to allow Christ to work in our lives. Jesus taught His disciples that if people desired to come after Him and experience His power working in their lives, they must deny their will and way and follow His way, no matter the effort or the cost (Matt. 16:24–26).

3. *The Holy Spirit Represents Christ in Our Midst*

Only Christ-centered support groups have a power that great that they can turn their will and their lives over to. And only Christ-centered support groups can experience the koinonia fellowship of the Holy Spirit unifying individuals into one body working together to overcome common struggles, and guiding and directing the group into the truth, which ultimately sets us free.

Jesus taught the disciples about the work that the Holy Spirit would do in their midst. He told them He had to leave so that the Holy Spirit could come. Jesus identified the purposes that the Holy Spirit will fulfill within the group fellowship (John 16:7–15). First, the Holy Spirit will glorify Christ and represent Him in our midst, taking those things that God has for us and disclosing them to us. Second, the Holy Spirit will convict us concerning sin and righteousness, showing us those things that we need to stop doing and those things that we need to start doing. And third, the Holy Spirit will guide us into all of the truth that we need to know to be set free.

Only Christ-centered support groups have access to this source of wisdom and truth. Only Christ-centered support groups can experience the deeper bonds and fellowship of the Holy Spirit. That fellowship of love can cover a multitude of sins (1 Pet. 4:8), and the kindness and patience of God reflected to one another in the fellowship of His Holy Spirit lead us to repentance and change (Rom. 2:4).

One fellow ended up in one of our support groups to impress a judge and avoid going to jail. He had a history of violent anger, abuse, and assault. I have watched that person change over the past several years and make peace with himself and with others. I have seen him restore a marriage and an alienated relationship with his children. I rejoiced with him when he came to know God as his Father through Jesus Christ. That person thanked me for the recovery ministry, which has become such a part of his life: "I have never before felt in my life the love and acceptance that I have experienced in group. It has allowed me to become open and honest with myself, God, my spouse, and my children. It has saved my life."

4. Reconciliation Takes Place

One last aspect of Christ-centered support groups gives them their unique power to affect people's lives in addition to their relationship with God, Jesus, and the Holy Spirit. It has to do with reconciliation.

I heard a statement attributed to Karl Menninger, the renowned psychiatrist and founder of the Menninger Clinic, that touches on this subject. He said that if people could forgive themselves and forgive others, he believed 90 percent of his patients could walk out of the hospital the next day. Approximately 10 percent of the emotional problems had their source in organic and biochemical disorders. The rest had to do with the nature of the patients' relationships with themselves and others, including God.

The process of reconciliation with self, others, and God is a powerful healing process that occurs in Christ-centered support groups. Christ provided our reconciliation with God and allowed us to be at peace with God (Eph. 2:13–16). God determined that reconciliation with Himself could come only through Jesus Christ and His sacrifice on the cross (Col. 1:19–23). Because of that reconciliation, we have been saved from the wrath of God, and we can now experience His love (Rom. 5:8–11).

Christ provided a way for us to be reconciled to God, and because of that reconciliation, we can be reconciled to ourselves. (We will see later how Steps Four and Five of the Twelve Steps lead us to that reconciliation.) But Christ also calls on us to be reconciled to one another. In the Sermon on the Mount He instructs us that we must be reconciled with one another before He can freely work in our lives (Matt. 5:21–24). (Steps Eight and Nine of the Twelve Steps lead us into that reconciliation with one another.)

Reconciliation is not the same as restoration. We are called on to be reconciled to others, but we have no control over whether they choose to be reconciled so that the relationship can be restored. As far as we are able, we are to pursue peace with others and not allow bitterness to take root in our lives, but we are not responsible for their response or the hardness of their hearts, which may prevent them from receiving our amends.

Paul recognized the power of reconciliation. Our reconciliation with God through Jesus Christ allows us to become reconciled with ourselves and become new persons, overcoming and leaving the old things behind. God now gives us that same ministry of reconciliation to share with others. Paul instructed the Corinthian fellowship,

If anyone is in Christ, he is a new creation; old things have passed away; behold, all things have become new. Now all things are of God, who has reconciled us to Himself through Jesus Christ, and has given us the ministry of reconciliation, that is, that God was in Christ reconciling the world to Himself, not imputing their trespasses to them, and has committed to us the word of reconciliation (2 Cor. 5:17–19).

The willingness to be reconciled is expressed through the willingness to offer forgiveness. Jesus taught that we are to be willing to forgive, even as we have been forgiven. In the Lord's Prayer we are taught to pray to God to forgive our debts only as we are willing to forgive the debts of others (Matt. 6:12). Jesus instructed the disciples about their need to be willing to forgive up to seventy times seven (Matt. 18:21–22). He shared a parable with them about a man who had been forgiven a great debt by his king but refused to forgive a lesser debt that another man owed him. The king was furious and then required the first man to repay his debt in full. Jesus indicated that God has the same expectation for us and forgives us as we are willing in our hearts to forgive one another (Matt. 18:23–35).

One of the most powerful moments that I have ever witnessed took place in a meeting of all our support groups. During a time of personal testimony, a group member confessed publicly to sexually abusing his child years before and asked for forgiveness. His spouse, who was in another support group, was present, and she came forward and tearfully embraced the abuser. As she did so, a woman who had been abused by her father came forward and testified. She had been carrying a deep resentment toward her father for years. He had never acknowledged what he had done and the pain it had caused in her life. When she heard the person confess his sin and ask for forgiveness, she said that God immediately healed her of that bitterness and put understanding and acceptance for him in her heart. She then embraced the abuser and offered him her forgiveness. All of that came about in a large room full of people. Later, three other sexual abuse victims told me privately of the healing in their hearts and lives as a result of what happened that day.

These four distinctive characteristics are vital to the purpose and function of Christ-centered support groups. Anyone who leads a Christ-centered support group must understand these distinctions. These differences should be stated in writing as a part of the group's structured format, which guides the group. They should be seen and read by all persons who become part of the group. They should be affirmed in prayer as a group opens and closes its sharing time together. More important, these characteristics should be modeled in the lives of group members as they share their experience, strength, and hope with one another. Ultimately, these four things determine whether the perfect and unlimited power of God will work in the lives of group members.

Before we move on to setting up and maintaining a recovery ministry, we need to arrive at an understanding of goals for participants in a Christ-centered support group. These goals allow a group to accomplish the purpose it has established for itself. We have already seen what a support group is and what makes it distinctively different as a Christ-centered group. Now we need to identify what support group members do as part of a support group fellowship.

Chapter
7

Goals and Expectations

Before we get into the specifics of setting up and maintaining a recovery ministry, we need to understand what a support group does. We do that by establishing goals and expectations for group participants. Each person in the group must meet these goals and expectations if the group is going to accomplish its purpose.

Each group, of course, will have an individual purpose. For example, the purpose of an addicts group would be to deal with chemical dependency. Or the purpose of a sexual abuse survivors group would be to come to grips with childhood sexual abuse. However, the goals and expectations for each group are the same. Each group insists that its members work toward three goals: (1) to be safe for one another; (2) to accept one another; and (3) to be responsible for ourselves. Let's explore each expectation.

1. To Be Safe for One Another

To facilitate recovery, members of a support group must be safe for one another. Unless a group is safe, members will not feel free to take the risks to reach the level of honesty required to know and be set free by the truth. David realized that God desired truth in his inmost being if he were to find the wisdom to cleanse his heart, renew his spirit, and restore his life to balance and sanity (Ps. 51). Some very definite things that we do or do not do in support groups create and maintain an atmosphere of safety.

To be safe for one another, group members maintain anonymity and confidentiality at all times. Group members are not to be identified to anyone outside the group at any time for any reason—not to friends, spouses, elders, or even pastors, no matter how interested and concerned they may be. Group members are to be careful in talking about the group with others if someone could be identified as a part of the group.

Maintaining confidentiality means not repeating anything that anyone shares in the group to anyone outside the group at any time for any reason. What is shared in the group stays within the four walls of the meeting room and in the hearts of those who share those experiences in common with one another.

There may be three exceptions to this expectation: (1) the person indicates a suicidal desire, (2) the person speaks of a homicidal intent, or (3) a minor child is being physically or sexually abused. Sharing that information in good faith with the appropriate person or authority to protect someone from harm should not be considered a breach of confidentiality.

Maintaining confidentiality also means that group members do not talk about another group member or his or her issues unless that person is present to respond. This avoids the danger of gossip and the possibility that someone may be misrepresented to others outside the group who may overhear a conversation between group members. Concern for a group member should be communicated directly to that person in a kind and open manner.

Obviously, members of the group are free to share anything about themselves that they are doing or learning from their involvement in a support group with anyone they choose to. That can even be part of recovery and is encouraged in Step Twelve of the Twelve-Step process of recovery. Biblically, that is the testimony we have to share, and Scripture states that Satan is overcome through the blood of the Lamb (Jesus Christ) and the word of our testimony (Rev.

12:11). We *cannot* share anyone else's testimony. We must allow others to share their testimonies when and where they choose.

To be safe for one another, group members do not minimize, criticize, judge, or condemn what another member may be thinking, feeling, or doing. It is the work of the Holy Spirit to convict. Our job is to reflect the kindness and acceptance of God, for Christ's sake, and allow Him to lead persons in the group to repent and change the thoughts, feelings, and behaviors that are sabotaging their lives. Christ said that He came into the world not to condemn it but to save it (John 3:17). The work of a support group is not to condemn members for anything they may be thinking, feeling, or doing but to offer salvation (safety) through Jesus Christ.

To be safe for one another, group members do not permit direct confrontation or physical or verbal attacks. Confrontation doesn't change behavior. It may stop it momentarily, but unless people choose to change, the new behavior will not be permanent. The desire to change must be internally rather than externally motivated. People change as the result of encouragement to change. (Keep in mind that we are referring here to the process of change in support groups. There are a time and a place for the confrontation of an intervention to get people to stop self-destructive behavior.)

Encouragement puts courage into hearts to change. Perhaps that is why God indicated to the prophet Ezekiel, "I will give them one heart, and I will put a new spirit within them, and take the stony heart out of their flesh, and give them a [new] heart of flesh, that they may walk in My statutes and keep My judgments and do them; and they shall be My people, and I will be their God" (Ezek. 11:19–20).

Under no circumstances are there to be physical or verbal attacks on group members. Physical attacks are not just physical blows but consist of any acts of intimidation through the use of force or the suggested or implied threat of force. Verbal attacks are judgmental statements, sarcasm, name-calling, or demeaning or belittling statements. Verbal attacks can also involve excessive, intimidating displays of anger or rage toward a group member.

Within the support group, confrontation always takes place *indi-*

rectly. As people assume responsibility for focusing only on themselves and sharing their experience, strength, and hope, they are forced to look at their lives. It is an internal confrontation.

Direct confrontation does have a place in a recovery ministry. It comes as we develop relationships of trust with particular individuals and give them the right to influence the way we see ourselves. It can take place as we choose someone to be a sponsor, or when we covenant with a person or group of people to work the Twelve Steps together or to be a part of a Family of Choice group (which will be discussed later). Bonds of trust have been established and tested over time that make it safe to give a person the right to influence how we view ourselves through direct confrontation.

To be safe for one another, group members do not attempt to fix other people's situations, give advice, take others' inventories, or tell others how to work their recovery programs. Using a support group to problem-solve situations is dangerous because it communicates a lack of confidence in persons' ability to think and decide for themselves. It inadvertently can create a sense of inadequacy and shame because it says, in effect, that they do not know the right thing to do and they need others to tell them what to do. Putting the group in the position of giving advice and being the source of wisdom for group members is dangerous because it creates an unhealthy dependency on the group as the higher power rather than on God.

Taking others' inventories refers to the inventory steps that are part of the Twelve-Step process of recovery. When we take others' inventories, we focus on what they may be doing or need to change rather than concentrating on what God needs to do in our lives. Jesus warned against this practice when He instructed us not to worry about the speck in another person's eye until after we first removed the plank from our own (Matt. 7:5).

Working others' programs of recovery happens when we involve ourselves in deciding how, when, and what they should change rather than allowing God to make everything appropriate in His time. The danger is that we set ourselves up as the higher power, which we are not. And a spirit of judgment and condemnation may come into play, which discourages others from becoming responsible for themselves.

It is safe when group members simply share experience, strength, and hope. Others in the group can then take what they need from what is shared as God's Holy Spirit shows them the truth they need to be free according to His timing for their lives.

To be safe for one another, group members follow the established format, guidelines, traditions, and principles. The format determines what takes place in a group meeting and provides an order to follow. The guidelines determine how things are shared in the meeting and the group's response to what is shared. The traditions protect the general purpose and the overall health, balance, and well-being of the group. The principles guide the group in dealing with specific situations that may affect the group and its functioning. All of these together create structured boundaries that protect the group and its members from anything detrimental or destructive. (They will be discussed in detail later, as well as the process through which they are established or amended.)

Recently, we had to address the question of profanity in the support groups. It had never been a big problem. Most group members were not comfortable using it, but we didn't want to be judgmental and insist that others clean up their act to get our support. Then a person new to our fellowship had to leave the group because of a panic attack brought on when someone used profanity. Even though it was not addressed at anyone and was just an expression of some very painful feelings, it proved to be very threatening to this new group member who had been constantly abused with profanity in her family and her marriage. The profanity made the group unsafe for her, and she was unable to return to it afterward. Other group members had similar experiences and feelings whenever profanity was used in meetings. When anything makes a support group unsafe, it becomes a group issue. Safety is vital to a group's well-being.

Group members must be safe for one another. But safety provides only the atmosphere for change. Acceptance encourages change, and it is the second expectation and goal that group members should actively pursue.

2. To Accept One Another

It is not enough for support group members to merely provide an environment of safety for each person to grow in; they must also actively work to be accepting of one another. The atmosphere of safety allows people to share openly and honestly about themselves, and the presence of acceptance encourages people to grow and change.

I believe the Bible has this kind of support in mind when it calls on the body of Christ to edify, or build up, one another. Paul instructed the early church that one of the goals as a fellowship should be to edify one another. He advised the church in Rome, "Let each of us please his neighbor for his good, leading to edification" (Rom. 15:2). He observed what was happening when the church in Corinth assembled and urged, "Let all things be done for edification" (1 Cor. 14:26). He exhorted the church at Thessalonica to continue to "comfort each other and edify one another, just as you also are doing" (1 Thess. 5:11). He taught the church at Ephesus to speak the truth in love so that the body of Christ would grow and build up (edify) itself in love (Eph. 4). He told them that they were to speak no unwholesome words but only say and do those things that resulted in edification so that others would receive the grace sufficient to meet their need at that moment (Eph. 4:29).

If support groups are going to provide people with the courage to change, members must be supportive and accepting of one another.

To accept one another, group members listen attentively with open minds and hearts to whatever others share. People must be unconditionally accepted where they are. It is the job of the Holy Spirit to convict and of God to change thoughts, feelings, and behaviors as people turn over their will and lives to Him. To close our hearts and minds to what others share is to abandon them and reject their needs, communicating to them that they are unacceptable.

To accept one another, group members ask questions only to clarify and understand. No one should ever feel put on the spot in a support group. There is a difference between questions that interrogate and questions that seek to understand better. Usually, questions that interrogate begin with the word *why* and imply that the person is stupid, wrong, or bad. They create defensiveness and close down communication between people. Questions that ask how a person feels or what an experience was like invite openness and indicate interest and acceptance that encourage a person to disclose more without fear of judgment.

To accept one another, group members affirm one another whenever anyone takes the risk of sharing and being honest. It takes courage to overcome the fear of disapproval or judgment that people may expect if they are totally honest. For some, sharing who they are means risking rejection or abandonment. Group members need to offer support to those who take that risk, no matter how small it may be. They may simply thank the persons for sharing, or they may express how they identify and relate to what the persons have shared.

One new group member had been so emotionally abused that she was unable to introduce herself for the first two or three meetings. The group welcomed her, thanked her for coming, and encouraged her to return. Finally, she was able to slowly and hesitantly introduce herself. It took a lot of effort and even some tears. When she finished, the group cheered and whistled and applauded the effort made and the risk she had taken to tell who she was and why she had come to the group.

To accept one another, group members encourage one another to change, grow, and overcome. It is vital to instill hope in group members that change is possible, and that it is happening, although it may seem a slow, difficult process. Others need to share their testimonies of how God is working in their lives through the support group. This is one time when it may be helpful to have people look back and see how far they have come rather than focus on how much farther they have to go. The group affirms that they can do all things through Christ who gives them strength. Group members must constantly encourage one another to put courage into the hearts of people to change.

To accept one another, group members identify and relate to one another's successes and failures. The group must notice and applaud any success a member experiences in the process of recovery. I have seen group members actually give someone a standing ovation for a change that has taken place. Even if the result is less than perfect, affirming the effort is important. Focus on the efforts people are making, not the results. The results will come if the efforts are continued.

Relating to failure in a similar manner is just as important. It is helpful to have other group members relate their experiences in failing before they learned how to succeed in an area of recovery. Group members must be reminded that recovery is an imperfect process and that failing is the normal process through which we learn to do things better. Group members affirm one another as perfectly imperfect and clarify that there is a difference between failing and being a failure. I am reminded of the man who asked Thomas Edison if his more than one thousand failed experiments in his attempts to make an electric light bulb had discouraged him. Edison replied that they had not. After all, he had learned one thousand ways *not* to make a light bulb! Group members support one another by reminding one another that the normal process of learning to do something involves *not* doing it well at first.

To accept one another, group members model recovery and are willing to sponsor others in their recovery. There is a saying in Alcoholics Anonymous that you can't keep what you don't give away. Group members must be willing to model the recovery that they have achieved for the sake of the persons still struggling to gain that recovery. Group members must be willing to sponsor other group members and help them along in recovery. More will be said about sponsorship later, but it is a basic biblical principle. Paul reminded the Romans that those who are strong ought to bear the weaknesses of those without strength and not just please themselves. Each is to please others to build them up (Rom. 15:1–2). Group members have an obligation to support others in the same way that they have been supported.

To accept one another, group members remind one another to be patient with the process of recovery and to be gentle with themselves and their mis-

takes. Encouragement is the key to support groups. God, in His sovereign wisdom, chooses to instantly deliver some persons from their afflictions. However, God's usual process for change is through growth over time. There is, indeed, "a season, a time for every purpose under heaven," as the writer of Ecclesiastes observed, and God has an appropriate timing for everything (Eccl. 3:1–11). Recovery follows the imperfect pattern of growth. This process must be understood to support one another and offer group members the acceptance leading to self-acceptance.

If Paul visited a support group, I think that he would remind us to

> glory in tribulations, knowing that tribulation produces perseverance [patience]; and perseverance, character; and character, hope [one of the three things we share with one another]. Now hope does not disappoint, because the love of God has been poured out in our hearts by the Holy Spirit who was given to us (Rom. 5:3–5).

If James were part of a support group fellowship, I think that he would urge group members to "count it all joy when you fall into various trials [mistakes], knowing that the testing of your faith produces patience. But let patience have its perfect work, that you may be perfect [mature] and complete, lacking nothing" (James 1:2–5).

To accept one another, group members do not interrupt or enter into side conversations while others are speaking. The most important thing taking place in a group is what a person is sharing. Each speaker must be given the undivided attention of the group to validate the significance of what is being shared. Interrupting or speaking to others while someone is sharing, even if it is only a brief side remark, sends a clear message that what is being shared is not as important as something or someone else.

To accept one another, group members do not determine what others think, feel, or need without checking it out with them. Acceptance is shown through being willing to understand what others think, feel, or need rather than determining for ourselves those things or judging the thoughts and intents of others' hearts and minds. Sometimes the favorite aerobic exercise of people in recovery seems to be jumping to conclusions. We should ask questions and understand clearly what others think, feel, and need instead of assuming that we know. A favorite saying in our support groups is, "When in doubt, check it out." It avoids a lot of misunderstandings. It shows respect by allowing people to have their unique reality as determined by God rather than by human beings.

To accept one another, group members do not interfere with the expression of painful feelings. This is a tough one for Christians who are oriented to comforting one another with the same comfort that they have received from God. What we are talking about here, however, is a question of timing. Ecclesiastes 3 refers to a time to mourn and a time to be comforted. One of the most supportive things that a group can do is allow its members to bring painful feelings out into the light where they can be accepted, learned from, and then released. Don't minimize hurt or sadness by comforting and attempting to remove them too quickly. Allow them to run their course, then comfort. In the Sermon on the Mount, Jesus taught that mourning was a blessed thing to do because it ultimately leads to comfort. But we must mourn first. We must dip into the deep well of feelings before we can pour them out.

In practical terms, that means sitting quietly and attentively while others share and process intense or painful feelings. God will take care of them and give them wisdom regarding what they need to do with their pain. Part of that wisdom may come afterward when another group member shares experience, strength, and hope about a similar situation. Don't interrupt the expression of the feelings. That would interfere with the release and the healing. Don't touch the persons while they are mourning, except perhaps with a light touch to let them know that someone is there for them while they are going through the feelings. That diverts the attention away from the feelings to the person attempting to prematurely comfort. If someone needs a tissue, place one quietly in the hand, but let the person continue mourning. The whole group should simply be there through the process and witness the feelings. The persons gain a tremendous sense of acceptance, which helps them to become willing to release the feelings to God.

The time to comfort is after the season of mourning. After the expression of the feelings has run its course, offer comfort through empathetic words or a reassuring touch. Comfort is vital, but it is the end result of mourning and requires special sensitivity and good timing.

I was in a group meeting, and a person said he had so much bottled up that he just wanted to scream and get it all out. The group members were so accepting and supportive that they gave the person permission to let go. What began as an anguished cry turned into deep sobs. After a few more minutes, the sobs turned to quiet tears. The group then went on with the sharing while the person continued to silently weep and mourn. After the meeting, many went to him to offer more acceptance and comfort for what he had expressed.

Even after people experience safety in a group and receive the acceptance of others, they will not change until they make a decision to be responsible for themselves. This is the third expectation that a group has as a goal for its members.

3. To Be Responsible for Ourselves

We must be responsible for ourselves if we are to be in control of our lives. When we make other people, things, or circumstances responsible for our happiness or unhappiness, our success or failure, our lives are out of our control and can be tossed around by any whim, accident, or passing fancy. When we focus on what someone else is doing or not doing to us, we feel helpless and powerless. We relate to life as victims.

God doesn't allow us to define ourselves as victims or martyrs or to invite others to our pity party. To give other persons, things, or circumstances that power is to make them our gods and give them power over us; instead, we must turn to the one true God, the living Christ, who has all power in heaven and earth.

To take responsibility for my life means that I have the ability to respond to things in new and different ways. There is a saying in recovery circles: "If I am not the problem, there is no solution." That doesn't mean I am to blame for all of the things that I may be experiencing, but I can control only my thoughts, feelings, and behavior, not those of others. I have to accept my powerlessness over other people, circumstances, or things.

Taking responsibility for ourselves is not the same as running our lives according to self-will. As Step One of the Twelve Steps shows us, that leads only to unmanageable lives. Taking responsibility for ourselves means focusing on what God's will is for our lives and what He desires for us to do, and leaving the rest for Him to take care of in His way and in His time.

To be responsible for ourselves, group members speak only from personal experience. We are experts only on ourselves. We know what we feel, think, and need, not what others may feel, think, and need. We know what God has done and needs to do in our lives, not what He needs to do in the lives of others.

Group members speak only from what I call the "responsible I" rather than the "advisory or accusative you" or the "generalized we." If I share what *I* think, feel, experience, or need, I am being responsible. If I speak in terms of what *you* think, feel, need, or have done or may be doing, I am giving advice or making an accusation and judgment about your thoughts, feelings, or behavior. If I refer to what *we* think, feel, need, or do, I am generalizing and implying that my experience is the same as yours. It is similar, but it will never be the same and I can't presume to speak for anyone else. I must let others speak for themselves. I am responsible to speak only from personal experience.

To be responsible for ourselves, group members are committed to keeping the focus on ourselves and our recovery. We accomplish nothing by talking about someone else who cannot be controlled. We are productive when we talk about ourselves and what we need to do differently.

I can't change my circumstances, but I can change my perspective about them and my response to them. By taking the responsibility to change what I can change, I find that I am no longer powerless.

As much as I am concerned about my parents, children, spouse, and friends, I am not and cannot be responsible for them unless I want to be their higher power and take God's place in their lives. (Understand I am not talking about minor children who are dependent on me. Even then, I am not in the group to work on them. By taking responsibility for myself and helping myself, I am ultimately helping them.) I am concerned about others, I pray for them, and I turn them over to God to work in their lives according to His will for them, not mine. My responsibility is to focus on finding and working out His will for me in my life.

To be responsible for ourselves, group members speak the truth honestly and appropriately. In recovery we tend to live in extremes, which is particularly evident in the way we communicate. We deny or indirectly express feelings, or we express them explosively and too directly. One aspect of communicating the truth responsibly requires that we learn to express thoughts and feelings directly to check things out and resolve conflict. Misunderstandings, overreactions, misinterpretations, and unresolved conflicts that have accumulated over a period of time are typically a major factor in the lives of people in recovery, and often are the source of the problem that brings them into recovery. A slogan often heard in recovery is, "You can't heal what you can't feel (and express)!"

A second aspect of responsibly speaking the truth is communicating it appropriately. The opposite of one extreme is the other extreme, not balance. The opposite of dysfunctional is still dysfunctional, not functional. As group members, we are to strive for moderate, appropriate expression of feelings. We may feel an emotion intensely, but we are expected to learn to be aware of timing, dosage, and form when it comes to expressing feelings to the group. Timing involves waiting patiently for our turn to share and the appropriate time to share. There will not be enough time for us to express all of the feelings we may have about an issue without depriving other members of an opportunity to share. Dosage means that we are both selective and concise in the feelings we express. Form involves the way we share feelings. Often, people in recovery have backgrounds of verbal abuse, and the way that feelings are expressed can seem threatening. For that reason, we must own our feelings (use the "responsible I"), not accuse, judge, or threaten in any way, and avoid profanity. Being aware of timing, dosage, and form will keep communication of feelings responsible and appropriate.

To be responsible for ourselves, group members are willing to risk being honest, vulnerable, and trusting of others and God in order to change and grow. One of my favorite posters shows a graceful sailboat anchored in a peaceful cove. The caption says, "Ships are safe in a harbor, but that's not what ships are for." Ships are meant to sail. We are meant to grow in relationship to others and to God. We must take risks if we are to change and grow. Earnie Larsen puts it this way: "If nothing changes, nothing changes."

It is the group's responsibility to be safe and supportive, but it is our responsibility to take the risk of being honest with the group about what is happening in our lives. We must be willing to be vulnerable and break the rules that say don't talk, don't feel, and don't trust. We must trust others and God that when we drop the denial and pretense and present ourselves honestly, the way we really are, we will not encounter criticism, shame, or condemnation. Instead, we will receive the acceptance and encouragement we need to face and overcome what is controlling our lives and keeping us from being the persons God created us to be.

It is risky and requires a giant leap of faith, especially for those who have developed walls to protect themselves from abuse. It is a giant leap of faith, but it should not be a blind leap of faith. Group members must take time to get to know one another and to feel safe in the group.

To be responsible for ourselves, group members put awareness and acceptance into action to take steps to recovery. I remember reading somewhere that awareness without action is like a parachute that opens on the first bounce! It doesn't help us. We will remain in our self-destructive patterns until we act on the awareness and acceptance that we gain from being in a support group and having others share their experience, strength, and hope.

To be responsible for ourselves, group members remain humble and teach-

able, being open to insight and wisdom from others and from God. Humility must be present if God is going to work in our lives. God declared through the prophet Isaiah that He dwells with "him who has a contrite and humble spirit, to revive the spirit of the humble, and to revive the heart of the contrite ones" (Isa. 57:15). The opposite of humility is pride, which maintains denial and defensiveness and prevents God from working in our lives directly or indirectly. It keeps us from seeing and accepting the truths of God's Word for our lives and the wisdom that others in the group can offer us concerning recovery.

Peter, perhaps more than anyone, understood the danger of pride. In 1 Peter 5:5-7 he shared what he learned about humility from his personal experience. Younger men are to be subject to their elders. Certainly, in support groups we must be willing to learn from those who have more experience and recovery wisdom to offer. That is the basis of sponsorship, as we will see later.

Humility is to characterize our sharing, for God is opposed to the proud but gives grace to the humble. Wisdom is to be both given and received with humility in support groups, knowing that God's grace is responsible for any good work that we are able to do. We are to humble ourselves and place our lives and our recovery in God's hands so that He may exalt us at the proper time. We are not to worry about how He may choose to work or when but trust that He cares and knows what we need and will do for us what we are unable to do for ourselves. Step Seven of the Twelve-Step process of recovery calls on us to humbly, on our knees, ask God to change whatever needs to be changed in our lives. The key to His giving us the grace that we need for recovery is whether or not we are humble and teachable.

To be responsible for ourselves, group members accept that God's timing is individual and perfect. It does no good to compare my recovery with the recovery of anyone else. My recovery is uniquely mine. Its order, progress, and timing will be exactly what I need for them to be. I will not be given more than I can bear. God knows my needs better than I can determine them by comparing myself to others in the group.

Conversely, I do not occupy myself with determining whether others in the group are recovering in the "right" way and at the "right" pace.

One person joined our groups for codependency and relationship addiction because she had a pattern of entering into desperate relationships that bordered on obsessions. Inevitably, the relationships would be sabotaged. The more she tried to hold on, the worse it would get. With recovery and our groups' support this person told me that she had backed away from a relationship because she knew it wasn't the right timing and that she couldn't pursue it any further until God worked out some things and gave her the green light. I couldn't believe she was the same person who couldn't eat or sleep or function at times without a relationship to depend on.

To be responsible for ourselves, group members do not try to fix one another or solve one another's problems. Two things happen whenever group members try to solve one another's problems. First, by focusing on your situation, I avoid the responsibility of facing myself and my situation directly and honestly. Second, if I try to fix you and solve your problems, I take from you your sense of responsibility, which is necessary to a healthy self-image, and I make myself your higher power, which creates a dependency on me rather than on God. Paul understood these two dangers and warned the Philippians not to depend on his presence with them to follow the Lord's will for them but to work out their own salvation with fear and trembling, knowing that God does the work in each of us, according to His will and His good pleasure (Phil. 2:12–13).

To be responsible for ourselves, group members do not try to convict or change one another's behavior. We focus on ourselves and what God needs to be doing in our lives, not what He needs to be doing in the lives of others. Our responsibility is to be open to the work of God's Holy Spirit convicting us of the things that need to change in our lives, and to allow the Holy Spirit to convict others in the group of what they need to be working on in their lives.

To be responsible for ourselves, group members do not blame others or circumstances for our problems, realizing that to do so makes us victims and leaves us powerless. Blame is a primary symptom of a life that is out of control and a person who feels powerless. If someone or something else is the problem, I can focus on that; I don't have to look closely at myself. I am a victim, and I don't have to take any responsibility for myself. The blame game helps me avoid the shame game where I come face-to-face with my human limitations and imperfections, but it makes other people and circumstances the higher power that controls my life. When I quit blaming, I begin recovering. Step One of the Twelve Steps calls on me to take full responsibility for what I am powerless over and the ways that my life has become unmanageable.

Taking responsibility for something is not the same as taking the blame for it. It does not deny the impact of other people and circumstances on our lives, nor does it mean that we cannot hold others accountable for doing what they have done. It simply is a decision to reclaim control of our lives by managing, with God's help and the support of others, what we have absolute control of and are responsible for: our thoughts, feelings, and actions.

About two years ago, a person walked into my office to offer me an apology. Several years before, he had walked into the church office high on cocaine. He was so obnoxious that I was immediately called to deal with him. At one point I considered calling the police. He was in a rage and bitterly attacked me, the church, God, our pastor, his spouse, his boss, and anyone else he could think to blame. I just kept saying to him that the problem was not with everything and everybody outside himself; the problem was what he was feeling about himself on the inside. I asked him when he was going to do something about that. When he came by to apologize for that day, he had been clean six months. Once he quit blaming and began to take responsibility for his thoughts, feelings, and actions, things began to change and he changed. I still shake my head in amazement whenever I see him and he shares with me what God is continuing to do in his life.

I can summarize the whole process of what people do in support groups in three instructions: (1) be safe, (2) be accepting, and (3) be responsible. You must do the first two for others so that they can recover. You must do the last for yourself so that you can grow and change. These three principles must be taught, understood, and constantly reinforced in the minds of group members if the group is to remain healthy, balanced, and effective in helping members honestly face and deal with those things that they are struggling with. As group members strive to accomplish these three goals, the proper balance is established between individuality and community so that self-responsibility does not become self-centeredness and caring for others does not become a way to avoid self-examination and self-growth.

Now it is time to determine a strategy for establishing a recovery ministry. In the next section we will look at organizing and starting support groups.

Section 3

DETERMINING A STRATEGY:

 How to Organize and Start Support Groups

I hope that by this time I have established a sound biblical basis for recovery ministry in the church and that you have developed a personal rationale for the need to establish some form of recovery ministry in your church. Please understand that when I speak of this ministry, I am not talking about providing a room in the basement for an AA meeting or allowing secular support groups to use church facilities. Most self-help support groups already do that. That is not recovery ministry. I am talking about groups that are distinctively Christ-centered and are offered from the church to its members and the community as part of its pastoral care ministry. The church is directly involved in providing support groups as part of the caring, healing ministry that Christ has called it to do. I strongly believe God has called the church to do this new form of ministry.

The difference between secular support groups meeting at a church and a church recovery ministry comes down to whether or not people are exposed to and experience the distinctive characteristics of a Christ-centered group. Secular support groups meeting at a church experience the love, grace, and unity of one another as they deal with life. In Christ-centered groups, people have the opportunity to experience the love of God, the grace of Jesus Christ, and the unity of the Holy Spirit as they face and overcome together their common problems. It is the difference between fellowship and koinonia fellowship. The church should be offering this incredible resource for salvation and healing to the world. By definition, *salvation* means "to make safe or save from harm or loss." Through Christ-centered support groups, the church can become a place of refuge and safety from a sinful and imperfect world.

If you are interested in your church becoming a part of the Christian recovery movement, how do you go about getting started? In this section we want to answer that question by considering a strategy that our church found to be successful in starting support groups. You will also need a model for a support group meeting and an understanding of the guidelines that must be followed within that meeting if it is to be a safe, supportive, and healing environment. Finally, we will examine the issue of denial on a congregational level that must be addressed if a recovery ministry is to be successful. So, let's get started!

Chapter
8

Starting
a Group

We have started about three dozen support groups at our church. The majority are still meeting, but a number failed to establish themselves beyond their initial beginnings. From our successes and from our failures, we have learned valuable lessons about starting support groups with a reasonable chance to flourish and grow. As a result we have developed a systematic process that we try to follow in starting new groups. Those that evolve through this process or a modification of it have, so far, done well as ongoing support groups over the long haul. Those that we started any other way ultimately failed after a short period (not that they didn't meet some needs during that time) or continue to struggle toward establishing themselves.

Problems to Avoid

Three things are deadly to starting a successful support group: (1) lack of response; (2) lack of leadership; and (3) lack of planning. I don't care how well you do any two, the one other thing will ultimately cause a support group to fail or struggle to accomplish anything healthy and productive.

First, you cannot have a support group if people do not attend it or not enough people attend consistently enough to establish that essential sense of koinonia community. Lack of response can result from a failure to identify accurately the needs in the congregation and/or community. You start a group only to find that there is no need or the need is not great enough to generate a significant response. Lack of response can also result from not establishing a path that people can easily follow to meet their needs or to discover that they have a need. Our model for setting up support groups takes into account both possibilities.

You may fail to anticipate some factors initially, but you can later allow for them. When we attempted to start a single-parent support group on a weekday evening, it never generated a response due to time demands on the single parent as well as the need for child care. Even with child care provided, the group did not generate the needed response. When we moved the group to Sunday morning and made it a Sunday school class rather than a support group, it succeeded. Child care was available, and Sunday was a time that the single parent generally had allowed to be at church.

We had different difficulties with a phobics support group. When we offered the group on a Thursday night in one room, it didn't work. The room wasn't close enough to exits and rest rooms, and it had only one door. Also, nothing else was available at the church that evening for the persons who brought the phobics, since many phobics are unable to drive themselves. When we moved the group to a room with two doors that was close to building exits and rest rooms and held meetings on Wednesday nights so that the phobics' support persons could participate in adult classes, the group worked.

Second, you may have a tremendous response and need for a support group, but a lack of leadership to give the group consistency and stability means the group will eventually fail. People go where needs are being met. A good support group is like a city on a hill or a light in a dark place. It will need no advertising to attract those who need it. God gets us where He can meet our needs.

Leadership is not a question of expertise in support groups. It is merely a question of commitment. All group members are experts about themselves and their experience, strength, and hope; each one is qualified to be a group leader in some capacity. But some people must commit to doing what needs to be done to provide the group meeting and to steer it within the established guidelines, using the group's traditions and principles as the compass. Anyone can be trained to be an effective group leader, but there must be a core of persons dedicated to the purpose and need for the group if it is to succeed. I always present the starting of a support group as a birth process. I look for people who are willing to go through a nine-month pregnancy, labor pains, and several years of nurturing the group. Without that commitment from a leadership core, it is difficult, if not impossible, for a group to succeed.

I am very hesitant to start a group without a leadership core of three or four committed persons. Putting that much responsibility on one or two people is not wise. It leads to burnout. It fosters a codependency because the group leader gets focused on meeting the needs of the group rather than working on personal recovery issues. It encourages the group to identify a leader in the group and look to that person instead of God as the higher power. The strategy that we will talk about for starting support groups identifies a committed leadership core that can guide the group until it becomes old enough and healthy enough to care for itself.

I made the mistake of trying to start a cancer support group when one person was very assertive about the need for the group and the willingness to lead it. The group didn't last three months. It wasn't the fault of the person who wanted to start the group. She didn't plan on her circumstances changing. But when they did, the group that was struggling to get started found itself with no one to take the lead and very quickly faded away.

I didn't make that same mistake with our homosexual recovery support group. There has always been a need for the group, but on three different occasions, I have been unable to start one because I couldn't find a leadership core. Finally, God's timing became perfect, and He brought together five persons who were committed to a recovery ministry to persons desiring to overcome homosexuality. The group has steadily grown and has been very successful.

Third, lack of planning can sabotage support groups. If time isn't taken to plan, the group may start prematurely. It then struggles, discouragement sets in, the group becomes unclear about its purpose, and the group may eventually fall apart. As I look at the life of David after he was anointed to be king of Israel by Samuel, it is clear that God always takes us through a time of preparation before He promotes us to do the work He has for us to do. Only after we have been faithful in the little things (preparing and planning) are we ready to be entrusted with much (the harvest of need).

Planning involves defining the group's purpose, setting up its format, establishing and understanding its guidelines and traditions, and becoming familiar and comfortable with the small group process. It entails adequate publicity to generate a response. Our model for starting support groups makes sure that adequate preparation and planning have been done before there is promotion.

Two groups failed for lack of adequate preparation. We started one for people dealing with learning disabilities and one for parents in pain over children who were out of control, in rebellion against authority, or in jail or coming out of it. We didn't plan and publicize the groups adequately, and both failed after three or four months.

So, what is the best way to start a support group? I can speak only from our experience. This model has been successful for us. We have experimented with other ways that have not done as well.

We start support groups by identifying and determining the need. You first must identify a *potential* need, then determine the *actual* need.

You can identify potential needs in several ways. Among people in counseling, I see common struggles, and I identify a potential need for a support group. Other pastors identify the needs that they are addressing. People from our church and from other churches ask if we have a support group for a particular struggle or suggest the need for one. As I watch the news or read newspapers and magazines, I notice the trends in society. The Bible indicates potential needs common to all people. Our chemical dependency group deals with drunkenness; our eating disorder group, with gluttony; our sex addicts group, with lust; and so on.

Next, determine the actual need. I want to know if people will actually be a part of a group working together on that particular problem. I make that step as easy for people to take as I can. The isolation, secrecy, and shame that people often live with regarding their needs make it very risky and difficult to take more than small steps at first.

The Initial Steps

Determine the Need

To determine whether the potential need is an actual need, we offer an introductory seminar and invite people to find out more about a particular topic. This first meeting is informational. We minimize the barriers to attending by asking people to commit only to one evening's attendance and by offering the seminar for no cost or a minimal cost. We minimize the shame and risk factor by advertising the seminar in a way that does not identify people attending the seminar as necessarily having the problem. We also minimize the risk factor by not requiring anyone to do anything other than listen to a speaker. We don't ask participants to share unless they volunteer to do so.

We call them Life-Skills seminars. Area Christian professionals are willing to conduct one-evening seminars at churches without charge to minister and also to do public relations work for their practices or agencies or centers. At the end of the seminar we invite those who would like to know more about the topic to indicate that interest on a sign-up sheet. Based on the interest displayed, we decide that the potential need is an actual need that we may want to meet. We proceed to the next step.

Identify Participants

The second step is to offer a short-term group to see who will make a greater commitment. These groups last from six weeks to six months, long enough to build up a sense of community but not so long that people hesitate to commit to that length of time. Ten- to twelve-week groups seem to work well. For these groups we locate someone with interest or expertise in the targeted area of need who would be willing to lead the group. We may impose a minimal charge for these groups since they often are led by professionals, but we have always been able to find persons willing to work with us in this regard so that the cost is more than reasonable.

These groups will ideally consist of eight to twelve persons plus the group leader. The group leader may design the agenda or may choose to work through a book on the subject. Another helpful resource is the Support Group Series published by Lyman Coleman and Serendipity House (see Resources). These seven-week series cover various topics related to recovery ministry and do not require a professional person to lead them. They can be facilitated by an interested layperson so that the only cost of the group is the minimal expense for the study guides. This series is especially useful for group building in the formative stages.

At the end of the short-term group experience, we consider whether to take the next step in the group development process. Would people like to maintain the group relationships that they have developed and continue to address the needs explored in the group? If there are three or four interested persons, we consider them a leadership core to build an ongoing group around. We decide to continue to offer the support of the group on an ongoing basis and make it an open support group available to anyone to enter at any time. If the leadership core is willing to make that commitment, we move to the last step.

Make Preparations

In the last step of the group development process, we make all of the preparations for the group to meet on an ongoing basis. These preparations involve developing a group format, training the leadership core, and publicizing the group's formation and availability. The first two can take place simultaneously. We do the publicizing only after the first two preparations have been thoroughly made.

We make our congregation aware that a support group to meet a particular need is being developed. We invite anyone who has experienced healing or recovery in that particular area and would like to be involved in helping to set up a group to express that desire. We want people to brainstorm and develop the group and be a part of the leadership team. That leadership team then makes preparations for beginning the group.

Developing a group format and undergoing leadership training are discussed in detail in the next chapter and in the section on maintaining a recovery ministry. As a general rule of thumb, trying to format a group, train leaders, and publicize the group in less than three or four months really rushes things and results in a premature birth.

Good publicity is vital. Here are some ideas that I recommend.

If your church prepares a weekly or monthly newsletter, include a major article the week or month of the grand opening announcing the group and explaining its purpose. For four weeks prior to the first meeting, run an announcement in the Sunday bulletin. The week before and the week that the group starts, make a special announcement from the pulpit about it.

Keep information about the support group or groups constantly before the congregation. At our church, all of our support group meetings are listed in a directory in the monthly newsletter. We also make available fliers listing all of the support groups wherever church literature is displayed.

Most community newspapers run a section entitled "Support Groups" or "Group Opportunities." They will publicize your groups for no charge. One word of caution: advertise that they are Christ-centered groups. You want people who come to the groups to be clear about their purpose up front. Many non-Christians have chosen to be in our groups. Ultimately, many of them come to accept our beliefs as their own, but there should be no attempt to hide or minimize the Christ-centered nature of the group to entice people to attend.

Radio stations, especially Christian-oriented stations, will often publicize groups as part of a public service announcement. Sometimes cable TV stations will do the same.

Make pastors in other churches aware of the support group, especially if they are involved in counseling. Contact Christian counselors and counseling centers in your area.

All of these things will publicize the group. The best publicity is generated when people come to the group and find a safe, supportive place where their needs are met. They broadcast the group to persons within their sphere of influence.

We try to follow this basic process now with all of the groups that we consider starting. Sometimes we may modify things a little, but our experience has not been good if we deviate too much. One variation that worked was a group of people with prior experience in other groups who wanted to set up a similar Christ-centered group in the church. That was how our group for chemical dependency began.

Once you have determined the need and identified a committed leadership core, you are ready to determine the purpose and goals of the group: why the group is meeting and what the group desires to accomplish by meeting. You then want to develop a meeting format that allows the group to fulfill its purpose and accomplish its goals. Let's take a look at what is involved in doing this in the next chapter.

Chapter
9

Developing a Group Meeting Format

The group meeting format guides the group. It is the road map that directs the group and keeps it on track. Groups may follow any number of formats. Our model format for our groups is suggested here, but don't hesitate to modify it or develop your own. Whatever format you adopt, it should be structured, short, and simple if it is to be effective.

Structured Format

One of the first tasks of the leadership core is to develop the group format. The format should be written out and printed up in a brochure that can be given to each member at each meeting.

People need to know what to expect to feel secure and safe enough to share freely and openly. To keep returning to a group, they need to experience and come to expect that something positive and helpful will be accomplished each time they meet. A structured format ensures that as the same process is followed in each meeting, there will be the same basic results, although the details may vary from meeting to meeting.

I have already mentioned the problems with our support group for addicts. Part of the difficulty was created when the group got away from following its written format. That format had evolved over several years of determining what worked for that group and strictly adhering to it. When a different agenda was instituted, the group quickly lost its effectiveness.

A group leader cannot come in, shoot from the hip, and hope to hit the target. Following a plan allows anyone to facilitate a group. With the written format, group leaders feel more secure and have a greater sense of competency and adequacy to lead a meeting.

Another reason to have a structured, written format available is that it orients newcomers to what the group is about and what is expected of them as they join the fellowship. The format contains the essential information that they need to know to begin to participate in the group.

One last benefit of the written format is that it publicizes the group. If you are a group leader, you can share brochures about the group with another interested church, agency, or counselor. Group members can take copies of the brochure and give them to friends or others.

Short Format

Group members and newcomers should be able to look over the information very quickly. Include only what is essential to orient people to the group's purpose and manner of functioning during meetings. Since all or part of this information will be read in the meeting, it must be short enough to be presented within the first fifteen minutes so that the group has well over an hour for sharing.

Our Adult Children of Confusion support group developed an excellent format, but it was too long. It took at least a third of the group's time to get into the sharing. People quit coming to the beginning of the meeting because they knew that if they came in a half hour late, they wouldn't miss anything. We rewrote the format so that we could accomplish our goal of being into the sharing within ten or fifteen minutes. People now arrive on time.

Simple Format

Present only the basics in terms that others can understand. We develop a recovery language over time that becomes a part of the communication process, just as we use a religious jargon when we talk about conversion, justification, transformation, and sanctification. Make sure that your format is understandable to the person who has never been a part of a support group before and may have little or no knowledge of the group's issue.

Sample Format

Let me share the basic format that we offer to those who want to help us develop a new support group. We try to present all of our formats on either an 8½-by-11-inch or an 8½-by-14-inch sheet of paper. An 8½-by-11-inch sheet can be folded so that there are six panels. An 8½-by-14-inch sheet will create eight panels and has room for more information. Some of our earlier groups tried to include so much information that they required stapled booklets, but they were time-consuming to print and much more expensive.

The first panel indicates the name of the group, when it meets, and where it meets. We also like to use illustrations and graphics to make the front cover appealing. The brochure opens up then to the inside panels where the group's format is laid out. Several key elements are standard.

A General Group Format Sample

Welcome to the meeting
Opening prayer
Purpose of the group
Introduction to the process
Greeting of group members and newcomers
Announcements and offerings
Meditation and group sharing and discussion
Affirmation and closing prayer

The first thing is *the welcome,* which is simply a call to order. It is very brief. Our groups typically declare, "Welcome, in the name of the Lord Jesus Christ, to this meeting of *(the name of the group)!* Let's begin our meeting this evening with a word of prayer. Let us pray."

Next is *the opening prayer* that defines the group meeting as Christ-centered and establishes our dependency on God to do for us what we cannot do for ourselves. You may develop an opening prayer, or you may rotate the opening prayer and allow group members to pray spontaneously. We have a standard prayer that we encourage all our groups to use. Feel free to use it:

Father God, we seek to understand and know You as our perfect heavenly Father who loves us with an unfailing, everlasting love that nothing can separate us from;

Lord Jesus, we desire You to be Lord of all and the power greater than ourselves and our situations, and we ask You to restore our lives to sanity and balance through Your grace;

Holy Spirit, we invite You to be present and unify us as one family of love and acceptance so that we may encourage and support one another in the process of growth and change. Amen.

The opening prayer may or may not be printed in the format. Printing it out clearly defines the Christ-centered nature of the group for persons new to the fellowship. Some groups do not print it because of space considerations.

The next item is *the purpose of the group.* The purpose is defined very specifically to establish what the group will talk about and do in the meeting. It also sets limits that will keep the group focused. The big temptation in any support group is to talk about important events in the lives of people. But the group must remain single-minded and stick to the task at hand. For example, the goal of a chemical dependency group is to help its members get clean, straight, and sober, and to maintain a chemical-free life-style, so it must stick to that purpose to have an effective meeting.

The next item is *the introduction to the basic process* of the group so that people know what is expected of them. Several basic elements should be included. Confidentiality is established. Risk taking is encouraged, but the right to pass is expressly given. Being safe, supportive, and trustworthy is emphasized. Individuals are expected to be responsible for their own thoughts, feelings, and behavior and speak only from personal experience. Blaming or judging will not be allowed. Speaking briefly and listening attentively are expected so that everyone has a chance to participate.

Remember, the format briefly introduces the group process. These things should be elaborated in other group literature, in welcome packets for newcomers, in orientation sessions for new group members, or in group conscience meetings. (More will be said about these things later when we talk about the group meeting.)

Next comes *the greeting of group members and newcomers*. We use the greeting process developed by Alcoholics Anonymous, which I will describe in detail later. You may want to create your own group greeting. This group ritual requires persons to identify themselves with the issue that the group is addressing and allows the group to respond to them and affirm them for being there. Establishing and experiencing a relationship with each person in the group and the common struggle are vital. This first step out of isolation, secrecy, and shame and into honesty and healing should be an introduction, not an autobiography. The time for more personal sharing comes later.

After the greeting comes a time for *the group offering and announcements*.

The meditation and group sharing and discussion are the heart of the group meeting. Very little needs to be said in the brochure, although our groups often include the Serenity Prayer here.

The last items are *the affirmation and closing prayer*. A closing ritual affirms group members for their honesty and desire to grow and commits what has been shared and is needed by each group member to God. Each of our groups develops its own brief closing ritual statement, which is read by the group facilitator, followed by the group praying the Lord's Prayer in unison.

Other Information

Other pertinent information may be included in the brochure. All of our groups include the guidelines so that members are constantly reminded of the expectation of being safe, accepting, and responsible.

If it is a Twelve-Step group that will be using the Twelve Steps in meetings, they should be included in the format.

Some groups note the characteristics or traits common to persons dealing with their problems, such as the characteristics of adult children or the traits of codependents. Others may list the core issues of the group. Often, defining key terms or stating the basic beliefs of the group in regard to recovery is a good idea.

Whatever is included in the format brochure should provide persons coming to the group enough information to determine if the group will be helpful to them, offer them a sense that the group will be safe and supportive for them, and give them an idea of what to expect from the group and what will happen in the meeting.

Once you develop the group format, your next task is to establish the guidelines that will give structure and safety to meetings. We'll talk about them in the next chapter.

Chapter
10

Establishing
Guidelines

As you develop your group format, you will also need to establish group guidelines to direct the meeting and how people share with and relate to one another. These guidelines allow each group member to experience the sense of safety and support necessary to trust and take the risks that are part of recovery and healing. The guidelines identify, promote, and maintain the qualities that ensure this will take place at each meeting.

For the first few years, each of our groups had a set of guidelines presented in its own way. The only common guideline was confidentiality. Part of our year-long evaluation process with the leadership of all of the groups included identifying and defining the guidelines essential to the welfare of groups. We discovered seven qualities that must be present in our group meetings and our interactions with one another within those meetings if recovery is to take place. We developed a short form and a long form of the guidelines. All of our groups follow these guidelines.

The Short Form

1. CONFIDENTIALITY
   We maintain confidentiality at all times in all areas having to do with the group and its members.

2. RESPONSIBILITY

We each take personal responsibility for our thoughts, feelings, behavior, and recovery, and speak only from our personal experience.

3. ACCEPTANCE

We offer one another the same unconditional love, acceptance, grace, and forgiveness that God has shown to us through Jesus Christ.

4. RESPECT

We treat one another with the utmost respect and value one another as individually and uniquely created by God, deserving of being heard and understood.

5. HONESTY

We are committed to rigorous honesty as a way of life and a fundamental principle in establishing and maintaining a healthy relationship with God, ourselves, and others.

6. OPENNESS

We are determined to be open and willing to gain new awareness and insight from the experience, strength, and hope of others, and to risk making positive and healthy changes in our attitudes and actions.

7. ENCOURAGEMENT

We seek to build up and affirm one another at all times: motivating one another to believe that positive change is possible, encouraging one another to persevere in new directions as God leads, and recognizing our achievements as we overcome and become new creations in Christ Jesus.

In the short form we describe these seven qualities as our basic group guidelines with one word and a positive statement of what we seek to do in our group interactions. In the long form we define these qualities more precisely in terms of what we do *not* do so group members know what is inappropriate. The one exception is the guideline on encouragement. It is expressed in positive terms of what we want people in the group to do to encourage one another.

The Long Form

1. Confidentiality. How do we maintain confidentiality at all times in all areas having to do with the group and its members?

We do not repeat anything that anyone shares in the group outside the group. What is shared in the group stays in the room and locked away inside our hearts and minds in a sacred trust. We do not share those things with our spouses, friends, counselors, pastors, or others who may know the people and what is taking place in their lives. We let each person be responsible for deciding what to share, with whom, and when. We may share our lives outside the group and offer a general testimony about the way the group is helping us. But we cannot reveal the details of what others share in the meeting without their permission.

We do not identify any member of the group to anyone outside the group. We avoid talking about the group when others may be listening and could identify persons as belonging to it. We may choose to identify ourselves as being in the group. That confession is often a part of our testimony and confirms the work that God has done in our lives. But each person must determine when to take that risk.

Be careful in talking with persons who may know that an individual is in a group and may ask you questions. The intent is usually well-meaning and one of concern, but you must maintain confidentiality. A good general response is, "It seems that you're really concerned about _____. Why don't you ask her how things are going? I'm sure she'd appreciate your interest. Obviously, confidentiality is vitally important to a support group, and I'm not at liberty to talk about people in the group or what they are sharing. I'm sure you understand." Most people will be understanding, and you will have encouraged them to talk directly with the person most in need of their concern and support. If they do not understand or have other motives, you have set a healthy boundary that they must respect.

We do not talk about other participants or what they have shared during the group at any time outside the group unless they are there or we have their permission. When we are with other group members outside the meeting, any sharing should focus on our issues and relationships, not on persons who are not there or what they may have shared in the meeting. If we have issues with other persons in the group, we go to them and include them directly. To do otherwise is to engage in gossip, which is a sin against them and against God. That does not mean we cannot express general feelings toward a group member with others within the group. The only exceptions would be an individual's checking things out with a sponsor to prepare for a direct confrontation or to make direct amends, or group leaders' discussing group members in regard to an individual confrontation or a group conscience about a guideline violation.

2. Responsibility. How do we each take personal responsibility for our thoughts, feelings, behavior, and recovery, and speak only from our personal experience?

We do not blame others by allowing their actions or behavior to control the choices that we have made or need to make. We make our own choices. Our choices and actions are the result of our thoughts and the meaning that we attach to what others have done or not done and the resulting feelings that we have about ourselves. We then act according to our thoughts and feelings. We determine; others can only influence. We blame because we do not want to look at ourselves and feel any sense of responsibility. We are afraid to be ashamed. But if we blame, our lives are controlled by others, and we are victims. Victims are helpless and cannot change.

We are not victims! We have choices regarding our thoughts, feelings, and behavior. We can realize and accept that we live in an imperfect world full of imperfect people, including ourselves. We do not focus on changing others or circumstances that we cannot control; we focus only on changing within ourselves and our circumstances those things necessary for our recovery, well-being, and serenity.

It is a waste of time and energy for us and the group to try to change those who are not in the group or may not be willing to change. We concentrate on those things that God is showing us that we can and need to change in ourselves.

With all of the time and energy available to us that we have freed up by letting go of others, we can recover, grow, and change. Regardless of what happens with others or circumstances, we can detach ourselves from feeling responsible for it and being driven to try and control it. We can experience serenity in the midst of things that we cannot control through surrendering the need to be in control to God. We can discover the secret that Paul learned about how to be content regardless of circumstances (Phil. 4:11–12).

3. *Acceptance.* How do we offer one another the same unconditional love, acceptance, grace, and forgiveness that God has shown to us through Jesus Christ?

We do not discount, minimize, or in any way criticize another person's thoughts, feelings, or experience. We accept one another unconditionally. Each person must be free to honestly bring thoughts, feelings, and behavior out into the light so that they can be exposed to the truth of God's Word and will revealed in the lives of others. People are accepted at whatever point they may be in their lives. People are allowed to determine when they are ready to share and change. They have the right to pass at any time when they are unable or unwilling to share. We trust God to bring about the changes that He desires in the lives of each of us. No one is shamed for being human and imperfect. God's kindness, revealed to us through the acceptance of one another, leads to repentance and change. Our responsibility is to listen to others and offer our experience, strength, and hope when it is our turn to share.

We do not confront others when their ideas, attitudes, or behavior differs from what we have experienced or our expectations for them. We do not set ourselves up as others' higher power by determining what they need or how they should be. We do not put God in a box and manipulate Him by insisting that He work in other people's lives according to our will. People do not change through confrontation. They change through acceptance and encouragement.

Direct confrontations are not allowed in a support group. We are all confronted indirectly when we honestly look at our own lives and face the truths that we learn from sharing our experience, strength, and hope. If someone in the group has an issue with another group member, that should be addressed outside the group meeting, privately and directly according to biblical guidelines for reconciliation and making amends.

The guideline governing confrontation applies to the sharing relationships within the meeting. It does not apply to individual relationships that we choose to enter into outside the group with a sponsor. We choose a person as a sponsor based on identifying with that person and experiencing a sense of acceptance. We allow that person to be a mirror for us, reflecting those things in our recovery process that help us change and grow. But even that confrontation always takes place within the context of an unconditionally accepting relationship in which we feel valued and supported.

We do not judge or try to convict one another of sin or shortcomings, knowing that we are all learning, growing, and changing together as God's Holy Spirit convicts and gives us the wisdom, desire, and courage to change. There is no room for judgment in a support group. We show one another the same acceptance that Jesus showed the woman caught in adultery. We do not cast any stones at what anyone else is doing. We allow God's Word and His Holy Spirit to convict. We have been given the ministry of reconciliation to God, others, and ourselves. We are graceful in our words and actions toward one another. We are quick to offer forgiveness as we have been forgiven by Christ, and to encourage others to be forgiving of themselves. We trust in the faithfulness of God to cleanse us and free us from all unrighteousness, and we show that same acceptance and faithfulness to one another when we sin or fail.

4. *Respect.* How do we treat one another with the utmost respect and value one another as individually and uniquely created by God, deserving of being heard and understood?

We do not interrupt one another or engage in side conversations when someone is sharing with the group. To interrupt someone is to indicate that what we have to say is more important. To not listen fully and attentively to what someone is sharing is to minimize the importance and value of what is being shared. It does not respect the risk that is taken whenever anyone shares openly and honestly. It is a violation of the trust that we place in one another to be supportive of the risks that we are taking by listening to and accepting what is shared unconditionally. If we have questions, we wait until the person has finished sharing before asking them. We ask questions that indicate a desire to know and understand a person better rather than questions that interrogate, attack, or judge.

We do not sermonize, moralize, or spiritualize, or tell one another in any way how or when to change. We leave that up to God and to the individual. Sermonizing, moralizing, or spiritualizing and giving quick, easy, general answers imply that others are doing something wrong, that there must be sin in their lives, and that they just don't have enough faith if they are still struggling.

This guideline does not mean we cannot share the truth of God's Word that He has revealed to us and that is setting us free. We can offer it only as our own experience, strength, and hope and allow others to accept it as God reveals it to them. We cannot force truth on others, nor should we get frustrated or impatient when they do not receive or believe it.

We do not monopolize the time and attention of the group while sharing our experience, strength, and hope so that all group members may have the opportunity to share and be heard. Sharing should be brief and concise. We limit our sharing to three to five minutes. By doing so, we respect the need that others have to share and the value of what they have to offer the group. If a person has a greater need for support than the group can offer in the meeting, we encourage the person to talk to someone after the group meeting, to seek out a sponsor to talk with outside the group, or to consider the need for individual counseling.

5. Honesty. How are we committed to rigorous honesty as a way of life and a fundamental principle in establishing and maintaining a healthy relationship with God, ourselves, and others?

We do not present ourselves to be something that we are not or expect perfection in ourselves. We fearlessly search out and face truth as we grow and change. We know the danger of maintaining pretense and denial in our lives. The truth, not denial, sets us free. The only people that Jesus directly judged were the religious leaders for the sin of hypocrisy. He accused them of maintaining an exterior image that covered up interior disorder and decay. After David was confronted with his sin of adultery and murder, and the elaborate schemes of pretense and deceit to cover them up and protect his image, he realized that he had learned a great lesson. God desires and requires truth in the inmost being if we are to receive the wisdom to overcome and recover (Ps. 51:6).

We are honest with ourselves and our imperfections. We accept that we are perfectly imperfect and that we are acceptable to God because of what Christ has done to save us from our imperfections. We are all in the process of choosing each day to allow God's grace to work in us and give us power and forgiveness.

We do not deny, repress, or run away from our feelings. Buried feelings do not die; they are simply buried alive. They continue to express themselves in other, more destructive ways.

In our meetings and in our interactions with one another, we are inevitably going to trigger feelings in one another, some of which may be quite intense. Our imperfections are going to grate against the imperfections of others. We want to be responsible for directly and honestly presenting our feelings to one another in a moderate and appropriate manner. We seek to be truthful and honest with our feelings so that we can then be reconciled to ourselves, God, and others.

A man asked Jesus to heal his son. Jesus wanted to know if the father believed, and the man confessed honestly, "Lord, I believe;

help my unbelief!" The Bible indicates that Jesus responded to the man's honesty and ministered to the boy (Mark 9:17–29). We are to have that same honest faith as we approach God for understanding and strength to deal with those things in our lives that we cannot understand. We are to be willing to share that faith with others instead of pretending to have all the answers.

6. *Openness.* How are we to be open and willing to gain new awareness and insight from the experience, strength, and hope of others, and to risk making positive and healthy changes in our attitudes and actions?

We do not present ourselves as experts on anyone other than ourselves or pretend to have all the answers, knowing that in His time God will provide insight and direction and that they often come through others. We must remain open and flexible to whatever way God chooses to work in our lives. We must not limit Him or His resources for us to certain sources; we must not insist that He work in the lives of others in the same way that He works in our lives. We are called upon to abide in Christ Jesus and His word and will for us.

We do not judge what others feel or express, nor do we feel threatened when others ask questions to understand us better or to help them with their recovery. Our need to protect ourselves and avoid any sense of shame about our thoughts, feelings, or behavior often causes us to overreact to things that are expressed, take them personally, and become defensive. Often, because we have been criticized by so many and have become self-critical, we may perceive interested, concerned questions as interrogative and judgmental. We must stay open to group members and be willing to distinguish between what we feel is happening and what is really going on.

We do not criticize or get impatient with the imperfect results of recovery efforts by ourselves or others. We help one another learn from mistakes. Recovery requires changing old attitudes and actions. We must be willing and open to taking the risk of trying, knowing that imperfect results usually follow initial efforts. It is the effort that is important; the results will come with consistent effort.

7. Encouragement. How do we seek to build up and affirm one another at all times: motivating one another to believe that positive change is possible, encouraging one another to persevere in new directions as God leads, and recognizing our achievements as we overcome and become new creations in Christ Jesus?

We identify with and relate to one another's experiences, struggles, and needs by responding to and affirming one another when we share in group. Whenever any group member takes the risk of sharing and being honest about thoughts, feelings, and actions, we want to encourage the person to continue to bring things out into the light.

We acknowledge and support the risks that we take and the small steps that we make in recovery. We may get impatient with the process of recovery or become discouraged because we do not see change or we are not making changes perfectly. When that happens, we remind one another that if we keep taking steps in the right direction, we will get there eventually. We point out to one another the things that have changed and the steps that we have already taken rather than obsess about the steps that lie ahead.

We celebrate and applaud the changes that we are making and the successes that we are experiencing one day at a time as we recognize together the accomplishments that each brings to the group. Some groups have special tokens that celebrate and mark significant moments in a group member's recovery journey. Twelve-Step groups frequently mark the taking of various steps in recovery with a symbolic chip; different colors mark various periods of growth. Some moments may be marked with a ceremony, a party, or even a special after-group activity. Whatever form it takes, we must mark significant moments of change and growth with a celebration of our accomplishments, expressing gratitude to God for the opportunity to become new creations in Christ.

Health-Preserving Guidelines

These guidelines are vital to the health and well-being of the support group meeting. Groups must actively and consistently work toward making sure that each member understands and follows the guidelines or the group will not function as a support group. These qualities make a Christ-centered support group unique, a special place of safety and healing. The guidelines may seem vaguely familiar because each guideline, except confidentiality, which is the cornerstone of any support group, reflects one quality of the koinonia fellowship mandated by Jesus Christ and the Bible as the way that God works in the body of Christ to bring wisdom and healing to His children.

We have found several ways to teach group members the meaning and importance of the guidelines. I encourage you to use any or all of them, or you may be creative in finding new ways.

Some groups have an orientation meeting for visitors and new members that takes place before they participate in the group discussion. The guidelines are discussed in detail using the long-form model.

All persons who are new to our support group fellowship are given a handout that welcomes them to the group and introduces the recovery ministry of our church. This handout provides information about the support group experience and includes the detailed information of the long form of the guidelines.

Our groups present the short form of the guidelines in their format. Some groups go through the short form prior to discussion.

Group leaders especially need to be trained in the significance of the guidelines. All group members should follow the guidelines, but the leadership should emphasize them.

If a group gets blatantly away from the guidelines or if it seems not to properly understand them, leaders should reinforce or reestablish them. A special discussion during the sharing time, known as group conscience, is basically a time for members to teach themselves about, reaffirm the importance of, and recommit themselves to following the particular guideline being discussed. Leaders guide this discussion by sharing the meaning and importance of the guideline to them from their personal experience, then allowing others to share their experiences and reaffirm the need to follow that guideline so that the group remains safe and supportive. The group puts pressure on itself and each member to practice and adhere to the guidelines.

The format and guidelines must be accomplished and established clearly, in writing, before the first official group meeting. Then you're ready to have your first meeting and start an ongoing support group. Let's take a look now at what happens when a support group meets.

Chapter
11

The Group Meeting

We've identified and determined the need for a support group. We've recruited a leadership core. We've developed a written format and established guidelines to structure the sharing process. We've publicized the availability of the group to the church and possibly to the community. Now it's time to have a meeting. We want to walk through that process and see what happens before, during, after, and outside the support group meeting.

This chapter is not intended to be a detailed description of small group dynamics and group interaction. It will not train you and make you an expert support group facilitator. But it will give you enough understanding, together with the information in the section on maintaining a recovery ministry, to get started.

I believe that anyone can lead a support group. You don't have to be an expert on group psychology or have a degree in counseling to be an effective facilitator. You do need to know your limits and the limits of the group, which the format and guidelines provide. Excellent books about group dynamics and group leadership are available. One that we provide to all of our group leaders is *RAPHA's Handbook for Group Leaders*. We use it in our group leadership training in addition to training materials that we have developed for our situation.

Ultimately, the best teacher is experience itself. You prepare, you offer yourself as a willing vessel for God to use in facilitating the group, and then you do the best you can leading the group, knowing that God is the One ultimately responsible for the success of the group. The koinonia fellowship of the group, not the wisdom or expertise of the leader, gives members what they need.

Before the official beginning date of a support group, we encourage the leadership core to have several practice meetings. The leadership core becomes a small group and meets for several weeks, letting each person direct the group from beginning to end. Your leaders will gain a sense of the flow of the meeting and learn what to expect when the meetings begin.

Before the Meeting

Several logistical points need to be taken care of before the meeting. Early on in the life of the group, the leadership core should try to get as many members involved as possible in taking on tasks to serve the group. (We will talk about this later when we look at the importance of servanthood within a group.) Group members should assume responsibility for various tasks. However, the leadership core may have to do the tasks initially until they can find others to take over.

The room should be set up for the meeting. Some groups have put a sign on the door indicating that a group is meeting inside. Sometimes the uncertainty of a closed door and the insecurity of walking into an unknown situation are enough of an excuse to keep people from taking that first step into the support group meeting.

Make sure the room temperature is comfortable or someone knows how to get the thermostat adjusted. Group members can easily become focused on the external temperature rather than the internal thoughts and feelings.

If possible, chairs should be set up in a circle so that members can maintain eye contact and fully attend to one another. Chairs set up in rows where people have their backs to one another do not foster community and connectedness.

A copy of the format should be placed in each chair so that as persons, especially newcomers, arrive, they can look over the purpose of the group and anticipate what is going to happen in the meeting.

We encourage each of our groups to have a book table in the room with books and literature pertinent to the recovery issues of the particular group. You could have one copy of each book for members to browse through before or after the meeting. Each person can then pursue purchasing a book through a local bookstore or the church bookstore if the church has one. Our church bookstore keeps the most frequently requested books in stock. Or you could have one copy to browse through and another copy in a group library that could be checked out. Some groups order several copies of the books that they have found most helpful and sell them at cost to members.

Book tables are good places for members to fellowship before the meetings. Talking about good books that we have read and can recommend to one another begins the sharing process. But be careful not to get into the bookstore business. The books can be written by secular and Christian authors, but the group leadership should be familiar with the contents and know that they specifically address the needs of that particular support group and that they are not incompatible with basic Christian beliefs. We trust our group members to be spiritually discerning about secular counsel. A great deal of it can be helpful since God is ultimately the author of all truth, but some can be confusing. We don't want to create any more confusion in the lives of group members. They are already experiencing enough of that.

Some of our groups provide refreshments before meetings as a way for members to relax and fellowship. Refreshments during the meeting are another matter, which will be discussed under group principles that maintain the recovery ministry. Someone must obviously plan and prepare ahead of time for them.

Designate a newcomer spotter and greeter to make sure that they are welcomed to the group. People who walk into the room and feel out of place and not noticed or welcomed may leave before ever experiencing the support of the group during its meeting. Notice and welcome people as they arrive. Eventually, each group member should assume the responsibility to be open, accepting, and friendly to all and especially to newcomers.

A lot of our groups provide child care during the meeting so that it is easier for members, especially single parents, to attend. A designated person who coordinates the child care may direct persons needing that service to its location and explain what is expected financially.

A group can do one last thing prior to the meeting that can be a special opportunity for ministry and fellowship. Some of our groups have made it a practice to take time before the meeting for prayer and praise. It can last from fifteen to thirty minutes. It is a time to express gratitude to God for what He has done in our lives and in the group and to join with others in agreement on the needs that we and other group members may have. We then ask God to meet those needs in some way through one another and through the meeting.

During the Meeting

Group meetings should always begin and end promptly. The facilitator of the evening's meeting is determined in advance, and that person should start the meeting exactly at the advertised time.

The group facilitator begins by declaring the welcome to the group, which calls the meeting to order. In a large group, it may be necessary to direct people to take a seat a few minutes before starting to give them time to settle down. Then the facilitator may read the usual opening prayer or may call on a person to pray. Remember, this brief prayer should focus on the group and its needs. Be sure to make arrangements in advance with a group member. Don't surprise anyone with a prayer request.

Following the opening prayer, the facilitator quickly reads

through the sections in the format describing the group's purpose and introducing the process that the group will follow in its sharing together.

After the group purpose and introduction, announcements are made while the group takes up an offering. All groups should be self-supporting by taking their own offerings. However, group members should be free to give as they feel led. The only exception is the expectation that group members who use the child care will give something to defray that expense. Our groups suggest a donation of two dollars per child, up to a maximum of five dollars per family.

Announcements should be directly related to the group's purpose. We suggest that our groups put up a permanent bulletin board or set out one at each meeting to publicize other items of interest. Some groups set up an announcement table to make available fliers about upcoming events.

Announcements should be as brief as possible. We don't announce all the details. Instead, we announce the what and when and indicate where additional information can be obtained.

If group members have difficulty being brief, designate one person to make the announcements each week. Anyone with an event to announce must get that information to the designated person before the meeting begins. The announcements are then edited and screened; those that need to be made during the meeting can be given and the rest posted on the bulletin board.

The sharing time should take up most of the meeting. Our rule of thumb is that it should take no more than the first fifteen minutes to get into the sharing time, so that an hour and fifteen minutes remain for the most important part of the meeting.

During the first part of the sharing time, group members and newcomers are greeted. A welcoming ritual permits persons to introduce themselves and be welcomed to the group, and it identifies newcomers so they can be especially recognized. Many of our groups use the traditional Twelve-Step group welcome. Each person says, "Hi, my name is _____," and then *briefly* (no more than one sentence) identifies the reason for coming to the group. Then the group responds with "Hi" and the person's first name. This ritual establishes a sense of community and trust.

If the group has gotten so large that it splits up into smaller groups for the sharing time, you may make the introductions all together and then split up, or you may split up first into the smaller groups and then let members of the smaller groups introduce themselves to those they will be sharing with that evening.

I learned about the power of the greeting from one support group member. She was new to a group, and I asked how she liked the meeting and whether she thought she'd come back. She told me that she really enjoyed the sharing and was sure it would be helpful to her, but she would definitely be back to experience the group greeting again. I was intrigued about why a person would come back to a group solely because of that. I learned two important things from her answer. First, there is an incredible sense of relief in admitting to a problem and finding out that you're not alone. Second, it is affirming to be welcomed to a group when you have struggled to belong or feel that you were appreciated by others in your life. That is what the newcomer to the group experienced when she shared her name and problem with the group and the group answered in unison with "Hi" and her name.

Next, a person shares an opening devotional or meditational reading that focuses the group's attention and feelings on the topic chosen for that evening. The topic can be any of the recovery issues that the group has identified as relevant to healing. For our Twelve-Step groups, the topic once a month is one of the Twelve Steps. The other weeks the group determines the topic.

The facilitator for the evening can choose the topic. Since the facilitator rotates among the leadership and the members from week to week, that allows for a good variety of topics. The facilitator may select the topic a week in advance and ask a member to prepare something to share with the group, or the facilitator may prepare the opening meditation.

Sometimes a group member will request a topic for a meeting. In that case, let the group member making the request prepare the opening devotional since it is a strongly felt need.

The person presenting the topic is the first to share thoughts and feelings about it since the person had the opportunity to reflect on it while preparing the opening reading. That reading may have come from any of a number of sources—recovery literature, other books, the Bible, or the written thoughts, observations, and personal experience of the group member. God can use many sources to reveal His truth to us to bring freedom and healing.

If the group is going to split up into smaller groups, presenting the devotional reading to the whole group seems to work best. Then a designated leader or member can begin each smaller sharing group with personal reflections on the topic to get the discussion going.

Once the discussion is started, the facilitator opens up the sharing to anyone who wishes to share his or her experience, strength, and hope. If the group follows the guidelines, the sharing flows easily from one person to another until all who want to share have had the opportunity. If time remains, the facilitator encourages additional thoughts and feelings or reactions to what has already been shared. Very seldom is it difficult to fill up the sharing time. Usually, groups run out of time.

There really is nothing complex about support groups and the sharing process. What heals is the process of walking in the light, seeking truth in the inmost being, becoming vulnerable and sharing (confessing) our sins and struggles with one another, and being known and accepted as we really are. God speaks to us through the collective voice of the group sharing and works in our lives as we learn from one another's experience, strength, and hope. Don't get impatient or try to force results. Trust the process. It works not because of what we do or don't do but because it is God's way for His power to be revealed and to work in koinonia fellowship. It is a simple process, but its power is unsurpassed in its ability to change lives.

The last five minutes of group time, whether in one large group or several smaller ones, should be spent in bringing closure to the experience. Closure means taking what has been revealed and offering it up to God to use in whatever way He chooses to bring about recovery and healing in our lives. Our goal is to become more and more conformed to the image of Christ and become who we were created to be, and less and less conformed to the world and the mold that it has squeezed us into.

Groups should always end in prayer. That ending may take many forms, but it should be a sacred closing ritual that takes place every time the group meets to share. Most of our groups pray together the Lord's Prayer. Some groups may precede this closing prayer with a time for *brief* prayer requests. The prayer requests must be personal (what I would like the group to be in prayer about for me during the coming week), and they must be brief (stated in one sentence). After a few minutes for prayer requests, the group dismisses with its closing prayer.

A closing ritual that we are striving to adopt in all of our support groups is one that I learned from Lyman Coleman and the Serendipity Support Group Series. For the closing prayer, group members form a circle and hold hands as a way to experience connectedness and affirm one another. As we do so, we place one empty chair that was not occupied that evening into the middle of the circle. Part of the closing ritual is an acknowledgment of the empty chair and the expressed desire for God to bring someone new who needs the support of our fellowship to the group to fill that chair. Two things take place, I believe, when we do that. God brings who He wants to be in our group to us, and group members become sensitive to sharing with others and inviting them to the group. In that way groups grow and flourish.

That's all that's involved in group meetings. Unless the group is made up of perfect people, which it isn't or they wouldn't be in the group in the first place, there will inevitably be problems within the meeting process. I will try to address many of them in the next section on maintaining your recovery ministry. While it is not difficult to start support groups, and the group process is basically a simple one, keeping a recovery ministry healthy and growing requires both commitment and effort.

The Overgrown Group

Let me briefly address two specific situations that may develop in the meeting. The first situation occurs when the group gets so large that the quality of the sharing experience is diminished. The second situation occurs when a small number of people take over the sharing.

The first situation is a wonderful problem to have, since it means that needs are being met, but a frustrating one to deal with if time runs out before all group members have the opportunity to share. We have found several ways to solve this problem.

One solution is to hold another meeting at a different time and hope that the group will split into two smaller groups. That may happen, but some people may go to both meetings so that the groups don't really become smaller. Another problem with splitting and starting another group is making sure that you have adequate leadership for both groups. Two of our groups split in this manner, and both groups have not been as strong ever since, primarily due to the loss of leadership.

Another solution is to begin the meeting with all members together but then break up into several smaller groups for the sharing time. The greeting and welcoming can take place either before or after the group breaks up, although it is usually best to do it afterward if the group has gotten that large. Otherwise, you take up most of your sharing time introducing one another!

A variation of this solution works well. Once a group regularly draws a large crowd and attracts a lot of newcomers, it develops a special newcomers group. Everyone meets together for the first ten minutes through the opening, purpose, introduction, and announcements. Then all of the newcomers go to an orientation meeting, and the other members form smaller sharing groups. Members then welcome and greet one another.

Our largest support group went to this format and, as a result, grew even more. Before we offered the newcomers group, many people attended the group a few times, struggled to fit in or understand what the group was about and how to participate in it, and then quit coming. Now, newcomers learn what the support group is about before they move into the general sharing group and they are much more likely to remain involved. People frequently comment about how helpful the newcomers group was to them.

Groups of four to twelve create the opportunity for intense intimacy and sharing. The ideal number is four, six, or eight; ten to twelve members stretch that intimacy to its maximum. A group of twelve to twenty permits intimacy but also provides just enough space to hide for people to feel safe and develop trust gradually. A group with twenty to forty members may break up into two evenly divided groups when it is time to share, or it may begin a newcomers group. A group of more than forty may be subject to the Rule of Forty. When a group has over forty members, it begins to lose the group dynamics of belonging and connectedness and takes on the dynamics of a class. Group members feel isolated and become passive spectators rather than active participants. At this point you *must* split up the group in some way or lose the momentum of the group and its ability to support members and help them change and grow.

The Dominated Group

The second situation, I have found, is much easier to manage. Your group may be dominated by the same persons sharing their experiences at every meeting. Others in the group sit back passively and are unwilling or unable to jump in and present their needs. Sometimes one or two particularly needy persons in the group immediately demand the group's attention when the floor is opened up for sharing, and no one else gets the opportunity to share.

In one of our groups a person very quickly monopolized the sharing time. Whenever she began to share, she wept hysterically and tied up the sharing time, often for the remainder of the meeting. Another group had difficulty with a person who always jumped in first when the floor was open for people to share and typically took up so much time that only a few other people had a chance to share. Other groups had difficulty with members who came with their own agendas and kept talking about the same things over and over again, even though the group was trying to discuss a different topic.

If any of these things happen regularly, the facilitator may need to become more assertive and direct the sharing rather than allow the sharing to just happen. The best way to do that is to declare that during the sharing time, the group is going to go around the circle instead of letting anyone jump in.

Circle sharing puts gentle pressure on group members who are afraid to share or who always let others share first because they think that what others have to share is more important than what they are experiencing. It make those who dominate wait their turn, which may come near the end of the group if you begin the circle sharing near them and go around in the direction away from them.

After the Meeting

After the meeting is over, logistical details may need to be taken care of. Chairs may have to be put up, or the room cleaned up and rearranged so that it is left as the group found it. The offering and any money from the book table must be accounted for and prepared for deposit. At some point the book table and announcement area must be cleared away and the group literature stored. Other details specific to each meeting must be attended to at this time. But the primary things that need to occur are fellowship and ministry.

The koinonia fellowship of the support group makes it a powerful healing experience in the lives of people. This occurs during and after the meeting as well as outside it. After the meeting, members should be encouraged to fellowship around the book table or over refreshments, or to continue sharing with one another. Members, and especially leaders, should actively seek out newcomers and make them feel welcome. That is vital to the group's continued growth.

As important as the fellowship is, the more important thing is the bearing of burdens and ministry to one another. Group members

157

may minister in prayer to individual needs that people have brought to the group or that have come up during the sharing. Groups may use another room set aside for this purpose, which affords a degree of privacy and quiet, or they may direct interested persons at the close of the meeting to the designated "burden bearers" who sit down with them in the group meeting room for one-on-one ministry and prayer. With all of the issues that support groups can stir up and bring out into the light, this time can be very powerful and healing.

Outside the Meeting

Events outside the meeting can contribute to the koinonia fellowship and can be a part of the recovery process. The possibilities are limited only by the group's creativity, time, and energy.

Three times a year all of our support groups get together for a covered dish supper that is open to all those in recovery and people significant to them that they wish to include in their recovery process. This meeting educates persons interested in the recovery ministry in a very real way. After the dinner, a speaker can exhort and encourage the group members to growth. Or a video or film related to recovery can be viewed. Skits and plays that dramatize recovery are effective. Group members can share with one another what the Lord is doing in their lives and has done through the support groups. Either before or after the sharing, there can be worship and praise celebrating what God is doing in their lives.

Once a year we hold a retreat for all of the recovery groups. A common recovery theme is selected, and the retreat becomes an extended opportunity for fellowship, sharing, and ministry.

A group may organize a seminar or conference and bring in a special speaker to address issues that the group desires to focus on more extensively than may be possible in a usual meeting.

Some of our groups have taken on service projects to do together. These projects have strengthened the bonds of group members as they unite to accomplish a common ministry goal.

Smaller groups have spun off some of the larger primary recovery groups. These groups of four to six people typically provide more accountability for persons who want to work on specific issues.

All of our groups are involved in our Support Group Ministry Awareness Sunday. Individuals in the groups share their experiences with others in the congregation who may be interested in the ministry for themselves or someone they know with a similar need.

These and other activities outside the meeting contribute to the group-building process. They deepen relationships, and group members minister to one another's needs.

Which Group to Start?

There is one last question to answer about starting a support group before we deal with the major hurdle to starting a recovery ministry. You know how to go about starting a group now, but which group do you start?

If your church is large enough, you may have enough interest from the very beginning to start groups to deal with a specific issue, such as chemical dependency, eating disorders, adult children issues, sexual abuse, or divorce recovery. Groups need only five or six people to get started. They will grow from that point if there is a need. Our largest group, which has consistently had sixty to eighty members each week for the past several years, began with four people.

Another way to start a group is to select a general theme and include people who share more similarities than differences. Three main groups can cover the majority of needs. An *addiction group*, for example, could include those dealing with a dependency on substances, such as alcohol, drugs, and/or nicotine, or experiences, such as eating, gambling, sex, spending, or working. The word *addiction* literally means "to favor." Whatever assumes the favored place in their lives and becomes the thing that they depend on to give them worth or power other than God can be considered an addiction. All of the group members could share powerlessness over their addiction, whatever addiction they may be struggling with. As the group grows, it could eventually split into more specific groups to deal with the individual addiction issues.

Two other general groups could be a *codependency group* to deal with dependency issues, such as living with someone who is chemically dependent, dealing with abusive relationships, or facing the pain and confusion of a dysfunctional family and a *loss group* to deal with grief issues, including divorce, death, loss of job, ability to function, and so on. Both groups may eventually split into separate groups for specific issues: divorce recovery, a grief group for those who have lost a loved one, an unemployed group, a group for those in relationship with someone chemically dependent or someone acting out sexually, those in abusive relationships, or adult children of dysfunctional families or sexual abuse survivors. Several of our groups began in this manner as I shared earlier.

One last way is to start only one group that involves anyone who wishes to be in a support group. The common denominator is the desire to be honest and accountable to walk in the light with other people who are willing to do the same. Even though people may bring many different issues into the group, using the Twelve Steps enables them to identify what they are powerless over and how their lives are unmanageable as a result. They can all then be part of a general recovery fellowship.

So, your written format is ready to go, and you've developed your group guidelines. You know what's going to take place before, during, after, and outside the group meeting. You've decided which group or groups you are going to start. But before you can really get things going well in your recovery ministry, you may have one last obstacle to overcome, or all of your efforts may be frustrated. That is congregational acceptance of a recovery ministry. In the next chapter we will discuss this issue.

Chapter
12

Congregational Acceptance of a Recovery Ministry

One key to a successful recovery ministry is congregational awareness and acceptance. The congregation not only contains potential group members, but it can and should be the greatest referral source for the ministry. Church members have spheres of influence extending to family and relatives, friends and neighbors, and people they work with or interact with on a regular basis. All provide an opportunity to bring others into a ministering relationship with the church through a support group. But there, lurking in the shadows waiting to sabotage a recovery ministry, is the dread enemy of the support group: denial.

I see denial revealed primarily in two attitudes that individuals and congregations take toward problems.

The first attitude is that there is no problem. We seem to fear admitting to being sinful and imperfect. We create such an atmosphere of guilt for people about their lack of faith or holiness that we deny them access to God's source of grace, which is meant to be supplied through the body of Christ, and to His truth, which will set them free. God already knows that we are sinful, imperfect, and struggling. That condition qualifies us for the saving grace of Jesus Christ. We are called upon to confess (admit to) sin to God and to others to be healed (James 5:16) and to be cleansed from all unrighteousness (1 John 1:9). In fact, the whole book of 1 John warns us against denial and calls on us to support one another in love in facing sin in all of its manifestations and in dealing with our human imperfections.

The second attitude admits that the problem exists but minimizes its impact on people or their need for help in dealing with it. But God works through koinonia fellowship. It's part of His plan for healing His people.

A sexual abuse survivor shared with me her story of going to her pastor and lay counselors for help in coming to terms with the memories and feelings overwhelming her. Instead of receiving comfort and acceptance, she was scolded for not having forgiven her abuser and for holding on to the past when she was now a new creation in Christ. Experiencing even more shame for needing to deal with and heal the reality of the abuse by a parent (who also happened to be a church leader), she became embittered at the church and God, who she felt had betrayed her. She turned to alcohol, food, and promiscuous sex to manage the pain that she was not allowed to talk about and release. I wish hers were an isolated story, but I hear it often from those who feel forced to leave the nurture of their church to find support in our groups.

Denial must be shattered if individuals and congregations are to know the truth and see people healed and set free. It must be directly confronted on a congregational level if a church is to have an effective recovery ministry. We have found several ways to do this.

The Role of the Pastor

I strongly believe that confronting denial must start with the pastor. The pastor models for the congregation the reality of being human and imperfect and depending on the power of God revealed in and available through the koinonia fellowship of the church. We are admonished in the Bible to not forsake coming together and encouraging (putting courage into) one another, especially in difficult times (Heb. 10:25). The pastor must give church members permission to need one another to deal with these imperfections.

When I began to attend some of our support groups to deal with my recovery issues, I was hesitant and cautious. I was concerned about my image and what people would think. After all, I was a pastor and director of counseling. What credibility would I have and how could they trust me if I was struggling and imperfect? To my amazement, the more honest and open I have been, the more people trust and respect me. One group member explained it to me by referring to the verse about Christ as our high priest who has been touched with our infirmities. The more real and vulnerable I have been, the more others seem able to relate to me and feel understood and accepted.

The pastor must also encourage the congregation to live truthfully and honestly before God and one another. Three tremendous sermons could be preached on Psalm 51:6 (actually, the whole psalm and the events surrounding it in David's life), John 8:31-32, and 1 John 1:5-10. But if people are going to be given permission to be truthful, they must feel safe to be truthful. There can be no shame or condemnation in Christ. There can be no one waiting to hurl stones of accusation. The congregation must also be taught how to respond to one another in love and acceptance, hating the sin and working together to overcome it, but loving, supporting, and reconciling the sinners to God, others, and themselves.

From the pulpit, the pastor can draw attention to the availability of the recovery ministry through announcements. That information can be printed in the bulletin or available in the pew racks or posted with other church announcements. In doing this, the pastor either directly or indirectly gives people permission to need and seek out the support of others. The pastor can also take advantage of other means to bring about awareness and acceptance of the recovery ministry, such as a pastoral letter to the congregation or articles for church publications.

The pastor can periodically allow support group members to share their testimonies with the congregation of what God has done in their lives through the groups. They can be done occasionally as brief praise reports to the congregation or regularly as part of a support group Sunday emphasis. It is always powerful when people share personal testimonies of the life-changing work of Jesus Christ. It gives the congregation permission to look at their lives and need for support.

The Role of Support Group Members

The pastor plays a large role in creating awareness and acceptance within the congregation. But people who are a part of the recovery ministry also play a vital role in its development. At some point in recovery to keep what we have, we must be willing to give it away. Overcoming Satan's destructive work in our lives involves the blood of the Lamb and what Christ has done for us and the word of our testimonies that we share with others (Rev. 12:11). In Twelve-Step groups this is part of Step Twelve and is known as "carrying the message."

Carrying the message can happen formally or informally. Sometimes support group members who are involved in other church fellowships and groups share their experiences. Other times they may be invited to speak and share their testimony. Each time of sharing helps others to understand and accept recovery ministry and gives people permission to consider whether they or someone they love needs the same help and support.

Our support group members periodically offer and lead educational seminars in our congregation or in other churches on topics related to their particular group. They minister by providing information, understanding, and encouragement to those who may be struggling in that area or know someone that they want to help. Our support group members have also trained those in our church who are in positions of leadership and ministry in understanding how to respond to and help persons with particular problems.

Our congregation has a recovery ministry awareness month. (It doesn't necessarily have to be a month; it can be one or two Sundays.) On designated Sundays, which are well-publicized, we set up an area in our main fellowship hall or narthex area with information about the support groups. On a table we have individual fliers that describe each group, what the group is for, and where and when it meets. We have copies of group literature and books. We tell people where they can purchase the books or have the church bookstore stock them. Support group members answer questions and share their experiences of being in the groups. Support group members give their testimonies in the service as a way to draw attention to the support group emphasis, and they invite the congregation to drop by the area and find out more about the ministry.

The key is to confront denial in the congregation and give people permission to be imperfect and struggle with the issues in their lives. There must be a regular, consistent, and clear message that the church is called to provide that support and is willing and able to do that through the power of God revealed in the koinonia fellowship of support groups.

Your Role

If you are reading this book because you feel a burden for this ministry, but your pastor is not entirely sold on it, you have a few options. One is to make this book a gift and pray that God will let it find favor in your pastor's heart! A second option is to get permission to try a recovery ministry and then make an evaluation. You will have to do all of the work in creating awareness and acceptance initially. Things will probably go slowly at first. But most pastors are interested in ministry that changes people's lives and in church growth, and when your pastor sees these things taking place, you may get the backing and pastoral endorsement that you need. A last option is to become involved with another church receptive to this new ministry. You don't have to leave your church to be a part of and participate in another church's recovery ministry. Later, perhaps, you can come back with more understanding and experience to share with your church. Many people came to our groups from their churches, then went back to their churches after they had developed a nucleus of people who were able and determined to start a similar group there. Whatever works for you and helps you to get a recovery ministry started in your church, do it!

Well, now you've gotten your support group(s) going. You planned well, did a good job of publicizing them, and got a healthy response to your efforts. People are excited, they're sharing with one another, and you can really see koinonia fellowship developing. But you need to make decisions that you hadn't thought about and solve problems that you hadn't anticipated. Don't panic! This is not the time to get discouraged, overwhelmed, or afraid of recovery ministry. This is the time to make the decisions to set up a structure that will allow you to maintain the ministry. For me, real discipline and effort come in at this point. It is easy to begin support groups. The challenge lies in maintaining them. If you're up to the challenge, we will take it on in the next section.

Section 4

DECIDING ON A STRUCTURE:

Maintaining a Recovery Ministry

D espite all of the time and effort that goes into setting up a recovery ministry, it is not starting the support groups that will be the most difficult task; it will be maintaining that ministry on an ongoing basis. I have always had two goals for our recovery ministry. First, I want the groups to be there for people to go through the whole process leading to recovery. A three-month or six-month or even one-year group will not provide enough support for some problems. I would like to think that long after those of us who originally started the recovery ministry at Mount Paran are gone, it will remain and continue to support people through those problems and experiences that are common to all people. For that to happen, the groups must be basically self-sufficient and self-sustaining, which is my second goal. The acquired wisdom and experience of the group must be passed along to a succeeding generation; that generation assumes it as a trust to be passed along to the next one, and so on.

To accomplish these two goals, we have developed a structure that safeguards and maintains the koinonia fellowship of support. In this section we will look at each essential aspect of this structure. We are still learning, but I will share with you what we have discovered so far.

We will examine six aspects of this structure. *Group traditions* preserve the purpose and goals of the ministry. *Group principles* protect the integrity of the meeting. The role of *group leadership* is outlined, and the importance of *servanthood and sponsorship* is established. The *Twelve Step program* disciples and matures individuals and groups, and *Family of Choice* groups provide more in-depth, intensive growth experiences for group members.

Chapter
13

Group
Traditions

Group traditions allow support groups to accomplish their purpose and meet the needs of members while avoiding things that would create confusion, conflict, or disrupt unity. They establish a proper sense of responsibility of members to the group, and of the various groups to the recovery ministry.

You may develop as many group traditions as you find helpful and necessary for your situation. I will share the ones that our groups have identified and adopted for themselves as a model. The twelve traditions of Alcoholics Anonymous influenced us as we worked to develop our own, but our traditions reflect our uniqueness as a Christ-centered fellowship and yours should do the same.

Our Traditions

Tradition 1: We are guided by and follow only one authority—a loving God who manifests Himself to us through the lordship of His Son, Jesus Christ—and the wisdom of His word as revealed in the Bible.

This tradition establishes Jesus Christ as the central and ultimate authority in any matters pertaining to the functioning of the support group. Any philosophy that is taught must be consistent with the

Bible. Guidelines, traditions, and principles must reflect the truth of God revealed in Scripture. We cannot and do not seek to control what others may think, feel, or express as long as they recognize and respect the authority that we follow. The opening and closing prayers of our groups acknowledge God as the ultimate source of love and healing and Jesus Christ as Lord, whose grace is sufficient to meet all of our needs.

One time we were taken to task by some group members who had grown up in the AA Twelve-Step program and wanted everything in the groups to reflect the philosophy of *The Big Book* of Alcoholics Anonymous. Our groups didn't always do what *The Big Book* said to do. We established this tradition because, although we use the wisdom of the Twelve Steps to structure and disciple those in recovery, we are not and do not desire to be AA groups. Much in *The Big Book* of AA is helpful, but the Bible is the Bigger Book that guides our fellowship.

Tradition 2: The unity of the group is of primary importance. The common welfare of the group is not based on individual needs or personalities but comes from the purpose and principles of the group as a whole.

This tradition recognizes the sense of safety that the unity of the group provides. It is necessary if group members are to be honest and vulnerable and take the risks leading to healing. In this atmosphere group members can be ministered to. Psalm 133 declares that this unity is good and pleasant and associated with God's blessings. No one person, need, or personality will be allowed to disrupt that unity. If a person cannot dwell with the group in unity, that person will be asked to leave its fellowship.

Of course, there will be differences in the group from time to time that can and must be worked through. But willingness, flexibility, and humble, teachable attitudes that allow unity to be restored and preserved must be present whenever conflict occurs.

In the past persons have come into our groups with their own needs, agendas, or theology that they wanted the group to accept or accommodate. The persons became disruptive to the group as they insistently demanded their own way. This tradition was established so that all individuals in the group and their personalities and needs are subservient to the overall purpose and process of the group established by its group conscience and expressed in its traditions, guidelines, and principles.

Tradition 3: Our fellowship is open to anyone who desires to change, grow, and heal and seeks our understanding, acceptance, and support. We require only a willingness to be open and honest.

This tradition reflects the unconditional love of God in Christ. We don't expect others to believe the way that we believe or to act the way that we would like for them to act. They have to please God, not us. Our fellowship is open to non-Christians as well as Christians. We ask and expect only that our beliefs be respected in the same manner that we respect their thoughts and feelings. We will not curtail the expression of our faith to make others comfortable, but we will not force our faith on them. We trust God through the Holy Spirit to convict and draw all people to Himself through Jesus Christ in His perfect time and way. We seek only to show the kindness and mercy of God to one another.

This tradition also allows us to accept people wherever they may be in the process of healing and recovery. We don't expect others to clean up their act first to be accepted into our fellowship. Jesus declared that He came not to minister to those who were perfect and whole but to those who were incomplete, sick, and needy (Matt. 9:12–13). We consider this church to be a hospital and our support group meetings to be the emergency rooms. All that is required to be a part of our fellowship is the willingness to be open and honest with ourselves, others, and God so that He can work in our lives to bring us to the truth that sets us free and heals.

I got a call one day from a person who wanted to know if we allowed Jewish people to attend our support groups. I assured him that all we asked was that he be honest, open, and respectful of our beliefs and that we would be the same with him. That person became an important part of one of our support groups and even took on a leadership role. Another person expressed the need for a group, but he wanted me to know up front that he was really angry with God and hated Him. I said that the best place for him to be with those feelings was in a group where God could work on them, and that as long as he was honest and open with his feelings and didn't act out in the group or blaspheme God, God and the group could accept him where he was. That person worked through those feelings in the group and now is an active member of our church.

Tradition 4: Our primary purpose is to carry the message of faith, hope, and love to those who are suffering and share our pain.

This tradition calls on us to be single-minded in purpose. All that we do and talk about in our meetings concerns the single stated purpose of sharing our experiences in that area with one another to give one another faith, hope, and love to overcome. Nothing is as important as bearing one another's burdens and ministering to those who share our struggle and our pain. This tradition keeps us from spending our time, resources, and energy as a group on anything that does not accomplish our purpose of providing support to one another for the specific problem that has brought us together.

Tradition 5: All groups should be self-supporting and responsible to meet their own financial needs and obligations through offerings and designated contributions by members.

This tradition establishes the responsibility of group members to invest in themselves as well as in the recovery of others. It is vital to our own well-being and sense of self-esteem and also to the well-being of the group that we assume an active responsibility for our lives rather than sit back passively, helplessly, and dependently. Each group takes its own offerings and pays for those things that it determines are necessary. They may include refreshments, literature, child care, activities outside the group meeting, seminars, benevolent situations involving group members, a group tithe to God through the church, and so on.

All group offerings are turned in to and accounted for by the church's business office as part of the group's commitment to fiscal responsibility. All group moneys are spent according to a consensus of the leadership, and a regular printout of receipts and expenditures is made available to the group.

Tradition 6: No worldly problems, intellectual arguments, or spiritual debate should divert us from our spiritual aim and group purpose.

This tradition ensures that the group will not get caught up in things that will distract from its basic purpose and its foundational spiritual truths. It is not that we are apathetic to world problems, but in the group, we understand that the only thing that we can absolutely control and change to accomplish something positive and constructive in our lives is ourselves. Intellectual arguments and spiritual debates are useless and fruitless in that context as well. We don't attempt to sway anyone to our point of view. We simply offer our support by sharing our experience, strength, and hope.

Tradition 7: The group wisdom comes from within its members as God works in us and speaks through us and should not be entrusted to outside speakers or those who are not part of our fellowship.

This tradition protects the group from confusion and division. No one is allowed to lead the group, advise the group, or determine the needs of the group who has not been a faithful and committed member. No one is presented as an authority to the group meeting who has not been a part of its fellowship. Visitors from other support group fellowships may share in meetings. And speakers are invited for retreats, seminars, and special events. But wisdom and guidance regarding the needs of the group and the purpose and function of its meeting can come only from those who are an integral part of its fellowship.

Tradition 8: Each group is self-determining and responsible for recognizing its own needs and conducting its own affairs and meetings.

This tradition places the responsibility to determine and meet the needs of the group on the persons who know it best: its members. Each group must determine its purpose for meeting and develop its format. Group members must attend to group activities, financial affairs, and practical needs. The church provides guidance and responsibility only to ensure that groups reflect the purpose for which they were created and remain consistent with church policy and doctrine about how that purpose is pursued.

Tradition 9: Our meeting together and the support and help that we provide to one another are paramount and should not be preempted by other meetings, events, or occasions, except as determined by group conscience.

This tradition ensures that group meetings will always be available to those who need them. Meetings are never canceled so that members can participate in another activity, no matter how appealing or relevant that activity may be. Regardless of how attendance at a meeting may be affected by other events, the meeting must be held for those who need its support. If a meeting is to be canceled, it must be anticipated in advance, discussed, and agreed upon through group conscience and consensus, and then publicized and announced to the group prior to the meeting that will be canceled. A notice should be posted outside the group room advising when the group will resume meeting.

Most of our groups meet on holidays, even Christmas Day, if the meeting night falls on a holiday. Some of the best meetings have taken place on those days with only three or four members present. One time the groups were asked not to meet for an evening in case their meeting rooms needed to be used for a conference that our church and our senior pastor were hosting. The groups developed a contingency plan. Since it was a pleasant time of year, they would take their chairs and meet on the church grounds. It turned out that the church was able to work around the groups, but meetings are that important to groups.

Tradition 10: Each group is a part of the whole of the recovery ministry of Mount Paran Church of God and accepts its spiritual leadership and guidance in matters pertaining to the common good and welfare of that ministry.

This tradition establishes the role and proper authority of the church in the affairs of the support groups that are a part of the recovery ministry. The unity and the well-being of the recovery ministry as a whole are of primary importance, not the needs of any one group. All leadership and responsibility for the groups is ultimately conferred by God through the fellowship of this church and those designated as its pastors. Any group that cannot operate under that spiritual covering will be discontinued as part of the church recovery ministry. Any group leader who cannot agree with and be spiritually accountable and loyal to the church's leadership will be asked to step down or be removed from a leadership role.

Tradition 11: We are nonprofessionals and provide no expertise other than our own experience, strength, and hope.

This tradition establishes the group's lay orientation. We do not provide treatment, counseling, or any professional advice or expertise to our group members. Professionals may be part of our fellowship, but they do not operate in any capacity other than as group members working on their own recovery. We do not attempt to give insight or advice about what group members should or should not do in their lives. We simply share our experience, strength, and hope with one another. God may use our experience to speak to others in the group, but it is their responsibility to choose and to carefully discern God's perfect will for their lives rather than looking to, asking for, and acting on the wisdom of imperfect group members.

Several times Christian counselors and therapists have joined groups and wanted to lead them. One counselor always wanted to reply after people shared and offer psychological insight into why they were doing or feeling what they were experiencing. Another wanted to lead the whole group on an inner healing experience. A support group is not for those purposes.

Tradition 12: We have no leaders, only trusted servants who do not control or govern from any position of authority over the group. The group entrusts them with the responsibility to maintain the safety of the group established in guidelines and preserve the purpose of the group according to traditions and principles.

This tradition protects the group from any person assuming too much authority, and it protects individual members from assuming too much responsibility for the group. Leadership of the group should be associated not with individuals but with the group as a whole. Each group member is to follow the guidelines, traditions, and principles. The role of leadership then becomes one of serving the group by facilitating the meeting and group functions. Trusted servants enable the group to carry out its purpose by maintaining the safety of the group according to its guidelines, traditions, and principles established by group conscience, and by insisting that the members follow them in all of their interactions with one another.

Tradition 13: Confidentiality is the basis of trust and safety within the group, and it is the cornerstone of our well-being and ability to fulfill the purpose for which God has called us as a group.

This tradition establishes confidentiality in every regard concerning the group and its members. Confidentiality has already been established in the guidelines for what is shared during the meeting, but by establishing confidentiality as a tradition, we reaffirm it as the single most important element in maintaining a healthy and safe support group. The inability to maintain this tradition and to follow the same guideline is so damaging and destructive to a support group fellowship that any violation calls for immediate confrontation according to group principles and may result in expulsion from the group.

Altering Traditions

Once group traditions are established, any additions or deletions can result only from consensus among the total recovery ministry, which should include representatives from each group as well as input from the designated church representative responsible for that ministry. Additions may be proposed from time to time as the nature of the recovery ministry changes and experience and wisdom concerning it grow. Carefully approach any attempt to delete traditions. They should not be discarded without serious consideration about the reason to do so.

Group traditions should be presented clearly and directly in the group literature. Our groups include them in the welcome literature given to newcomers. Group leaders must understand the traditions completely and have the ability to present them within meetings should the need arise. This understanding is a key component of leadership training, which will be discussed in more detail in a later chapter.

Your traditions preserve and protect your recovery ministry and each group in it. Consider carefully what they need to be to ensure the ongoing health and balance of your groups.

Traditions and guidelines are significant, but they do not tell you what to do in specific instances where problems affect the safety and ability of the group to function properly and pursue its purpose. To do that, you need to develop specific principles that outline the group's position on various situations. In the next chapter we will look at developing group principles and talk about the specific ones established in our groups.

Chapter
14

Group Problems, Group Principles, and Group Conscience

I wish I could say that if you planned your support group properly, established your traditions and guidelines clearly, followed your format precisely, and stated your goals and expectations plainly, everything would automatically go smoothly in group meetings, and your recovery ministry would be an instant and overwhelming success. In recovery we learn to be rigorously honest. So, as much as I would like to, I cannot offer you that assurance. My experience has been that wherever two or more imperfect people are gathered together, there will be problems in the midst. Expect them. Plan for them. Allow for them. Don't allow problems to sabotage the group or use them as an excuse not to take the time and effort to deal with them.

Groups grow and mature as they struggle. It is part of God's natural plan for growth. The caterpillar must struggle for a season in its cocoon before it bursts forth and takes to the air as the butterfly. We struggle with lifting weights to build up our muscles and our strength. The strength of a group comes from the struggles that it overcomes. From the lessons of what not to do, the group learns what to do.

The Chinese language uses symbols to represent words and

meanings. The symbol representing the word *crisis* is actually two symbols connected together. If you separate the two symbols, the first symbol represents the word *danger*; the second, the word *opportunity*. The Chinese understand that any crisis contains both danger and opportunity. That is the way to approach group problems and crises. An element of danger may seem overwhelming and threatening to you and to the group, but you also have the opportunity to learn from the crisis, seek and gain the wisdom that it offers, and establish that wisdom in principles allowing the group to proceed stronger and more sure of itself and its purpose.

I remember when I was in graduate school taking group counseling classes. My professor taught us that there is a process of group development. First is the *forming stage*; group members are excited just to be together, and everyone is overaccommodating and on best behavior. No one is quite sure what to expect. Group members cautiously sit back observing and making sure that they fit in. The second stage is the *storming stage*; group members exert their individual needs and pressure the group to measure up to their expectations. It is a time of testing to find out the limits and boundaries. There are power struggles to define the group's purpose and influence the way that the group goes about accomplishing that purpose. This stage is often full of confusion, chaos, and conflict. It will force the group into the third stage, the *norming stage*; the group will have to identify and adopt the basic principles that will allow it to function constructively and productively. The common welfare of the group is established as more important than any individual need or personality through the collective process of group conscience. The group then can move into the fourth stage, the *performing stage*; it can function as a whole despite the individual imperfections. The established norms, or group principles, keep the group self-correcting whenever it runs into any problems that would otherwise create confusion, chaos, or conflict.

Self-correction takes place through the group conscience, which we will discuss later in this chapter. For now let's look at some common problems that our recovery ministry has already struggled with and the principles that we have established to deal with them. Establish principles in writing so that the group conscience is clearly voiced and can be presented directly to individuals whenever it needs to be enforced. Present these principles to newcomers in their orientation meeting or welcome packet. Make them part of the leadership training. If it is necessary, select them as the topic of discussion and reaffirmation in the group meeting. These norms (principles) allow the group to weather the storms.

Group Problems and Principles

Group Problem: Who may attend our groups? Are they open to non-Christians?

Group Principle: Our groups are open to anyone who desires our understanding and support and is willing to be both open and honest. That is a tradition. We don't force our beliefs on anyone, but we don't apologize for the Christ-centered nature of our groups. We will not compromise our beliefs to accommodate any group member. We will not judge anyone for not believing as we do, knowing that the Holy Spirit convicts us and brings us into all truth, but we do insist that others respect our beliefs and follow our traditions, guidelines, and principles.

Early on, our groups debated this issue. Some non-Christians attending our groups were uncomfortable and defensive about our beliefs. But we felt strongly that our groups should be accepting and provide a place where others could be exposed to the light and see the unconditional love of Christ through us.

Group Problem: What if someone becomes very angry and acts out in a group meeting?

Group Principle: We expect very intense emotions during recovery. We will accept any intense emotions honestly expressed as part of the healing process of bearing one another's burdens and casting our care on God. We do expect persons to be controlled by the Holy Spirit of God and able to own and present their feelings responsibly in a way that does not directly threaten anyone in or outside the group or make the group unsafe.

A lot of hurt and anger is expressed in meetings. One group member had been so severely physically and sexually abused for most of her life that all she could do in the meetings was cry and rage. We allowed the rage to be expressed and the wound to drain. At times we had to firmly set limits when she threatened to harm other people or things with her rage, but as long as she was angry and didn't sin, we provided a safe place and encouraged her to express the hurt.

Group Problem: What about the use of profanity to express feelings?
Group Principle: We don't judge anyone inside or outside the group for the use of profanity. We understand that in some cases it may be an expression of the depth of the pain inside a person. However, we believe that there are other ways to express feelings just as intensely, and we don't allow profanity in our meetings. Meetings are meant to be a safe refuge. Profanity often brings up fear for those who have been verbally abused. It may bring on a sense of shame for those who are trying desperately to leave the old life and life-styles behind. Profanity that takes the name of God or Jesus in vain shows a lack of respect for those of us who seek to honor God and make Jesus Lord of our lives.

No one has shown disrespect for our beliefs by taking the name of God or Christ in vain. But I know that we lost at least a dozen group members before someone was brave enough to say that he felt unsafe when people were using profanity and others finally expressed that it reminded them of the old selves they were so ashamed of. The groups then addressed the problem.

Group Problem: What about smoking at group meetings?
Group Principle: Smoking is not allowed in any group meetings or within the church facilities. We understand smoking to be destructive to our lives physically; it is an addictive-compulsive behavior that controls lives and medicates emotions. It is threatening and unsafe to group members who do not smoke, and it prevents the honest experience and expression of feelings in meetings. We do not judge people who may be still struggling to gain control over this

aspect of their lives. We accept that God must convict them of His desire for their lives to be controlled only by His Holy Spirit and give them the power to overcome in this area.

One reason that people in our church started the alcoholics and addicts support group was to get away from the smoke-filled AA meetings they had been attending. Our groups have never allowed smoking.

Group Problem: What about eating or drinking during meetings?
Group Principle: Groups may have refreshments before or after meetings as a way to fellowship together if they choose. However, we recognize that caffeine and sugar are mood-altering substances, and that eating and drinking during meetings can be a way to distract from feelings and avoid reality. For this reason, we do not allow eating or drinking during the meeting itself so that we can be fully present for others and rigorously honest in dealing with ourselves and our feelings.

Group Problem: What if people have used drugs or alcohol before the meeting and are obviously under the influence?
Group Principle: We understand the nature of addictive-compulsive behavior to be cunning, baffling, and powerful. We do not judge one another as we struggle to overcome its strong hold. We would rather the persons be with us, surrounded by our love and the truth of God, than for them to be alone, isolated, and ashamed. As long as their behavior while under the influence does not distract or disrupt the group, they may remain in the meeting. Only if they interfere with the group process as a result of being under the influence should they be asked to leave.

One person fairly regularly comes to meetings under the influence of alcohol. He sits quietly, and we just keep loving him. He has been coming back for almost two years now, so he must feel loved and accepted. We do not ignore the problem. We continue to encourage him to get help. But there is no judgment or condemnation or exclusion from the group. On the other hand, another person regularly came to meetings under the influence of prescription medication that she was abusing and interfered with the group process. We ultimately had to ask her to leave. It was a difficult time for us and for the person, but the pain of it helped to break through the denial and clarify her problem.

Group Problem: What about people who continue to relapse?
Group Principle: We understand and accept the imperfect process of growth. We do not expect perfection, only effort. We support one another as we make the mistakes we will surely make and encourage one another to depend more on God and others and less on ourselves and our own ability to control and manage our lives and overcome our problems. As long as we take responsibility for our relapses or mistakes and are willing to confess them to ourselves, God, and one another, we believe that Jesus continues to offer us an unlimited grace that will ultimately be sufficient to meet all of our needs, and that He expects us to offer the same grace to one another (Matt. 18:21–35).

One person kept relapsing for several years, but we kept encouraging her, and she kept coming back and trying again. Finally, as our senior pastor is fond of saying, the vaccination took! She now has almost three years of recovery and has rebuilt her life. That might never have happened if we had quickly given up on her and condemned her for repeatedly making the same mistake.

Group Problem: What about group members who are always trying to give advice or tell others what they should think, feel, or do?
Group Principle: Although usually well-intentioned, offering advice to one another about what to think, feel, or do is not helpful. Advice giving takes personal responsibility away from individuals and may create an unhealthy dependency. Advice giving sends a subtle but powerful message implying that persons are incapable of seeking God's wisdom for themselves and of acting on that understanding. We do not presume to know what others need, so we do not give advice. We simply offer our experience, strength, and hope.

Group Problem: What about group members who want to confront others about personal issues or recovery issues?

Group Principle: Direct confrontation of individuals is never appropriate in a support group meeting and will not be allowed. Confrontation may stop behavior, but it does not help people change. Encouragement gives us the courage to change, and that is all we allow in meetings.

Two people in one group especially felt that they had to confront what a man was doing or not doing in recovery. Their frustration and anger toward the person who would not change would inevitably get the group off track. I was surprised that the person being confronted didn't leave the group. In another situation, two group members tried to use the group to take sides in their personal disputes.

Group Problem: How should the group approach the person who continues to deny that there is a problem and pretends that everything is fine?

Group Principle: It is not our responsibility to make anyone see the truth. It is only our responsibility to seek truth in ourselves and share that truth with others. We believe that people will see the truth when they are ready and prepared to do so and God reveals it to them. We understand that denial has a protective purpose, and we would not harm one another in any way by attempting to remove it forcibly or prematurely. We recognize that each person must be allowed to let go of denial when ready to do so. By truthfully sharing our own experience, strength, and hope, we provide one another with the opportunity to confront the denial that is in all of us.

When we first started one support group, a person attended a while but never could see that he had a real problem. Eventually, he dropped out of the group. Four years later he came back. After continuing to make the same mistakes and getting the same results, he finally admitted that there was a problem and it must be something in him rather than in everyone and everything else.

Group Problem: What about the person who wants to spiritualize everything and preach to the group about trusting Jesus and praying more?

Group Principle: This problem is the same as spiritual advice giving and is treated in the same way. We trust that the love of God and the grace of Jesus Christ are the ultimate sources of our safety and healing. We pray and present ourselves as living sacrifices, desiring only the knowledge of His will for our lives and the power to carry it out one day at a time. We know, however, that it is our responsibility to seek truth in the inmost being and to expose everything to the light, confessing our faults and our sins to one another so that we can be healed. We have found recovery to be a question not of trusting Jesus more but of being more honest with God, ourselves, and others. This we seek to do. We may share the spiritual truths that God reveals to us. We do not preach to others about what God needs to do in their lives. We show by example what He is doing in our lives that others may see and choose to follow.

One group member shared with me her struggle to overcome a particular sin. For years she had attended church service after church service, responded to altar call after altar call, and prayed daily for deliverance from the problem. But she had never brought the problem out into the light and confessed it to anyone else. When she finally became part of a support group and admitted to God, to herself, and to other safe, supportive people the exact nature of her wrongs, the power of the shame, secrecy, and isolation was broken, and she was able to find victory.

Group Problem: What about the group member who wants to talk about other people and circumstances and blame them for personal problems?

Group Principle: We understand that God has given each of us a free will, and that we have the right to our own thoughts, feelings, and behavioral choices and the responsibility for them. We are influenced by things outside ourselves, but we are not determined by them. They are not our higher power. Jesus Christ is our higher power whose grace is sufficient and who can supply all our needs.

We are not victims. We always have options and choices. To blame other people or circumstances is to give up the control of our lives to things that we are powerless over. We do not have time to blame. We are to focus on what we can control, and we turn over to God what we cannot control. We learn to pray the Serenity Prayer for the wisdom to know the difference between the two.

One person came to our groups to get help to deal with a spouse who was an addict. He was terribly depressed and suicidal. All he wanted to talk about was what his spouse was doing to make him miserable and how bad the marriage was. Months later I ran into him at church and almost didn't recognize him. He was relaxed and smiling. When I asked him what had happened, he said, "Nothing." When I asked him if anything had changed in the situation with his spouse, he said, "No, she hasn't changed, but I have, so everything is different now." That was several years ago. The situation still hasn't changed, but he is no longer controlled by it because he chose to change in spite of it rather than to blame and remain helpless.

Group Problem: What about group members who get into conversations about their experiences while the rest of the group sits and listens to them?

Group Principle: This is known as cross talk and is not allowed in meetings. The group learns and grows as everyone has the opportunity to share his or her experience, strength, and hope. In this way, the needs of the whole group are met. When just a few members talk with one another about their experiences, the whole group suffers. If we relate to group members and what they have shared in a special way, we should approach them after the meeting and talk one-on-one.

Before we understood the problem with cross talk, in some meetings three or four group members would get a conversation going, and the rest of the group would sit there for an hour or so just looking and listening. The same people would dominate the sharing every week. The group dwindled. When the principle about cross talk was implemented, the opportunity for people to share increased significantly, and the group began to grow again. People have to feel involved if they are going to remain in a group.

Group Problem: What about the person who monopolizes the time so that others do not get to share?

Group Principle: Group members grow by learning from one another's experience, strength, and hope. When more people have time to share, the opportunity is greater for the needs of all group members to be met. This principle relates to our traditions. Group members are responsible for being direct and concise and limiting their sharing to no more than three to five minutes each. If everyone who chooses to share has done so and time remains, the group may offer the extra time to people who feel they need it. Monopolizing the time because of extreme need is addressed in another principle.

In some situations one person talked for the whole meeting, and no one else was able to share. One person kept talking even after the time had come for the meeting to end and many people got up and left. If people have more to share, we encourage them to talk to others after the meeting or during the week.

Group Problem: What about the group member who is always judging what someone else is doing or not doing?

Group Principle: The Bible clearly instructs us not to judge others. All of us are God's children, deserving one another's respect. We do not judge others' thoughts, feelings, or behavior. Judgment brings on condemnation and shame, which only further alienates us from ourselves, others, and God and makes the group unsafe. Kindness leads to repentance. We are kind to one another in thought, word, and deed.

Group Problem: What about group members who are determined to be martyrs and victims and will not or cannot change?

Group Principle: We understand that we cannot change others. Only God can change us as we yield our will and our lives to Him. We realize, however, that if nothing changes, nothing changes. We are responsible to make new choices and try new behaviors. We cannot force group members to change, but we also do not have time to waste over things that we are powerless over. We accept the problem, but we focus on the solution and what we are capable of doing in Christ and encourage others to do the same.

One of the most miserable human beings I have ever met was determined to hold on to a wrong that was done to her years before. She was convinced that her whole life was ruined and that things could never be different. All of the persons involved were dead. The person was so full of bitterness that no one wanted to be around her. Yet she refused to forgive, let go, and take the responsibility for getting on with life. The people who were dead and gone continued to abuse and control her because she refused to exercise the healing power of forgiveness and not let what someone else had done determine who she was.

Group Problem: What about the group member who is excessively needy and overwhelms the group with problems?
Group Principle: We are not a counseling group. We are not to solve anyone's problems. We are to support one another as God gives each of us the wisdom that we need through the sharing of experience, strength, and hope. If a group member needs more support than the group is designed to offer through the sharing, we encourage that person to seek one-on-one ministry after the meeting or individual counseling outside the group.

Group Problem: What about the group member who wants to talk about other group members or gossip about people outside the group?
Group Principle: In meetings we are not allowed to talk about anyone other than ourselves. We realize that we are powerless over the lives of others and are responsible only to God for what we are doing with our lives, not what someone else does. We understand gossip to be a sin in the sight of God. It judges and devalues His children. We are learning to value ourselves and to love others as God has

loved us and is teaching us to love ourselves. We do not allow anyone to say or do anything in our meetings that would diminish that
sense of worth in any way in ourselves or in others.

Some groups form smaller groups so that there is plenty of time
for everyone to share and so that close friends and spouses can be
separated and feel free to talk openly and honestly without the other
being present. After one meeting, two facilitators were discussing
how their groups had gone. Both indicated problems with spouses
wanting to talk about and blame the other spouse for all their problems. It turned out that a couple had come to the meeting that night
and separated when the group broke up into smaller groups for
sharing. The wife wanted to talk about the husband in her group,
and the husband tried to talk about the wife in his group!

Group Problem: What about the group member who is constantly
violating confidentiality?
Group Principle: The group must be safe, and members must be able
to trust if the group is going to experience the koinonia fellowship
that God works through to deliver and to heal. The violation of confidentiality destroys that safety and trust. It will not be tolerated. It
will be dealt with promptly, directly, and appropriately. The group
will not allow anyone to remain who is not able or willing to maintain absolute confidentiality.

Group Problem: What about group members who are getting romantically involved with one another?
Group Principle: We are not responsible for making decisions for
group members and cannot control the choices they may make. We
cannot forbid people to become romantically involved. If one or both
are married, we will not encourage the relationship and enable sin
in any way. Honesty and personal responsibility are the basics of
our program, and we will lovingly and privately confront members
who are violating a covenant relationship. If members are unmar-
ried, we can only encourage them to understand that relationship
building, like recovery, is a process, and God must be the higher
power who prepares us and promotes us in a relationship in His

time and in His way. If relationship issues between two group members interfere with the function and well-being of the group, one or both will be asked to leave the group until they can resolve the conflict and can participate in the group without bringing the relationship into it.

This problem has been a tough one. On the one hand, there is no better place to meet someone who is committed to open and honest relationships than in a support group. I have counseled with and married couples who met in our support groups and were able to develop healthy relationships. On the other hand, support groups can be places to find other needy, insecure people to develop relationships with. I have had to intervene and help people get out of destructive, abusive relationships that they had entered into with other support group members. We cannot control people's choices, but if recovery teaches group members nothing else, it should teach them that nothing good usually happens quickly. I encourage group members to take things very slowly and make sure that God is building the relationship between them and that it is a safe and healthy one. That takes time. There are no shortcuts to intimacy.

Group principles are established whenever a group encounters an issue that becomes a problem or is considered a potential threat to accomplishing the group's purpose. Group principles come into being through a process that Alcoholics Anonymous called group conscience. Also, group principles are maintained and enforced through group conscience. Since it is such a vital force in the life of a group, we must understand how to establish, maintain, and conduct group conscience.

Group Conscience

The book of Proverbs contains great wisdom, and much of that wisdom applies to support groups. According to Proverbs 11:14, a support group will fail if there is no guidance, but safety will be found in the wisdom of many counselors. Group conscience is based on this idea. A group must have trusted servants to perform leadership tasks, but its safety and health depend on the group's taking responsibility for the way it functions. It must not depend on any one person or authority within the group.

Group conscience can be initiated by the membership or the leadership. If it is initiated by an individual, the trusted servants should determine if a group conscience is needed to deal with the issue and set an appropriate time to address it with the group.

Leaders can initiate group conscience and bring issues to the group's attention for approval or disapproval. All matters pertaining to the group's purpose and functions are initially established in this manner. Group conscience establishes its format, its guidelines, its traditions, and its principles, and group conscience makes any changes to these things.

One of our groups got off track when it ignored this process. Group leaders decided to abandon the format and to change the focus and the way the group went about accomplishing its purpose. The matter was not brought before the group to allow the group conscience to speak. As a result, the meetings became unstructured and confusing, and the group became almost ineffective within a short period of time.

When a group is part of a recovery ministry involving other groups, an additional level of wisdom protects the group. While each group develops its format and the principles that uniquely apply to the group, the recovery ministry as a whole establishes common guidelines, traditions, and principles that keep the ministry healthy. Decisions of a group may not contradict or conflict with the group conscience of the total recovery ministry. Individual group conscience decisions that concern recovery ministry guidelines, traditions, or principles must be presented to the ministry leadership for final approval before they can be adopted by the group.

The ministry leaders can come to one of three decisions concerning individual group issues. They may override the individual group conscience on the basis that it is not in keeping with the common welfare of the recovery ministry. They may decide that the issue needs to be addressed by the total recovery ministry. Or they may decide that the issue is applicable only to that group and does not affect the well-being of the ministry as a whole; then they may allow the group to make its own decision on that issue.

When one group presented the issue of profanity for group conscience at a meeting of the recovery ministry leadership, other groups expressed the same concern. They were seeing new group members who were used to secular support groups and expected our groups to function in the same manner. The recovery ministry acted to establish the principle regarding profanity so that it would apply to all groups.

Raising issues for group conscience within the recovery ministry takes place in the same manner that it does in the support groups. A group representative can raise an issue for consideration by the ministry, or the ministry leaders may address issues affecting the common purpose of the ministry as a whole. If the ministry leaders decide to address an issue, they must send back each representative to hold a group conscience and determine how the group feels about that matter. Then a consensus is reached by the ministry leaders representing the collective voice of the groups.

Once group conscience establishes the guidelines, traditions, and principles for the group or the recovery ministry, it also maintains them through the same process. The Bible indicates that the enforcement of group conscience should follow a proper order and have the goal of forgiving, reconciling, and restoring members to the fellowship of the group (Matt. 18:15–17; Luke 17:3). This process involves three steps, but before you can hold group members accountable and subject them to group conscience, you must make sure that the group's guidelines, traditions, and principles were directly presented to persons when they joined the fellowship. They must be stated in writing and explained or given to group members as part of orientation.

Maintaining Group Conscience

Group members are expected to take personal responsibility to abide by the group's guidelines, traditions, and principles. We recognize that we are imperfect and will make mistakes from time to time because of our humanness and our need. At these times a gentle, nonconfrontational reminder of the appropriate guideline, tradition, or principle may be all that is needed to correct the situation; a member or leader should attempt that within the meeting. If the member is not willing or able to respond appropriately, the first step is taken in the process of group conscience confrontation.

In the first step of confrontation, an acknowledged group leader confronts the individual directly but gently in private as soon as possible after the violation has occurred. No leader should presume to initiate this confrontation without a consensus of the group leadership that a violation has indeed occurred. The leader presents the guideline, tradition, or principle in question to the person and discusses its importance to the safety and well-being of the group. Then the leader explains what the person did that was inappropriate and what would be considered the appropriate thing to do in the future.

At the same time that this confrontation is taking place in private, a general group conscience meeting is held to reintroduce and reinforce the tradition, guideline, or principle that has been violated without revealing or focusing on the person who has violated it.

If the group member repents, the issue is resolved, and the person is forgiven and reconciled to the group. Group conscience has been upheld, and the matter is closed. If the person does not accept the private rebuke and is not willing to repent, or if the person is not able to be responsible and continues to consistently violate guidelines, traditions, or principles, the second step of confrontation is taken.

In the second step, several group leaders, including the one who first attempted to correct the group member's actions, meet with the person. Again, this meeting is private, and the rebuke is gentle and respectful but firm and direct. The additional group leaders affirm the importance of the issue. While they are concerned about the member's needs and would like for the person to remain in the group, they must also protect the interests of the group and preserve the tradition that establishes the primacy of the group's welfare and needs. The member is expected to take full responsibility for his or her actions, propose changes in the future, and identify the accountability that will be required to follow through on that commitment.

With the agreement of all concerned, the matter is considered resolved and closed with the member, and the member is forgiven and can be reconciled to the group based on the full acceptance of personal responsibility to the group. The member makes public confession and apology to the group in general in its group meeting and private amends to anyone in the group who was specifically harmed. Biblically, the group is called on to forgive and to restore, and the apology should be accepted. This experience can be a positive one for the group by using it as the basis for a group conscience meeting to discuss and reaffirm the importance of the guideline, tradition, or principle that has been violated.

If the person still chooses not to take responsibility for the actions or continues to consistently violate guidelines, traditions, or principles, the process of confrontation moves to the third step.

In the third step, biblically, the person is to be brought before the church. In support groups, our guidelines, traditions, and principles do not allow us to use the meeting to make judgments. This step should never publicly shame or embarrass a group member by putting the person on the spot in front of the whole group. That is contrary to the purpose of a support group. Instead, this meeting takes place with the full leadership of the group. Again, it is a private confrontation that is respectful but increasingly firm. Leaders discuss what has taken place, what is expected, and what the consequences will be if there is any further unwillingness or inability on the part of the member to be personally responsible for maintaining the guidelines, traditions, and principles. The traditions have clearly established the consequence.

If the individual acknowledges that responsibility and accepts that consequence, the individual must make the private amends deemed appropriate and a public apology to the group once again. The person must ask the group's forgiveness and pledge that if, for any reason, personal responsibility to the group is not maintained, the person will voluntarily leave the fellowship of the group. (Later, the person can petition the group for restoration.) The individual is to be forgiven and reconciled to the group on that basis.

If the individual continues to reject the private rebuke of the group's leadership and refuses to take the personal responsibility outlined by group conscience, that person should not be allowed to return to that group or any group of the recovery ministry until the individual petitions the group leadership for restoration and is willing to accept full responsibility and carry out the steps necessary for restoration.

Conducting Group Conscience

Conducting a group conscience is actually simple. At the time in the meeting when a topic would be shared and discussed, a group member or leader presents the guideline, tradition, principle, or problem that needs to be addressed or reaffirmed. That person should begin the discussion by sharing his or her thoughts and feelings. After that, the meeting is opened up to allow members to express their thoughts and feelings about the issue, according to the regular guidelines for sharing, and a consensus is reached as to the will of the group. At the end of the sharing time, leaders should bring the discussion to a close by summarizing the group's feelings and reaffirming the guideline, tradition, or principle, or by noting the group's desire to establish a new guideline, tradition, or principle and determining to implement it as soon as possible or after taking it to the total recovery ministry for consideration and approval. The leader should then remind the group that it is self-governing and its collective voice has spoken. Each individual is expected to hear and heed that common voice.

One last thought about group conscience. How often do we continue to address problems with group members and allow them to be forgiven and reconciled to the group? I believe that Jesus has given us the answer in the passages cited earlier. We are told that if a group member makes a mistake seven times and repents seven times, we are to forgive seven times (Luke 17:3–4). Peter asked that question and thought that seven times was a more than reasonable number until Jesus indicated an unlimited amount of forgiveness was in order (Matt. 18:21–35). If there are willingness and repentance, the group accepts one another's imperfections and mistakes and offers acceptance and grace to one another.

The only exception to that principle is continued violation of group confidentiality. Confidentiality is so vital to the sense of safety in a group and the ability to trust that it is the only issue established as a guideline, a tradition, and a principle. Individuals who understand its importance and continue to violate it may be turned out of the group to protect the group.

So, now the group has its format, guidelines, traditions, and principles to guide it, and a way to preserve and protect them. But another element is necessary to guide a support group and to maintain a recovery ministry, and that element is group leadership. In the next chapter we will develop a model for group leadership because the continued effectiveness of a support group depends on the group's assuming responsibility for its leadership and being able to govern itself.

Chapter
15

Group
Leadership

I think the most important factor in whether or not a support group maintains a consistent ongoing ministry is that of leadership. Recovery ministry should be a lay ministry. It is the body of Christ using the power of koinonia fellowship to minister to one another. It is not someone coming in every week and doing ministry to a group of people. The group's ability to assume the responsibility for maintaining its ministry will ultimately determine the success or failure of the group. Leadership must come from within the group and be perpetuated by a process that allows the group to pass its collective wisdom on to succeeding generations of support group members.

When we speak of group leadership, we are talking about people who govern according to the guidelines, traditions, and principles that the group has established for itself; they do not dictate to the group what it should or should not do. Group leaders facilitate and guide the group; they do not control or run the group. They are members who have been entrusted by the group for a period of time to provide for its well-being by doing whatever is necessary for the group to pursue and accomplish its purpose. In this regard we choose not to refer to them or acknowledge them as group leaders, although they perform leadership functions. Instead, they are known as the group's trusted servants, which more accurately portrays their role and status. (In earlier chapters, I did refer to them as leaders to avoid confusion since I had not yet fully explained this distinction.)

Although the role of leadership is critical to the group's well-being, it also presents several potential problems. The group may become dependent on one member or a limited number of members to lead it rather than exercise its responsibility as a whole to determine its needs and govern itself accordingly. A group member may assume too much control and responsibility for the group's function and its success. Or a group member may separate from personal accountability to the group and not continue to honestly and openly work through recovery and face personal issues.

We will discuss in detail what it means to be trusted servants and the criteria that a group uses to determine who should occupy those roles. Then we will look at some leadership responsibilities of trusted servants in our recovery ministry. Finally, we will examine the model that our recovery ministry has developed for selecting, training, and nurturing trusted servants on an ongoing basis so that they feel confident and competent to function in those roles; it anticipates and minimizes potential leadership problems or addresses and corrects them as they may arise.

What Does It Mean to Be Trusted Servants?

Several years ago I met with several dozen people who had been or were trusted servants in our groups and had been part of the recovery ministry from the very beginning. I asked them to define what it meant to be trusted servants to their groups. Here is what they shared with me:

Trusted servants are group members called by God and recognized by the group to

- carry a message of recovery to others in need through sharing their experience, strength, and hope.

- serve the needs of others by giving their time, talent, and attendance to the group.
- facilitate the group and its adherence to its traditions, guidelines, and principles in order to accomplish the stated purpose of the group and maintain its continued welfare.

The people then made ten statements about being trusted servants.

1. Trusted servants are called and committed first and foremost to do the will of the Lord Jesus Christ pertaining to the group. We do not seek to impose our own will on the group. We turn our will and our lives over to the care of God and consider it a sacred trust and calling to give back to others in some way what we have received from God and the group so that they may receive the same comfort that we have received from God and one another.

2. Trusted servants are committed to the group and can be trusted to carry out any of its affairs pertaining to meetings and functions. The group's continued well-being depends on our willingness to perform those tasks necessary to keep the doors to the meeting open and the affairs in order. We are only as effective as we are efficient in our responsible attention to those details. We do not expect perfection, but we strive for consistency and dependability in all of our efforts.

3. Trusted servants set a consistent example of recovery by working honest programs and modeling the group's traditions, guidelines, and principles. We are not perfect. God is not through with us. We are always seeking truth in the inmost being and desire God to actively work in our lives even as we serve the group. We seek to be an example of honesty and transparency by taking the risks that we ask group members to take and showing them the meaning and importance of our traditions, guidelines, and principles through our actions and not just our words.

4. Trusted servants put the welfare of the group before personal interest. That does not mean we fail to use the group to meet our recovery needs and help us deal with and overcome our issues. We simply recognize that if the traditions, guidelines, and principles of

the group are not honored and maintained above all else, the group will ultimately fail in its purpose to provide support and the opportunity for each of us to get what we need. We know that our recovery depends on the group's welfare, and we are determined to protect it at all personal costs.

5. Trusted servants give in a healthy, balanced way so that others may live. We know that as God perfects His strength in our weakness, He calls on us to bear the burdens of those who do not yet have the strength that we have been given. We are clear that it is our responsibility only to help bear one another's burdens, not to assume them or take them away. We support the healing, overcoming work possible in each person's life, but we turn the responsibility for that work, along with our will and lives, over to God.

6. Trusted servants can be depended on to lead the group according to its purpose and format. We do not determine the needs of the group, nor do we impose our agenda on the meeting. We provide the group with structure and focus by following the format, and we ensure that each meeting will be productive by insisting that the group deal only with issues directly related to its stated purpose.

7. Trusted servants facilitate and govern according to the traditions, guidelines, and principles entrusted to us by the group through group conscience. We have no power to manage the group except what has been granted us by its members. We have no wisdom that the group should believe and follow that has not been established by group conscience. The authority that the group respects and follows is found not in its individual leaders but in the wisdom and power of its group traditions, guidelines, and principles.

8. Trusted servants are responsible and can be depended on to provide and maintain a safe, supportive environment for meetings so that honest sharing can take place. The group's traditions, guidelines, and principles create this environment. It is the responsibility of each member to honor the group's traditions and follow its guidelines and principles, but it is the role of each trusted servant to model adherence to them and to insist that they be upheld by the group. The authority to do so comes from the group who entrusts its servants to ensure the safety of the whole from any individuals who

may be unwilling or unable to follow its traditions, guidelines, and principles.

9. Trusted servants are not experts; we simply carry a message of hope, demonstrate the love and acceptance of Jesus Christ, and believe God to do the work in the hearts and lives of group members. We are not counselors. We do not try to do therapy or provide insight to others. We are not trained to lead group counseling, and we do not pretend to know all that there is to know about recovery. We are expert about our own experience, strength, and hope and can facilitate the group in sharing our lives with one another. We can provide the love and acceptance that offer the support necessary for God to give each group member the wisdom and courage to change.

10. Trusted servants do not stand alone. We realize that our strength lies in our relationship with others and with God. Just as we need accountability and a power greater than ourselves to recover, so, too, do we need that same accountability and power to serve the group in a trustworthy and effective manner. We are quick to look to other trusted servants and group members when we need help. We easily accept and admit any shortcomings and mistakes that we will surely make in leading the group. We trust God as the ultimate leader and guide for the group and depend on Him to perfect His strength in the group in spite of and through our weaknesses.

The Roles of Trusted Servants

We recognize and commission two kinds of trusted servants based on the roles they play in the functioning of the group. The first kind, *ministering trusted servants,* meet the practical needs of the group that allow it to accomplish its purpose. There can be as many ministering trusted servants as there are group needs and people willing to meet them. Someone may be faithful in arriving early to arrange chairs, set up the book table and announcement area, or put out the group literature. Some persons may greet and meet newcomers and welcome them into the group. Someone may be responsible for coordinating refreshments. Other people may plan and work on special group functions, such as retreats, seminars, and parties. Some people will be called on to facilitate the meeting by leading the group through its format. Any group members who function in these roles, or any other leadership roles that the group determines to be essential to its purpose and functions, are ministering trusted servants and should be recognized and acknowledged as such.

We have determined five general criteria for becoming a ministering trusted servant. Anyone who meets the criteria may freely approach the group about functioning as a ministering trusted servant in some desired capacity, or the group may encourage someone to take on a task. The general criteria for ministering trusted servants include the following:

1. They are willing to serve others and not just their self-interests.

2. They regularly attend meetings and are actively involved in the affairs of the group.

3. They desire to work an honest program of their personal recovery; they are willing to share with others their successes and their failures.

4. They exhibit a humble, teachable, and cooperative spirit in working with other group members.

5. They are committed to go the second mile and attend special meetings as needed to maintain the purpose and function of the group.

Any member is capable of meeting these criteria after just a short time in the group.

The second kind of leaders, *administering trusted servants*, guide the overall affairs of the group for a period of time. They assist the ministering trusted servants as well as all group members in maintaining the traditions, guidelines, and principles. Groups may have numerous tasks for their ministering trusted servants, but we have identified three essential roles delegated to administering trusted servants.

The first role is that of *program coordinator*. The program coordinator is responsible for what takes place during each regular meeting of the support group. This person does not necessarily lead each meeting but assigns those who do. The program chairperson also ensures, with the assistance of the other trusted servants and group members, that the traditions, guidelines, and principles are followed so that the meeting remains safe, healthy, and balanced.

The second role is that of *group representative*. The group representative is responsible for interaction between the group and the church, or between the group and any of the other support groups in the recovery ministry. This person leads meetings of the group's trusted servants and helps to coordinate functions or activities involving other support groups or organizations outside the group.

The third role is that of *secretary/treasurer*. The secretary/treasurer is responsible for the group's finances, its records, and materials or supplies. This person takes the group offering and deposits it properly, manages the group announcements, communicates and coordinates with the church in placing orders, and handles the payment of expenses.

Since these three persons essentially guide and direct the group, its meeting, and its affairs for a period of time, more is required of them than the ministering trusted servants. The specific criteria for administering trusted servants include the following:

1. They display the general criteria for ministering trusted servants.

2. They make a one-year commitment to serve the group in their position.

3. They confess and demonstrate a personal relationship with Jesus Christ as Lord of their lives, are committed to the recovery ministry, and are willing to be accountable to the church and its doctrinal statement.

4. They are working and model an honest program of recovery and are willing to be accountable to the other group administering trusted servants and the director of recovery ministry in the event that they should be unwilling or unable to do so.

5. They understand and accept responsibility for facilitating the group according to its stated purpose by maintaining its traditions, guidelines, and principles.

6. They ensure that all persons involved in their group as ministering trusted servants are properly trained and continue to nurture them to be effective in meeting the needs of the group.

7. They have been active, faithful, and committed to the fellowship of their group for a period of at least six months prior to being designated as administering trusted servants.

8. They can be called on by the church to meet special needs and reach out to others in the church and community when asked to participate in an intervention or to represent the group.

9. They attend additional meetings and activities as determined by the recovery ministry of the church to maintain the well-being of their group and the overall recovery ministry.

10. They are responsible for coordinating the planning and implementation of special group meetings, activities, or functions.

11. They select and train the persons who will take their position for the next year and act as their mentors and advisers for a period of time.

A smooth transition process of leadership is vital, and those who are in any position of group leadership, whether they are ministering or administering trusted servants, must be well-trained and supervised to feel confident and competent. When that does not happen, a support group will very quickly flounder, and there will be a leadership void or leadership will not be equipped to maintain the group's traditions, guidelines, and principles. The group will be vulnerable to losing track of its purpose and becoming unsafe and unproductive. To minimize this possibility, we encourage our groups to follow an orderly process of transition in leadership, and we require that all trusted servants go through a leadership training process. Let's consider what is involved in each process.

Leadership Selection

Obviously, as a group forms and begins, no group members meet all of the specific qualifications of administering trusted servants. Initially, a core group of people will be responsible for handling the meeting and taking care of the affairs. Over a period of time, the group will grow and mature; it will move into a more formal leadership structure. Group members can volunteer or the group can designate them to fill the three administering trusted servant roles. Moving into a more formal leadership structure as soon as possible gives the group consistent guidance and the opportunity for ongoing growth that comes with stability, order, and continuity.

The group's first administering trusted servants begin a process that should continue to provide consistent leadership with minimal disruption in transition periods. During the first quarter after someone becomes an administering trusted servant, the person identifies and recruits one other group member who meets the specific criteria for that role. That individual becomes the administering trusted servant's assistant. Each of the administering trusted servants should seek someone to become an assistant during that time frame.

During the second quarter, the administering trusted servant continues to lead the group while the designated assistant observes and learns what is involved in fulfilling that role. The assistant may even fill in occasionally. The administering trusted servant actively works with and teaches the assistant.

During the third quarter, the administering trusted servant turns over group responsibilities to the assistant while continuing to serve the group. The trusted servant is present and can still take over if needed, but as much as possible, the trusted servant shares the role with the designated assistant.

During the fourth quarter, the administering trusted servant completely turns the position over to the assistant but remains available as a mentor and adviser throughout the person's tenure as an administering trusted servant. The new administering trusted servant identifies the group member who will become the designated assistant, and the cycle of leadership perpetuates itself.

Group members are allowed to move into and out of any of the various ministering trusted servant roles as they desire to, as long as they meet the general criteria or follow the process that the group may set up for filling these positions.

Once this cycle is set in motion, the selection of group leadership becomes a fluid process. The group becomes self-governing from within its ranks. All group members who fit the general and specific criteria for leadership are qualified to take on any of the ministering or administering trusted servant roles and are expected to do so as part of their service to the group. This idea will be explored further in the chapter on servanthood and sponsorship.

Two of our largest and strongest groups, our addicts group and the group for family members of addicts, developed a solid core of leaders over a period of several years. Over time, various circumstances took almost all of those persons out of the fellowship. They left behind a new generation of leaders who did not have or were not able to pass along the vision for the group as well. As these people grew more and more weary and discouraged, they left the group. Very soon both groups were struggling to maintain an effective ministry. We are currently working to rebuild both groups that are so needed.

Leadership Training

Trusted servants must be properly trained to understand their role and how to carry it out. For the first few years of our recovery ministry, we left this to each group to accomplish. It was often done very informally with the end result that leadership training was frequently inadequate and inconsistent from group to group and within the total ministry. Now we have standard structured leadership training, and all support group trusted servants are required to go through it.

The training sessions are offered twice a year. They take place on a Friday evening and all day Saturday, concluding with a dinner and a Saturday evening service. Anyone who is a trusted servant may attend, but all ministering trusted servants are required to attend the first training offered after they assume that role in a group, and all administering trusted servants are required to attend all trainings during the time they function in that role. Even though they may repeat the training several times, we feel that they must be there to model the commitment to trusted servanthood for the new leaders and to affirm the importance of that office to the continued well-being of the group and the recovery ministry.

We designed the training with the assistance of about a dozen persons who had been involved with the groups since their beginnings and had been trusted servants and another half-dozen persons who were trusted servants in newly formed groups. We asked them what they felt that trusted servants needed to know and understand to feel adequate for the task. We then categorized all of the ideas and identified nine main themes, which became the bases for the nine sessions. We arranged the sessions in a logical order and set an agenda.

Then we assigned three or four trusted servants to work together on each session, developing a written presentation and materials to be used. They were given about four months to accomplish the task. During that process, I consulted with each group and provided resources. These groups became the first faculty. They were to have handouts and present the information in whatever way they felt was most effective in the hour- to hour-and-fifteen-minute-long session that they were responsible for.

At the end of the first training weekend, all of the session presentations and handouts were put together into a training manual for support groups in our recovery ministry. We continue to fine-tune our training, and I'm sure that it will continue to change to meet the needs of the group leadership. But the basic core curriculum is set up so that a structured training experience ensures consistency to the groups and to the recovery ministry. According to the specific criteria established for trusted servants, administering trusted servants lead the training, although other trusted servants can be faculty members. As the pastor in charge of recovery ministry, I play a significant role in that training, leading some sessions, but trusted servants teach one another in the other sessions.

Let's consider now the model for training our trusted servants. We'll briefly talk about the goals of sessions and some sources for the information presented.

Trusted Servant Training Agenda

Friday Evening (7:00–10:00)
  First Session 7:00
     "The Vision for Recovery Ministry"
  Break 8:00
  Second Session 8:15
     "The Foundation for Recovery Ministry"
       Group Traditions
       Group Guidelines
  Closing Devotions 9:45
  Dismissal 10:00

Saturday Morning (9:00–1:00)
  Third Session 9:00
     "How Support Groups Work"
  Break 10:15
  Fourth Session 10:30
     "How to Handle Group Problems"
       Group Principles
  Break 11:45
  Fifth Session 12:00
     "Group Conscience: How to Establish, Maintain, and Conduct It"
  Lunch 1:00 (Everyone brings a lunch. Drinks are provided.)

Saturday Afternoon (2:00–6:00)
>   *Sixth Session* 2:00
>   >   "What It Means to Be a Trusted Servant"
>   >   >   Expectations
>   >   >   Responsibilities
>   >   >   Commitment
>   *Break* 3:15
>   *Seventh Session* 3:30
>   >   "The Relationships of Trusted Servants: To Self, Group, and Other Trusted Servants"
>   >   >   Personal Recovery Issues
>   >   >   Modeling
>   >   >   Accountability
>   *Break* 4:45
>   *Eighth Session* 5:00
>   >   "Developing Servanthood and Sponsorship"
>   *Dinner* 6:00 (Trusted Servant Banquet)

Saturday Evening (7:30–9:00)
>   *Ninth Session* 7:30
>   >   "The Sacred Trust: The Commissioning of Trusted Servants"
>   >   >   Communion Service

Let's briefly look at what is accomplished in each training session.

Session One. In "The Vision for Recovery Ministry" we examine the biblical mandate for recovery ministry and establish the importance and effectiveness of the ministry from God's perspective by understanding the meaning and purpose of koinonia fellowship.

Session Two. In "The Foundation for Recovery Ministry" we discuss guidelines and traditions to make certain that trusted servants understand and are clear about their meanings and purpose. We will talk later about maintaining them in the sessions on group problems and group conscience.

Session Three. In "How Support Groups Work" we seek to understand the dynamics of what makes support groups work and how to facilitate a meeting so that the group is able to accomplish its purpose. Two resources that we draw from in this regard, along with our experience and the information I've given in chapter 11, are the books published by RAPHA on group leadership and facilitator training (see Resources).

Session Four. In "How to Handle Group Problems" we anticipate problems in meetings and equip trusted servants to respond to those situations. We refer here to our own experience and group principles as well as to the RAPHA resources used in Session Three. In addition, numerous secular and Christian resources on small group dynamics and leadership can provide valuable insight in both sessions.

Session Five. In "Group Conscience: How to Establish, Maintain, and Conduct It" we teach the trusted servants to use the power of the group to regulate itself and be responsible for maintaining its guidelines, traditions, and principles so that the trusted servant does not stand alone as the group enforcer or decision maker. The information on group conscience in chapter 14 and the secular Twelve-Step literature are useful in preparing for this session.

Session Six. In "What It Means to Be a Trusted Servant" we draw from information discussed in the earlier parts of this chapter as well as from AA to firmly impress upon participants the importance of their role. We want to make sure that they are clear about what a trusted servant is (and isn't!) and that they understand their responsibilities to their group and to the recovery ministry.

Session Seven. In "The Relationships of Trusted Servants: To Self, Group, and Other Trusted Servants" we again draw from earlier parts of this chapter to establish healthy limits, boundaries, and expectations for trusted servants. They are to continue to work on personal issues, model an honest program of recovery, and interact with the group and other group leaders in an appropriate manner, especially in owning and expressing feelings and in dealing with conflict. Trusted servanthood is a life-style that is lived and recognized by the group rather than a status that is sought and attained.

Session Eight. In "Developing Servanthood and Sponsorship" we establish the importance of servanthood to the growth of the group and sponsorship to the growth of individual members. Trusted servants are expected to develop specific ways that these two things will be encouraged and promoted in their groups. The AA literature is helpful as well as Keith Miller's book on the Twelve Steps (see Resources). Chapter 16 "Servanthood and Sponsorship" was written especially with this session in mind.

Session Nine. In "The Sacred Trust: The Commissioning of Trusted Servants" the service gives trusted servants a sense of being ordained by God and by their groups and the recovery ministry to fill this special office. The biblical ideals of servanthood are applied to their roles in their groups as well as the model of servanthood that Christ presented to His disciples. We incorporate footwashing and Communion into our commissioning service as well as laying hands on the trusted servants and sending them forth to their calling.

Once you have selected and trained your trusted servants, you must continue to nurture their motivation and commitment to their calling.

The Nurture of Trusted Servants

It is important to maintain the motivation and commitment of the trusted servants by continuing to nurture them and provide them with periodic supervision and ongoing training. Encourage accountability to the other leaders in their group as well as to the other trusted servants in all groups of the recovery ministry.

Quarterly VHS meetings. Every three months we have a VHS meeting for all small group leaders in our church, including the support group trusted servants. Ministering and administering trusted servants are asked to participate in this monthly meeting as long as they function in a leadership role. VHS stands for vision/huddle/skills. The vision segment typically lasts thirty minutes and often is led by our senior pastor. He imparts the biblical vision of ministry to one another through the koinonia fellowship of small groups. In the huddle time group leaders form small groups to share with one another their concerns for their groups as leaders as well as personal concerns in their lives and recovery. This part of the meeting concludes with individual and group prayer for those needs. This segment usually takes about forty-five minutes. After a short break, the total group reconvenes for the last session, which focuses on skills training for group leaders. After this session, which also lasts about forty-five minutes, the meeting is dismissed with prayer.

Administrative council meetings. On a quarterly basis there is an administrative council meeting, which brings together all of the groups to discuss business matters, make plans, or address issues that may be affecting a group or the recovery ministry. Only the administering trusted servants of the groups and their assistants attend this meeting.

Group check-ins. Twice a year I meet with each group's leadership to discuss concerns and issues specific to that group and its leaders. I learn how each group is doing and what it needs and address problems before they reach a crisis stage.

Lay Ministry Appreciation Dinner. Once a year we have a Lay Ministry Appreciation Dinner to express our gratitude to all of those who have been trusted servants for the past year. We recognize and affirm them for giving their time and effort so that others may live.

Special group conscience meetings. Periodically, I will feel the need for input from the groups on decisions or plans that I anticipate needing to make, or a group may want feedback or approval for a decision that it is considering making, especially concerning a tradition, guideline, or principle. At those times I will call the group representatives together to give me feedback based on their understanding of their groups' needs or ask them to go to their groups and get an opinion for me. The group representatives help me to make decisions concerning the overall recovery ministry, which they then take back to their groups.

In addition to the things that involve the total leadership and recovery ministry, we encourage each leadership team to do things together to build up one another and provide opportunities to be accountable to one another. This may take place in their trusted servant meetings after the group meeting once a month or at other periodic group planning meetings. Some of our groups have had leadership retreats so that they can get to know one another better as well as make plans for the group.

You can be as creative as you need to be as long as you regularly provide opportunities to encourage and nurture group leaders as well as supervise and provide accountability for the manner in which they serve their groups. A word of caution: these are laypeople and volunteers. Be aware of the pressure of other commitments in their lives and do not demand too much of their time. You want to have reasonable expectations for them as group leaders, but you do not want to wear them down.

Two key attitudes are necessary to develop in group members if you want to maintain your groups and see them continue to grow, and if you want to maintain their individual involvement in the group and their personal growth. In the next chapter we will look at the concepts of servanthood and sponsorship.

Chapter
16

Servanthood
and Sponsorship

Ultimately, the best indicator of a successful recovery ministry is growth. When I look for growth in a support group, I am not necessarily looking at the number of persons attending the group. Instead, I look for the accumulation of experience, maturity, and wisdom that comes when a group is able to maintain itself effectively over a period of time and develop a core of recovery "veterans" who are able to disciple newcomers to the group and lead them through the recovery process. I look for growth in the lives of individuals. I want to see people whose lives are actively and dynamically changing. I am not so concerned about how and when the changes take place, since growth is an imperfect process and God is responsible for the preparation and timing that we need before we are able to change. But I want to see people whose lives are different as a result of being in the group.

I have observed our support groups and individuals in them for several years. I have watched groups grow, and I have seen groups fail to grow. I have seen groups start and enjoy success and growth early on but later fail to maintain that growth past a certain point. I have seen people grow tremendously in a short period of time in a group, and I have seen people attend a group for years and still continue to struggle to overcome the same basic problems in their lives. I have observed two people enter a group at the same time: one flourished and grew while the other soon became discouraged and eventually gave up. I began to ask myself and others in the group a simple question: Why?

Why do some groups grow and remain active and dynamic while others fail or stagnate into meaningless meetings? Why do some people grow like weeds in a support group setting while others struggle to maintain their growth? I discovered that it all boiled down to two essential elements. For the group, the element was *servanthood*. For the individual, the element was *sponsorship*.

Servanthood

When we consider the importance of developing servanthood in a group, we are not talking about trusted servants and leadership roles. We are referring to an attitude that all members have something valuable to offer to the group as well as the responsibility to put back into the group what they have received from it. Trusted servants naturally arise out of a group that has a well-developed sense of servanthood.

What happens in groups where no sense of servanthood is created and nurtured? The group forms and is sustained initially by its leadership core. After a period of time, which may be several months to several years, those persons gradually exit the group for various reasons, leaving a leadership vacuum. In the best-case scenario, that vacuum forces new leadership to surface so that the group can continue. Usually during this time, however, the group loses momentum and may drift aimlessly until a new sense of direction emerges and the group begins to grow again. In the worst-case scenario, the group rapidly disintegrates into stagnant and meaningless meetings, discouragement takes hold, and the group finally dissolves.

A sense of servanthood creates the expectation that everyone in the group has something to offer and that everyone needs to be doing something to make the group a better place for other members.

When this expectation is created, members continuously seek or are sought after to move into leadership roles. As they do so, they gain confidence in their ability to serve, which leads them to take on other leadership roles, and they also gain a new commitment to the group. It is their group, and they are invested in its continuing welfare. They are needed, so they remain in the group long enough to ensure that others are left to carry on when they do eventually leave the group.

Creating a sense of servanthood in the group ensures an even circle of continuity in the affairs of the group rather than the cyclical ups and downs of a group going from a leadership core to a lack of leadership to a new leadership core. It preserves the accumulated wisdom and experience by making sure that others in the group possess them and will pass them along to succeeding generations of group members.

I think Jesus was creating that expectation when He rebuked James and John for arguing over who would occupy the positions of status on His right and left. He made it clear that those who would lead must be those who would serve, and that we are all to follow His example of servanthood (Mark 10:35–45). In a group where everyone seeks to serve the needs of others in some way, everyone's needs are met. It is no secret and it is not surprising that people will be attracted to and continue to be a part of something that meets their needs.

The danger to a support group's continuity comes from what I call hit-and-run group members. They come in, unload on the group, use the group's time and energy to meet their needs, and then move on to some other group where they do the same thing again.

The founders of the Twelve-Step movement were very much aware of the need for servanthood if the fellowship was going to fulfill its purpose. Step Twelve specifically calls on persons who have benefited emotionally and spiritually from the support of the group to seek to serve others in need in the same way that they have been helped. Step Twelve creates an expectation of a lifetime commitment to give away what has been received so that the same help that was available to us will also be available to others when they need it. Paul establishes this expectation within the church when he points out that God "comforts us in all our tribulation, that we may be able to comfort those who are in any trouble, with the comfort with which we ourselves are comforted by God" (2 Cor. 1:3–4).

As needs are met and as people receive comfort, they should desire to give the same comfort to others. People in a group should be willing to do their part out of a profound sense of gratitude to God and others for the gift of unconditional love and support that they have received so that the group can continue to minister to the needs of others. A group exhibiting servanthood will remain a dynamic, growing force. Wisdom and experience accumulate, and the group matures into a strong, active fellowship. A group with little or no sense of servanthood withers and eventually perishes as its members move on and take with them what they have received from the group without putting anything back in.

Servanthood is not something that we do easily or naturally. Jesus indicated it was something that we must learn to do. Our own neediness often demands so much of our attention that we do not think about what we need to give to others. But I believe that in His example of servanthood, Christ gave us a model to follow.

Creating a Sense of Servanthood

First, we have to *establish the expectation* of servanthood. Christ did that in the Upper Room when He gave His disciples specific instructions regarding how they were to serve one another. In our support groups that expectation is presented in writing in our newcomer literature and communicated verbally in our orientation meetings. We continue to present the concept of servanthood and its importance to the group as part of our topical discussions or as a group conscience meeting.

Next, we *provide the example* of what we are asking each person in the group to do. Just as Christ provided a concrete example to His disciples by showing them what He expected when He washed their feet, we provide specific examples to group members by the way we serve. We invite them to watch and learn to do what we are doing for them.

Then, we *encourage the effort* by directly asking members to take an active role in some aspect of the group's meeting or functions. Get people involved in the affairs of the group as soon as possible. Give them a sense that they are needed. Reassure them that their efforts will always be adequate, accepted, and appreciated. Ask them to do things for the group, and assign them to work with someone who is doing that task now or has done it in the past. Jesus directly assigned His disciples tasks of servanthood and gave them the authority and the confidence to go out and do them. As an example, He told them the story of the good Samaritan and told them that they should go and do the same (Luke 10:1-37).

Finally, we *reinforce the result* by acknowledging and appreciating all who give so that others may live. There should be a regular time to applaud people who have served the group through their efforts. Jesus indicated God's pleasure with those "good and faithful servants" in the parable of the talents. Those who used what they had been given were rewarded. Those who did not reinvest what they had been given were chastised (Matt. 25:14-30).

One of the original trusted servants who helped to start our addicts and alcoholics fellowship excelled in this area. After people had been coming to the group for a few months, just long enough to get to know the group and feel comfortable, she would find some task to ask them to do for each meeting—from making the coffee to turning out the lights after the meeting. She made people feel so important to the group that they had to keep coming back. The group grew from a handful to hundreds as a result of her example and nurture of servanthood.

Sponsorship

Just as servanthood ensures that a group will continue to grow, sponsorship is the element necessary for individuals to continue to grow in recovery. Coming to support group meetings doesn't change people any more than coming to church changes people. The Holy Spirit convicts people of the needs in their lives, changes their hearts and minds, and gives them the wisdom and courage to become new creations in Christ. I see this as a three-step process.

First, people must have an *awareness* of their needs. If denial and rationalization are powerful and pervasive, they will be unable to see their true problem and desire to change. My experience has been that God continues to use various crisis points, whether minor or major ones, to break down walls of denial and bring people to that point of awareness. This is Step One of the Twelve Steps and leads into Steps Two and Three.

Next, people must have an *acceptance* of that awareness, which is the essence of Steps Four and Five of the Twelve Steps. The Bible talks about those who look into the mirror of God's truth and then turn away from it, immediately forgetting what they have just seen. I believe that people do so to protect themselves from the sense of condemnation and shame that they feel. But God's grace allows us to accept ourselves with all of our imperfections. The authors of the book *Facing Codependency* refer to this as being "perfectly imperfect." This acceptance allows us to look at ourselves honestly and intently, accepting our reality and determining with God's help to effectively do things differently and change (James 1:23–25).

Awareness and acceptance can come from many sources. They often come from support group meetings as others share their experience, strength, and hope. They come as we read the excellent recovery books and resources now available, many of them being written from a Christian perspective. Real-life experiences can provide us with valuable insight into ourselves. And there is no better source of awareness and acceptance than God speaking directly to our hearts through His Word. The Bible is a remarkably accurate textbook of the basic human condition. Whatever the source, awareness and acceptance must lead to the third step of change.

The final step is *action*. The passage from James just noted urges us not to just be hearers of the Word but to be effectual doers. We will need time, effort, humility, patience, and perseverance to change old thought patterns and learn new behaviors. Steps Six through Nine of the Twelve Steps are about things that we do to regain control of our lives.

Our Adult Children of Confusion group actually goes through

three stages. In the Newcomers Stage we ask new members to listen and develop their awareness of what it means to be an adult child. In the Growth Stage we ask members to participate and share with one another to identify and accept their individual issues affecting their lives. And in the Family of Choice Stage we ask those who are ready to do so to take the Twelve Steps and apply them to their lives to change what they have identified in Growth.

To act differently, we need two things that are the essence of sponsorship. The first is *accountability*. There are no Lone Rangers in recovery. If we could have recovered alone and changed ourselves by our own efforts, we would have done that long ago. We discover what God already knew. Self-will is ultimately futile. We must deny our self-will and look to God and others. Sponsorship provides us with accountability. Accountability helps us to change.

I remember times that I set goals for myself but was unable to act on my decisions until I found someone interested in what I was doing and would do it with me. Suddenly, I found the resolve and discipline to follow through. I knew I was going to have to answer to someone for what I was doing or not doing. That is why sponsorship and the accountability that it provides are absolutely essential to individual growth in recovery.

The second element that sponsorship provides is *affirmation*. If people are discouraged and do not believe they can accomplish anything, if their efforts are not recognized, or if they are not encouraged to keep trying, they will grow weary with the process of recovery. Sponsors are not just individuals to be accountable to. They provide the affirmation and encouragement to continue, like Paul, to press toward the mark of our high calling in Christ Jesus, which is that our lives be controlled by the Holy Spirit of God, and that is the essence of recovery (Phil. 3:12–14).

Sponsorship can be equated with discipleship. It is one person helping another person to grow and mature in all aspects of life. The Bible is filled with stories of sponsorship. Jesus is the ultimate example. He chose to sponsor twelve men and show them the way. He was their example for three years. They were accountable to Him to the extent that they left their homes and careers to follow Him completely. He constantly affirmed their ability and efforts to change their old natures and encouraged them to follow God's way. When His earthly relationship with them ended, they were prepared and equipped after they received the power of His Holy Spirit to go and change their world.

Certainly, Paul sponsored people in the early church and helped them grow. The most well-known relationship was with young Timothy. Paul specifically instructed the Thessalonians not to follow those whose lives did not reflect growth and recovery in overcoming their sin nature but to follow his example and imitate him (2 Thess. 3:6–9). He was to be their model. Paul was constantly affirming the early churches on the one hand, while on the other holding them accountable for what they were doing or not doing and pointing out areas where they needed to change and grow.

From these two examples alone, we see the biblical importance of the sponsorship necessary to change and growth. Now we need to consider and more clearly define what sponsors are, what they do, and how to choose them if we are to introduce this concept to our groups and encourage members to seek sponsors as well as be available to sponsor others.

What Sponsors Are and Do

Sponsors have something that we can see and need. They have something that we want them to teach us how to get. We desire to be like them.

Sponsors can see our value even when we are unable to and will believe in us until we can believe in ourselves. They are more than just friends; they are brothers or sisters in Christ who will reflect His love to us through the mirror of their acceptance and love. They should be "God with skin on" in the way that they love, accept, and value us.

Sponsors will walk with us through the recovery process. They should also be on the same journey so that they can relate to and empathize with us along the way. Their recovery process does not have to be complete. In some cases they may have only a little more recovery experience than we have, but they have some idea what to expect and what they have already experienced and know.

Sponsors are people to be accountable to. They know what we are doing in concrete and specific ways to recover. They must know and celebrate with us when we succeed. They help us learn from our mistakes and encourage us to keep trying when we fail.

Sponsors can mirror to us the things that we may have difficulty seeing or not want to face. When we lose touch with reality or fall back into trying to manage and control things ourselves, they point out where we have gotten off track. Although confrontation is not helpful or allowed in group meetings, caring confrontation is a valuable and necessary part of sponsorship. It comes out of the relationship and never has any blame or criticism attached to it, only gentle understanding and patient acceptance.

Sponsors give us feedback. There is not enough time in group meetings to do this for each individual if we are to have the opportunity to learn from others' experience, strength, and hope, but in the one-on-one relationship with a sponsor, we have time to explore our thoughts, feelings, and actions in detail. Sponsors may make suggestions that we are free to take or leave. Sponsors do not give advice.

Sponsors guide us along the path to recovery but do not try to control what direction that path may take or attempt to impose their will on our thoughts, feelings, and actions. They understand, as God does, that if we are to grow and mature, we must be allowed to make choices, good ones or bad ones, and experience consequences, even if they may be painful. Sponsors help us weigh pros and cons and think through consequences to make better choices, but they understand that we must learn to make our own decisions, which reflect an increasing understanding of God's will for our lives.

Sponsors do more listening than talking. Their job is not to fix anything. Their job is to let us be who we are and feel what we feel, then help us decide what we can control and change. This acceptance allows us to courageously face ourselves and our lives and

227

come to grips with what we discover. We are able to bring every-thing out into the light where we can see it clearly and expose it to God's truth, which heals and sets us free.

Sponsors are available to us when we need to call on them and get things out, check things out, or work things out, but we have the responsibility to let them know what we need.

What Sponsors Are Not

Having said what sponsors are, let me say a bit about what they are not.

Sponsors are not counselors or therapists. Support groups and sponsors are not substitutes for good Christian counseling and ther-apy when they are indicated.

Sponsors are not experts or authorities on anything other than their personal recovery experiences. We cannot expect them to offer us anything more than that or be something that they are not.

Sponsors are not pastors. They in no way replace the spiritual guidance provided by the church and the person that God has raised up to lead and guide His people. They should not seek to assume any spiritual authority over us.

Sponsors are not shepherds. They have no authority over us.

Sponsors are not just good friends to hang out with. Of course, there are times of fun and fellowship, and deep friendships de-velop. But time spent with sponsors is time to be redeemed doing the hard work of recovery.

Sponsors are not replacements for the fellowship of group meet-ings. It is possible to try to hide out in a relationship with one other person to avoid having to take the risk of sharing and being vul-nerable with others. Growth takes place in recovery as both our meetings and our sponsors become a part of the discipline of our lives.

Sponsors are not perfect human beings or perfectly recovered hu-man beings. They will fail. They will be limited in what they have to offer. They will inevitably let us down, disappoint us, or even hurt us. That's part of the risk of life. It is imperfect and filled with imperfect people. We must acknowledge that God is still in control, know that the intent of the sponsors was not to fail or hurt us, deal with our feelings, and move on.

How to Choose a Sponsor

I think the first question to answer concerning how to choose a sponsor is *when* to choose one. And the answer to that question is another question: How fast do you want to grow? The sooner you can become rigorously honest with yourself, God, and others, the sooner you can get better. The more that you are able to bring things out into the light and be accountable to someone, the more God is able to do in your life. I think the biblical principle established in the book of James applies here. When you confess your sins to someone who does not criticize or condemn but listens and prays, healing begins to take place (James 5:16).

Having said that, I don't think you should get into a support group and try to find a sponsor at your first meeting. Take time to become familiar with the group and to identify your personal recovery issues. As the group helps you to do that by sharing experience, strength, and hope, you should have a sense of being safe and of being where God wants you to be to recover and grow. Then you can identify someone in the group to become your sponsor.

On the other side of the coin, you shouldn't wait too long to find a sponsor. When you first attend a support group, you will likely go through an initial period of relief and excitement at being part of a group where you are understood and accepted. If that initial breakthrough is not nurtured and directed, discouragement and denial may set in and cause you to give up or walk away from your problem. Growth is not so much a problem of planting a seed but of nurturing it. I think that this relates to Jesus' parable about the seed that fell, sprouted, but then perished for lack of nourishment or was choked by weeds (of denial). But the seed that fell and was nourished produced an abundant harvest (Matt.13:3–8).

We encourage people *not* to wait until they think that they are ready for a sponsor to get one. Recovery requires that we begin to do things differently in our lives. Denial is a powerful force that prevents us from seeing our own need. When we think we don't need a sponsor is probably when we need one the most. Our greatest enemies are isolation, secrecy, and shame. Sponsors are God's warriors in doing battle with these giants in our lives.

How, then, do you direct people to find sponsors? You must first establish very clearly and directly the understanding and expectation that sponsorship is essential to growth. Before we began to emphasize sponsorship in our groups, some people intuitively knew what they needed and established such relationships with other group members. Most, however, continued to attend meetings and sit around waiting for something magical to happen in their lives. They got some relief and a limited degree of change but didn't experience the sustained growth that they desired and God desires for their lives.

Emphasize sponsorship in the group in the literature for newcomers. Present it in orientation meetings. Model it in meetings when people refer to a sponsor and share what they are learning from that relationship. Make sponsorship a group topic for discussion on a regular basis.

When you establish the expectation concerning sponsorship in the group, state that it is the responsibility of each group member to find a sponsor. Begin by looking and listening in group. Whose experience do you especially relate to? Whose strength do you need? Whose hope inspires you? Who seems to have the kind of recovery that you would like to have? Trust God to draw you to the person that he will use in your life as a sponsor to disciple you through the healing process of recovery. Make any decision a matter of prayer rather than an impulsive or desperate act just to find a sponsor.

Some of our groups maintain a list of persons who are available and willing to be sponsors. Although it is best for group members to take the initiative and find a sponsor, not everyone will be able to do that for various reasons. When sponsorship is mentioned, group members who need a sponsor can then be instructed to see a trusted servant for the list.

When you ask a person to be your sponsor, sit down and discuss together what will be involved in the relationship before a decision is made. Be direct and specific about your expectations for the relationship and what you think you need from a sponsor. The potential sponsor should be direct and clear about the willingness and the ability to do or not do what you need. If the expectations are realistic and both of you are agreeable, prayerfully commit to each other, and offer the relationship to God to use in nurturing the recovery process He desires in both lives.

As you make a decision about a sponsor, you should follow some definite guidelines to ensure that the experience will be healthy, balanced, and productive.

Guidelines for Choosing a Sponsor

A sponsor should be of the same sex. Sponsorship is based on trust, honesty, acceptance, and support—all qualities that are part of an intimate relationship. Opposite sex sponsors are extremely vulnerable to emotional entanglement, which may lead to what is known in Twelve-Step circles as Thirteenth Stepping—having sex with a sponsor. If you are single, it may prove to be too tempting. If you are married, it creates an uncomfortable situation for your spouse when the sponsor is of the opposite sex.

Unfortunately, some group members have ignored this guideline, and inevitably, the result is an unhealthy, destructive emotional or physical relationship. We have seen marriages and families almost destroyed as the result of the inappropriate choice of an opposite sex sponsor.

A sponsor should have similar issues. You don't want someone with opinions or textbook knowledge about what it's like and what you need to do. You want someone who has been there and can empathize. You want someone who knows what it takes to recover and has paid that price and is experiencing recovery.

Some people have been unable to find a sponsor because in a new group others have not had enough recovery or because their issues are so unique. In these situations it is possible to establish a good sponsorship relationship with someone who may not share the same issues but at least shares an understanding of recovery, such as a person in another Twelve-Step group, and has shown personal growth.

A sponsor should not *be a spouse or family member.* A spouse or family member will tend to be either too lenient and hesitant when confrontation is called for or too critical, controlling, or responsible for your recovery. You need someone who can be detached and neutral while caring.

Two sisters attempted to share a sponsorship relationship. When it affected their personal relationship, they realized that the best thing for both of them was to find someone who was uninvolved enough to be effective in helping them.

If you are part of a Twelve-Step group, a sponsor should have worked and be continuing to work a Twelve-Step program. A sponsor who hasn't been where you are going is not going to be able to take you there. You want someone involved in your recovery who has developed the honesty and demonstrated the courage required to take the Twelve Steps.

A sponsor should have a sponsor. You don't want to be accountable to someone who doesn't understand what sponsorship means or see the personal need for it. You want someone to help you walk in the light whose life is also in the light.

A sponsor should be willing to listen to you. A good sponsor will not interrupt, criticize, judge, or become impatient with your imperfect process of recovery. Most of the time your sponsor will listen and then make observations or ask questions that will allow you to look at things and choose what you need to do.

A sponsor should not be a controlling person. Your sponsor should not attempt to tell you what to think, feel, or do, or how you should be recovering. Your sponsor should encourage your dependence on God as your ultimate source and authority.

One person chose a sponsor who wanted to tell her who to date, where to go to church, and even whether to change jobs or not. The relationship was controlling and too much like shepherdship to be healthy and helpful. Eventually, the person had to terminate the relationship, although even that proved difficult to do because of the control involved.

A sponsor should be direct and honest, capable of loving confrontation. A sponsor must be able to speak the truth in love. Your sponsor must be able to lovingly hold a mirror up before you and help you see yourself clearly, not to shame you but to encourage you to be all that you can be and were created by God to be.

A sponsor should be unconditionally loving and accepting. No matter what you do or say, your sponsor should continue to see you as God sees you and love you with all of your imperfections. Your sponsor should always treat you with the utmost respect, even when you struggle and fail. You should know that your sponsor accepts and values you.

A sponsor should be humble and grateful. A sponsor's recovery should reflect dependence on God and others rather than on personal wisdom and effort. An attitude of gratitude is a mark of a person who is no longer a victim. This person has learned that God can turn what was intended for evil into good and work all circumstances of our lives into something that will accomplish His purpose for us.

A sponsor should be available. A sponsor is human and can overcommit, or circumstances can interfere when you are in need. Some things cannot be anticipated or controlled, but a sponsor should have enough time to give you what you need regularly and consistently enough for your growth.

One person attempted to sponsor several people even though his job, which required a great deal of travel, and some personal issues prevented him from being as available as he wanted to be and those he was sponsoring needed him to be. Eventually, he had to terminate some of those relationships and become realistic about what was manageable for him.

A sponsor should be willing to share with you. That means your sponsor is willing to share his or her successes and failures to help you grow. This willingness comes out of the person's acceptance of limitations and imperfections and helps you come to grips with your own.

A sponsor should be encouraging. A sponsor should help you see every crisis as an opportunity to grow. Every mistake should be one more lesson in how not to do something that you need to learn to be prepared to think and act differently. A sponsor should help you focus on the efforts that are being made, not on the results.

These guidelines make it seem impossible to find anyone to measure up to them. That's absolutely correct. So, you look for someone who offers you the most of what you need and whose life is growing in the other areas. There's also nothing wrong with having more than one sponsor. Different sponsors can help you work on different issues at different times in recovery. Don't have so many sponsors, however, that you get confused by all of their input. At that point you may need to simplify your recovery. Remember, recovery does not depend on having perfect sponsors, only willing and available ones.

What happens if you make a mistake in choosing your sponsor? Perhaps the person just isn't helpful, or major issues arise in the relationship. You should have no sense of failure in acknowledging that the relationship is not working out. That is how you learn. You make a mistake, see more clearly, and make a better decision the next time. But you continue to take the risk, and you do not quit trying just because the world and people are imperfect. You are free to change sponsors at any time and for any reason.

Before deciding to change a relationship with a sponsor, take some time and do not do anything impulsively because of what you may be feeling. Maybe you need to deal with and come to grips with the issues in the relationship. The same guidelines that apply to group sharing apply to sharing with a sponsor. As long as these guidelines are being followed in the relationship, what better place to work through things and resolve them? They are not going to disappear by accident. If they are your issues, you will probably carry them with you into the next relationship, so why not deal with them now? Ask another group member or a trusted friend to help you do a reality check on what is really happening in the relationship, then make your decision when you can separate your thoughts from your feelings.

A sponsor may choose to terminate a relationship. A sponsor's time and energy to spend in another person's recovery are limited and must be treated as a wise investment. If a sponsor doesn't see appropriate desire and effort to change in the life of the person, the most loving and helpful thing to do may be to terminate the relationship, which will force the person to do an honest self-evaluation.

You may raise one last question: What do you do early on in a group when there are not enough people with enough recovery to sponsor other group members? You do the best you can, and you function together as prayer partners for one another or burden bearers. If you cannot determine together what needs to be done, call on other group members to help you, or look to another group or other people who may have the experience that you need. The important thing is to be in a relationship with accountability. God can work through people, including group members with little or no experience, if their lives are yielded to Him and their hearts are honestly and earnestly seeking His truth.

Unfortunately, little material is available on the meaning and nature of sponsorship, especially from a Christian perspective. Keith Miller, in his book *A Hunger for Healing,* has an excellent chapter on sponsorship, which gives a good overview. Alcoholics Anonymous and Al-Anon provide literature on sponsorship from their perspectives. The main thing about sponsorship is not so much *how* it's done but *that* it's done. I think that as the recovery movement matures, more and more understanding and wisdom will be available to all of us on this vital aspect of group and personal growth.

The next chapters will examine the path of the Twelve Steps. Let's see how they can play a vital role in the maintenance of a recovery ministry.

Chapter
17

The Twelve Steps

The goal of any support group is recovery. Groups differ in the substance, state, or experience being recovered from and the process typically followed by members in reaching this goal. More and more support groups, regardless of their recovery issues, are using the Twelve-Step model. Most of the support groups in our ministry are based on the Twelve-Step model.

You need to understand how the Twelve Steps work and why they work, and I will make some suggestions about working them in general. It is not my intent to thoroughly explore the meaning and application of each step. That would take at least another book. For a more specific understanding of the steps and their application, I refer you to Keith Miller's *A Hunger for Healing*. He has done a marvelous job of presenting the Twelve Steps theologically as a model for Christian growth. (See Resources for other books, both Christian and secular.)

I would like to help you see the Twelve Steps as God's truth revealed in a process that ultimately can set us free from those things that would control our lives and separate us from ourselves, others, and God. To do so, I believe we must start with the origin of the Twelve Steps.

The Origin of the Twelve Steps

Perhaps the two best resources on the origin of the Twelve Steps and the beginning of Alcoholics Anonymous, the group that has birthed the Twelve-Step movement, are Ernest Kurtz's *Not-God: A History of A.A.* and the writings of Bill W., the original founder of Alcoholics Anonymous. They relate the history and earliest beginnings out of which the Twelve Steps were birthed.

Bill Wilson was a stockbroker in the 1930s. His life, career, marriage, and family had been nearly destroyed by his seemingly hopeless alcoholism. Despite his doctor's warnings that he would be dead in less than a year if he did not stop drinking, he was not able to maintain sobriety for more than brief periods. He tried and failed to stop drinking numerous times.

One day, while he sat at home half-drunk, he was visited by an old drinking buddy, a man named Ebby T. (the tradition of anonymity in AA specifies that no one's identity is revealed by using the full name). It was evident that Ebby had changed. He had been able to stop drinking and stay sober. When Bill W. asked him how it had happened, he told Bill that he had been to a meeting of the Oxford Group, headed by the Reverend Sam Shoemaker, and that he had "found God and got religion."

Ebby T. had originally been taken to the Oxford Group by Roland H. Roland H. was an extremely successful businessman who had been unable to overcome his own drinking problem. He had sought out Carl Jung, the famous Swiss psychoanalyst, for help with his problem, and Jung told him that only a religious conversion could deliver him from his alcoholism. Roland H. then sought out the Oxford Group and Sam Shoemaker, and through their ministry, he was converted and was able to overcome his alcoholism. Roland H. took Ebby T. to the Oxford Group, where he, too, was converted and delivered from his addiction to alcohol.

Later, Bill W. again checked himself into a treatment facility to try to overcome one more time the addiction destroying him. While in the hospital, he was visited by his old friend Ebby T. Bill W. recorded what happened after he left:

> When Ebby was gone, I fell into a black depression. This crushed the last of my obstinacy. I resolved to try my friend's formula. . . . Immediately, on this decision, I was hit by a psychic event of great magnitude. I suppose theologians would call it a conversion experience. First came an ecstasy, then a deep peace of mind, and then an indescribable sense of freedom and release. My problem had been taken from me. The sense of a power greater than myself at work was overwhelming, and I was instantly consumed with a desire to bring a like release to other alcoholics. The spark that was to become Alcoholics Anonymous had been struck.

In 1935, Bill W. sought the help of the Reverend Sam Shoemaker and his church in taking the same help that he had received to other alcoholics. Sam Shoemaker's church was the foremost of a group of churches which collectively made up the Oxford Group. The Oxford Group was a nondenominational, theologically conservative, evangelically oriented movement that emphasized the principles of self-examination, confession, restitution, and service to others. All of these principles greatly influenced Bill W. and found their way into the earliest AA traditions. Churches that were part of the Oxford Group were concerned with recapturing the spirit of early Christianity and were governed by four absolutes—honesty, purity, unselfishness, and love. These absolutes also are reflected in the early writings of AA's founding fathers.

In 1937, Bill W. split with the Oxford Group and Sam Shoemaker's church because of the mounting tension between "Wilson's group of drunks" and the philosophy and style of evangelism practiced by the church. The church did not regard drunks as attractive converts and worth the trouble. The recovering alcoholics struggled with the Oxford Group's rigid structure and insistence on absolutes when the newly converted were still occupied with learning how to get and stay sober. Finally, Bill W. felt forced to remove his fellowship of alcoholics from the church and launch what shortly became formally known as Alcoholics Anonymous. In his later writings he expressed his sadness at having to leave the fellowship that he enjoyed with Sam Shoemaker, who had introduced him to the Christian life-style and helped him to deal with failure, understand the unbounded grace of a loving God, and know the power of prayer.

Between 1937 and 1939, Bill W. and his AA group developed the formal traditions of their fellowship. The influence of the Oxford Group was profound. On the positive side were the understanding of the joy of a sober life and a relationship with God that was experienced in rich fellowship with others. AA maintains that rich fellowship today. Also, the purpose of each meeting was to assist one another in the practice of a true moral Christian life. Although AA today avoids affiliating with any religion, it still holds to a high moral standard of truth and honesty. Finally, it was accepted that apart from a conversion experience and a changed life, referred to in AA as a spiritual awakening, people could have no ultimate victory over the power of alcoholism.

Bill W. drew on six basic assumptions of the Oxford Group in developing the early traditions that are still the foundation of AA. First, people are sinners. Second, people can be changed. Third, confession is a condition for such change. Fourth, the changed person has direct access to God. Fifth, God still does and will do miracles in the lives of people. Sixth, those who have been changed must try to help others change.

The Oxford Group is also responsible in a negative sense for other vital contributions to the traditions of AA. Their fellowship steadfastly and consistently rejects the attainment of absolutes. They are to have goals, with the understanding that imperfect people will be able to achieve them imperfectly. The AA fellowship does not aggressively evangelize to seek new members but allows others to be drawn to the fellowship based on their need. The group does not want anyone to be offended by its beliefs and thus be deprived of the benefits of its help, so any and all beliefs are welcome and God is as a person understands Him to be. Finally, the cornerstone of the AA group became the importance of anonymity. In AA, no one knows and it does not matter who you are, and no one's involvement with

AA may ever be revealed outside the group by anyone other than that person.

In 1939, Bill W. wrote the essential steps that he and others in the group had learned were necessary to overcome their dependency on alcohol. He was exposed to these steps during the two years when he was involved directly with Sam Shoemaker and the Oxford Group. The Oxford Group drew some of its emphasis on living out the Christian life-style from the writings of John Wesley and his "methods" of personal holiness, as well as the writings of the early founders of the Christian faith, and encouraged Bill W. to follow these as he overcame his addiction to alcohol.

Bill W. never claimed that he developed anything original when he developed the Twelve Steps. He simply took what he had learned from the Oxford Group and the methods of John Wesley and others and put those steps into a language alcoholics could understand and practice. Most of the key phrases and concepts put forth in the Twelve Steps are taken directly from the Oxford Group teachings. Bill W. reworked them, but knew the result would be the same: revival (spiritual awakening) and maturity (sanity and balance) that could only come from conversion (making a decision to turn one's will and life over to God).

The steps were expanded and rewritten into the Twelve Steps as they are basically known today. In chapter 5 of the 1939 version of *Alcoholics Anonymous,* or *The Big Book* of AA as it is more popularly known today, those Twelve Steps* are presented with this introduction:

Rarely have we seen a person fail, who has thoroughly followed our path. . . .

Remember, we deal with alcohol—cunning, baffling, powerful!

---

*The Twelve Steps are reprinted and adapted with permission of Alcoholics Anonymous World Services, Inc. Permission to reprint and adapt the Twelve Steps does not mean that AA has reviewed or approved the content of this publication, nor that AA agrees with the views expressed herein. AA is a program of recovery from alcoholism—use of the Twelve Steps in connection with programs and activities which are patterned after AA, but which address other problems, does not imply otherwise.

Without help it is too much for us. But there is One who has all power. That One is God. May you find Him now!

Half measures availed us nothing. We stood at the turning point. We asked His protection and care with complete abandon.

Here are the steps we took, which are suggested as a program of recovery.

Step One: We admitted we were powerless over alcohol—that our lives had become unmanageable.

Step Two: Came to believe that a Power greater than ourselves could restore us to sanity.

Step Three: Made a decision to turn our will and our lives over to the care of God as we understood Him.

Step Four: Made a searching and fearless moral inventory of ourselves.

Step Five: Admitted to God, to ourselves, and to another human being the exact nature of our wrongs.

Step Six: Were entirely ready to have God remove all these defects of character.

Step Seven: Humbly asked Him to remove our shortcomings.

Step Eight: Made a list of all persons we had harmed, and became willing to make amends to them all.

Step Nine: Made direct amends to such people wherever possible, except when to do so would injure them or others.

Step Ten: Continued to take personal inventory and when we were wrong promptly admitted it.

Step Eleven: Sought through prayer and meditation to improve our conscious contact with God as we understand Him, praying only for knowledge of His will for us and the power to carry that out.

Step Twelve: Having had a spiritual awakening as a result of these steps, we tried to carry this message to alcoholics, and to practice these principles in all our affairs.

The impact and influence of Sam Shoemaker and the Oxford Group movement on Bill W. and the roots of the Twelve-Step movement are obvious. The church helped to begin and offer to the world one of God's most life-changing ministries, one that has done miracles in the lives of millions of individuals and families, and let it slip away because of its judgmentalism and legalism. Jesus issued a strong warning against this happening (Matt. 23:13–36). His desire is for all to enter into the kingdom of God, into the very presence of God to find His grace and help in time of need. I believe it is time for the church to reclaim and restore the truth of Scripture reflected in the Twelve Steps, and to offer once again the life-changing power of Jesus Christ that they point to and offer to all people.

The power of Christ-centered Twelve-Step groups is unique. The principles work in secular groups because God honors His promise and is faithful, even when we may not be. But following His principles and experiencing His presence in our lives in the relationship with Jesus Christ make available to us the full resurrection power of Christ Himself to do what we cannot do for ourselves. As Christians, we should readily understand why and how the Twelve Steps work and desire to follow them, for in following them we are following Christ Himself. It is my belief that the Twelve Steps are basically a form of discipleship, reflecting Christ's teaching in Matthew 16:24–26. They call on us to deny ourselves, take up our cross, and follow Christ. They reveal the futility of trying to control and save our own lives; they indicate what is possible when we surrender to God's will and are entirely ready for Him to work in our hearts and lives. They set before us a way, a straight path that leads us out of the bondage of whatever is controlling our lives and into the freedom of God's grace and love.

There is nothing sacred about the Twelve Steps. Their principles do not hold any power to change people's lives. Lives are changed by the One who established the principles and declared them to be His eternal truth for all people—God, as He has made Himself known through His Son, Jesus Christ.

Why the Twelve Steps Work

I believe the Twelve Steps work because they allow Christ to work fully in our lives to accomplish His purpose for us and overcome the things that Satan has used in our lives to separate us from God's love and disqualify us from experiencing His grace. Jesus summed that up when He declared Satan's purpose is to kill, steal, and destroy, but He had come so that we might experience life fully as God intended it to be (John 10:10).

Sin is about death and separation from God, ourselves, and others. Addictions and compulsions, dependencies and codependencies, are sin. They are about death—not necessarily physical death, although they often lead to depression, suicide, or living life so recklessly and dangerously that lives are lost. Even more common than physical death are emotional death, relational death, and spiritual death. We are separated from our true selves, from others, and from God. Satan's way is to lead our lives into this death-style and to see us destroyed physically, emotionally, relationally, and spiritually.

Three powerful weapons bring about this death: shame, secrecy, and isolation. In my counseling I constantly see people whose lives are being destroyed by these three things.

Shame is not the same as guilt. Guilt is the understanding that something we have done has violated our chosen values and leads us to correct it and be reconciled and restored to ourselves and to others, including God. The Holy Spirit convicts us of sin. That conviction and guilt do not separate us from God but draw us to Him, through confession, for forgiveness and cleansing from the effect of our unrighteousness. Shame, on the other hand, is a judgment we make about ourselves. We feel shameful (filled with shame!) and believe that we cannot be filled with God's Holy Spirit and be qualified for His love and grace. We condemn ourselves and believe ourselves to be embarrassments to God, others, and ourselves.

The Bible is very clear that there is no condemnation (shame) in Christ (Rom. 8:1). Satan is condemned for being the one who continually attempts to accuse (shame and condemn) us before God (Rev. 12:10), while Jesus declares that He came not to condemn the world but to save it and reconcile it to God (John 3:16–17).

This sense of shame then leads to secrecy. We are unable or unwilling to be honest with ourselves and with others. We don't want to see clearly and feel directly that sense of shame. We don't dare to reveal our true selves to others for fear of what they may think or say. We can't bring those things out into the light for fear that we will be exposed to be what we fear we are—shameful to God, others, and ourselves. Denial sets in, and our true selves become choked and ultimately die in the depths of secrecy.

We must protect our (shameful) selves at all costs. Isolation sets in. By isolating ourselves, we minimize the risk of exposure to condemnation by God, others, and even ourselves. We separate ourselves from fellowship with God, just as Adam and Eve did in the Garden when they felt naked and ashamed. We isolate ourselves from others through distance or pretense. Through denial, rationalizations, and elaborate justifications, we are isolated from our own selves and the part of us that desperately yearns to follow conviction to confession and repentance.

Eventually, our lives break down, and in the end there is only one result of this death-style. At that point the Twelve Steps become a way out. They take us out of this death-style into a new life-style one step at a time, one day at a time. When we don't know what to do, they tell us what we need to do, what we can do, and what we can't do and must completely rely on God to do. As my dear sister Sandy LeSourd is fond of saying, they are a lifeboat sent by God to carry us back through the storms in our lives to the safety and refuge that can be found only in Jesus Christ. That is the spiritual awakening, or reawakening, acknowledged by Step Twelve.

The Twelve Steps work because they destroy the power of the three weapons of shame, secrecy, and isolation that Satan has used against us to kill, steal, and destroy our lives. Once their terrible power has been neutralized and their bondage broken in our lives, we are free to enter into that new life-style and leave the past behind and become new creations in Christ.

The isolation is destroyed immediately. The Twelve Steps are based on the power of the koinonia fellowship that Bill W. experienced in the Oxford Group. They came out of that sense of fellowship, and they derive their power from the fellowship of people struggling together to overcome their common sins and shortcomings, whatever they may be. The Twelve Steps destroy isolation because they cannot be worked alone. They must be worked with others, and they bring us back into fellowship with ourselves, others, and God as we work them.

The secrecy begins to crumble with Step One when we have to admit what we are powerless over and in what ways our lives have become unmanageable. It continues to crumble through the rest of the steps until it has been removed completely from our lives. Step Five calls on us to admit to ourselves, God, and another person the exact nature of our wrongs. Steps Eight and Nine direct us to admit our wrongs in writing and make public amends to those we have harmed by our death-style. Steps Ten and Twelve call on us to continue to practice this same rigorous honesty and openness on a continual basis to maintain the new life-style that we have gained as a result of the steps we have taken. We realize as David did that God, indeed, desires truth in the inmost being, and that only by being truthful can we find the wisdom and truth that will set us free. We begin to walk in the light and to experience the freedom of God's grace and mercy.

As we work through the steps in fellowship with others, we discover that shame soon gives way to self-acceptance. As we confess our sins and shortcomings in Steps Five and Nine, we find forgiveness and cleansing from all unrighteousness. To me, one of the greatest miracles of healing is the healing of shame as we realize that we are forgiven and acceptable to God and to others and become acceptable to ourselves as well. This is the antidote for the toxic shame that Satan seeks to destroy us with. Forgiveness and self-acceptance are possible only because of what Christ has already done for us that we could not do for ourselves, and they can be fully experienced only in the koinonia fellowship of a Christ-centered group.

I believe that is why the Twelve Steps work and bring about miracles in people's lives. Of all places, Christ's church should offer and experience freedom from this death-style of shame, secrecy, and isolation. Unfortunately, in the past the church often encouraged judgment and condemnation. I see that changing now as Christ-centered support groups in the church follow the Twelve-Step path and embrace the principles that it establishes in the hearts and lives of its followers. Let's walk down that path now and see where it takes us.

How the Twelve Steps Work

This is *not* an attempt to describe how to work the Twelve Steps. You work the Twelve Steps in your own way and in a time that is right for you. What is important is not *how* you work them but *that* you work them. As you work them, God will give you the wisdom to work them better. It is also helpful to learn from the experiences of others. That is why in our Twelve-Step groups one of our monthly meetings is designated as a step study so that we can share with one another our experiences with that step. That is why you need a sponsor who has been through the Twelve Steps and can work through them with you. Numerous books relate experiences of other Twelve Steppers in working their recovery programs (see Resources). I encourage anyone desiring to understand and follow the Twelve Steps to read their stories and benefit from their wisdom.

The order and completeness of the Twelve Steps describe for me how to begin and how to live the Christian life. Each step accomplishes an act of biblical discipleship and leads to the next step. Trying to work the later steps without working the earlier steps is like trying to build a house without first establishing its foundation. Each step is also balanced by the steps surrounding it. There is a blend of faith and works, of hearing the Word and doing the Word. Together, the steps lead to a depth of spiritual awakening, the sum of which is much greater than any one of the parts.

The Twelve Steps reflect the central message of the Bible and the gospel of Jesus Christ. Where once there was alienation from God, ourselves, and others because of our sin and its manifestations (addictions, compulsions, dependencies, and codependencies), now there can be reconciliation and restoration. Where once there was death (physically, emotionally, relationally, and spiritually), now there can be life. In Steps One through Three, we become reconciled to God, and our relationship with Him is restored to one of a loving Father, full of grace, mercy, and help in our time of need. In Steps Four through Seven, we become reconciled to ourselves and experience the restoration of the right spirit within us that David prayed for (Ps. 51) as our sense of shame is removed by God and others. And in Steps Eight and Nine, we become reconciled with others as we seek forgiveness and are cleansed from all unrighteousness and released from the guilt that has been a burden. Steps Eight and Nine also provide for restoration of relationships but cannot guarantee it since it depends on the grace of others to accept the amends we offer.

Steps Ten through Twelve are the maintenance steps. They maintain the health and freedom that we have worked with God to accomplish in our lives through the first nine steps. They continue the growth that we have begun by maintaining the Twelve Steps as a daily discipline. They safeguard our hearts and minds from slipping back into conformity to old thoughts and habit patterns and encourage the continual transformation of our lives through the ongoing renewal of our minds (Rom. 12:2). As we do so, we continue to find and experience God's good, perfect, and acceptable will for our lives.

With that general understanding of how the Twelve Steps work, let's now look at each step and see where our Twelve-Step journey will ultimately take us.

Step One

Every journey must begin with the first step. Step One is the step of awareness and insight into our true condition. Taking this step requires that we admit to ourselves what we are powerless over and what now controls our lives. In the original AA Twelve Steps it was a substance—alcohol. In our groups we simply substitute whatever substance or experience is controlling and destroying our lives and our relationships for the word *alcohol*.

Admitting to this in general terms is not enough. We must also see just how unmanageable our lives have become as a result of the control that we have tried to exert over them. The second part of this step asks for an honest and specific accounting of how our lives are *not* working in accordance with God's will for us. When the price that we pay exceeds the perceived benefit that we are experiencing, we will be motivated and truly desire to change.

The admission of that insight must be public. It is an act of confession. That is why Twelve-Step groups often begin their introductions by saying, "Hi, my name is _____, and I am an alcoholic," or "I am a food addict," or "I am powerless over the confusion in my family and my life created by my parent's mental illness." That confession is Step One and the beginning of the healing and cleansing process that takes place in the Twelve Steps. It is also the admission that my own effort and will are inadequate to overcome the power of what is controlling my life. The denial of my self-will and the acceptance of my inability to control and manage my life lead me to Step Two. I clearly hear and understand the words of Christ when He calls on me to deny myself and accept my inability to control and save my life (Matt. 16:24–26).

I spoke to one group member who told me that before he joined a Twelve-Step group, he had been trying so hard to maintain his image as the "perfect Christian" and not admit what was controlling his life that he had begun to have severe panic attacks. Whenever he came to church and was around others who were important to him but did not know what he was struggling with, the shame would trigger an overwhelming sense of panic. When he finally took Step One in a Twelve-Step group, the shame dissipated and the panic attacks ceased.

Step Two

We are ready to believe and trust that a power greater than ourselves can and will restore us to sanity. This is the step of faith. Jesus declared that all power in heaven and earth had been given to Him by God (Matt. 28:18). The same power that raised Christ from the dead is certainly sufficient to raise us up from whatever death-style has taken control of us.

A group member related to me that of all of the steps, this one was the most difficult for her. Because her father had physically abandoned the family very early in her childhood, she had a great deal of difficulty coming to believe and trusting. Because her mother then struggled to provide her with even the most basic needs and would get upset and angry when she would ask for anything for herself, she struggled to accept that God would do the same thing for her that He did for anyone else.

Step Two promises restoration to sanity. By definition, *sanity* is "the ability to proceed (in life) with a sound mind and judgment, free from overwhelming pain and disease (dis-ease)." Our lives become insane, controlled by the pain and dis-ease that we experience internally as a result of external circumstances. We are unable to see ourselves or our lives clearly, and we lack the soundness of mind needed to see our way out of our death-style. Second Timothy 1:7 promises that "God has not given us a spirit of fear, but of power and of love and of a sound mind." That assurance leads us from Step Two to Step Three and allows us to act on that faith.

Step Three

We begin to act on what we have come to believe and have admitted. We make a decision, a conscious act of our free will, to completely turn over our will and our lives to God. In the AA Twelve Steps, our will and our lives are turned over to God "as we understand Him." This wording allows people to come to know God as He reveals Himself to them and as He works in their lives. In our Christ-centered Twelve-Step groups, we acknowledge "God as we know Him through His Son, Jesus Christ." It is a step of repentance for those who are coming to God for the first time. For those who have already accepted Christ, it is a call to discipleship: to deny our self-will, take up the cross of what we need to deal with in our lives, and follow Christ, knowing that His way is better than our way and leads to the truth, which will ultimately set us free.

This step is not only about turning from our own will and way to God's will and way; it also removes others as our source or those who would control our lives. I do not trust myself with my will and my life, nor do I trust others with my will and my life. I trust God and God alone to be the ultimate authority about what is best for my life. I present myself to Him as a living sacrifice, knowing that this is holy and totally acceptable and pleasing to Him and is the highest form of worship that I can experience (Rom. 12:1). Paul certainly understood Step Three, as did Jesus when He prayed in the Garden of Gethsemane, "Father, if it is Your will, take this cup away from Me; nevertheless not My will, but Yours, be done" (Luke 22:42). This, to me, is the essence of a Step Three prayer. AA has a Step Three prayer, and I encourage group members to develop their own to pray in times when they are faced with choosing their own will and way or God's will and way.

We are turning our will and our lives over to a caring God, not a distant, arbitrary, or punishing God. God, as many people understand Him, is the product of religious experiences that have been judgmental and shaming. Or God is one (or both!) of their earthly parents with a mask on. They hear and expect to receive from Him the same response to their feelings and needs that they received from their earthly parents. We turn our lives over to the God who has revealed Himself to us through the life of His Son, Jesus. If we have seen Jesus, we have seen the Father. If we have heard the words of Christ, we have heard the Father heart of God speak (John 12:49; 14:10). He is a God of grace, full of mercy and compassion, who will not turn us away. He wants us to cry, "Abba, Father!" and to come boldly and fearlessly into His presence to find grace in our time of need (Heb. 4:16). To the care of the one, true God, we can confidently turn our will and our lives and face ourselves and our situations honestly and fearlessly as we move on to Steps Four and Five.

"I have spent all of my life doing things for others and having to do things for myself. To make a decision to let go and let God was the most terrifying thing that I have ever done. I am a Christian, and I thought I had already done this. When I realized I hadn't and what I would have to do to deny my own will and let God have His way, I almost froze, the anxiety was so great," said a perfectionist in a group meeting coming face-to-face with his imperfection and need to let go.

Steps One through Three describe how to begin and live the Christian life-style. They describe the process of conversion. Conviction (Step One) plus faith (Step Two) plus repentance (Step Three) equals conversion.

We cannot start, nor will we complete, the Twelve-Step journey without the conversion experience(s) of the first three steps. But conversion is not the same as transformation. Transformation is the process by which God then turns what we are into what we were created to be. Steps Four through Nine take us through that process of transformation.

Step Four

In Step Four, we make a searching and fearless moral inventory of ourselves. We prepare to bring everything out into the light as 1 John 1 encourages us to do. To do so, we take an inventory—a literal listing of anything that is keeping us from following God's will for our lives. It is anything that we have done or may be doing that is hurting God, others, or ourselves. It includes the ways that we have become self-sabotaging and destructive to ourselves and others. It is important that this be a written admission, to see and face ourselves the way that we are in black and white.

Lamentations 3:40 gives us this instruction: "Let us search out and examine our ways, and turn back to the LORD [and His way]." We must be completely and thoroughly honest. We want nothing to remain hidden in the darkness of denial. God declares His faithfulness and His desire to cleanse us from the effect of *all* unrighteousness (1 John 1). This inventory is not to shame or punish us but to set us free from the burden of guilt that we have carried and to cleanse us from any way that shame has contaminated our lives. With this awareness and the knowledge that God loves us unconditionally, we can make this inventory fearlessly. When we have completed our inventory, we move immediately to Step Five.

Step Five

In this step, we complete the work of Step Four by admitting what we have already admitted to ourselves and to God to another human being. Making a written inventory allows us to clearly see the unmanageability of our lives and admit that to ourselves and God. The list specifically details the exact nature of our wrongs. We fully see the impact of our self-will and sin and our need for God to work in our lives.

Step Five calls on us to do what James 5:16 instructs: "Confess your trespasses [the exact nature of your faults] to one another, and pray for one another, that you may be healed." Step Five (and later Step Nine) leads directly and immediately to healing and freedom from the bondage of guilt and shame. Step Five is a public step. We must experience being totally known and fully accepted as we really are. Another human being must hear our full confession. It is a point of no return in the process of healing.

I can't tell you how many times I have seen people, especially Christians, just breeze through the first three steps only to hit a wall when they get to Steps Four and Five. Either they avoid these steps completely, or they do a selective inventory, not fully facing themselves and being completely, fearlessly searching and honest. From people who have truly taken these steps, I inevitably hear words like *freeing, cleansing, healing,* and *enlightening.* I listen to them describing experiences of having a heavy burden unloaded, of having the joy of being totally known and accepted, and of having the sense of shame washing away and being replaced by a quiet peace. It is the healing power of confession. It is the cleansing of all unrighteousness that 1 John 1:9 promises.

So far, the Twelve Steps have established two major theological truths in our lives and called us to follow them as acts of basic discipleship. Steps One through Three have led us to conversion, while Steps Four and Five have called us to confession. Steps Six and Seven represent another basic theological truth.

Step Six

We become entirely ready to have God remove all of the defects of character that we identified and listed in the inventory. Once again we admit that it is not by our might or by our spirit; only by the spirit (and grace) of God are we able to overcome those things in our lives that we are powerless over (Zech. 4:6). We totally surrender our will and completely accept what God desires to do in and through our lives, how He will accomplish that work, and when He will bring it to pass.

Becoming entirely ready is often a process. It may require that we experience additional consequences in our lives as we take back control and seek to reassert our will.

Step Seven

We humbly ask God to remove our shortcomings—whatever He sees that needs to change, whatever we need to do to change. We know that only God can do what we have so miserably failed to do. In the original Twelve Steps, this step actually read, "Humbly, on our knees, asked God to remove all of our shortcomings." Total dependency is now placed in and on God. God's job is to accomplish His will in our lives. Our job is to abide in Him and allow His Word and will to abide in us.

Step Seven brings with it incredible freedom. We cannot change ourselves. We are not supposed to. It is not our responsibility how and when we change. God will show us how to change and give us the power to change. When it is time to change, we will change. Our responsibility is to be entirely willing to do what He shows us to do, humbly ask Him to do whatever He wills in our lives, and gratefully acknowledge His amazing grace extended to us that enables us to do His will.

One group member described to me what he had experienced and learned about change. With some areas in his life he could clearly see the top of the mountain, and he knew that he was changing as he struggled to climb and reach the top. The top got closer and closer, and he finally reached it. In other areas he did not see himself changing at all. It was as if he was just walking along an endless flat plateau with no end in sight. Then one day he suddenly found that he had walked up to the very edge of the plateau and fallen into new thoughts, feelings, and behavior. I think all of us have both mountain and plateau experiences of God bringing about change in our lives as we take Steps Six and Seven.

Steps Six and Seven establish another major theological principle in our lives: transformation and sanctification. God now works in our lives to remove anything that is contrary to the purpose for which we have been created. A craftsman once explained why his woodcarvings of birds were so lifelike by saying that all he did was carve away everything that wasn't a bird. Sanctification is the process by which God removes the impurity and sin from our lives so that we become more and more like His Son, Jesus. He carves away everything else as we become entirely ready and humbly ask Him to work in our lives.

As we follow Steps Four through Seven, we become reconciled to ourselves. More and more we discover our true selves. We see and experience our true worth and value in Christ. We increasingly realize the death and destructiveness that existed in the old self and how much we may have hurt and damaged others whose lives were touched by that person. Steps Eight and Nine bring us into reconciliation with others. I believe that after we are reconciled with God and ourselves, reconciliation with others naturally and willingly comes. When we are not reconciled with God and ourselves, we remain defensive and continue to blame others to avoid the condemnation of the guilt and shame that we would then fully experience.

Step Eight

We make a list of all persons we have harmed, and become willing to make amends to them all. What a powerful step! If Step Five removes the sense of shame about who we are, Steps Eight and

Nine complete that process by removing the guilt for what we have done. Step Eight begins that process by having us make another list and fully admit to ourselves the harm we have done to others as a result of the ways that our lives have gotten away from God's will for them and become unmanageable.

This list must be as searching and as thorough as the inventory in Step Four. We must list *all* persons that we have harmed and what we have done to harm them. We include attitudes as well as actions. Jesus said that the attitude of the heart was just as important as actions (Matt. 5:27–28).

Developing the willingness to make amends may be difficult and take time, but we must be willing to become willing. We cannot continue to maintain the denial that we are not responsible if we are to truly walk in the light of truth and experience its freedom and healing, and we cannot continue to blame others for what we have done if we are to experience the grace of God in our lives and avoid having our lives contaminated by bitterness (Heb. 12:15–17). Our willingness takes us on to Step Nine, which calls on us to act on that willingness.

Step Nine

Step Nine is an action step. We make direct amends to such people wherever possible, except when to do so would injure them or others. To make direct amends is to acknowledge our responsibility so that the person harmed knows of our repentance and desire to change. This can take place in person, on the phone, or by letter, but it is to be *direct* amends wherever possible. The only exception would be a situation where the person is unaware of the harm that we have done and would be hurt, privately or publicly, by its revelation. In that case we make indirect amends by confessing to another person. Either way, the act of public confession is again the crucial issue. We cannot avoid our responsibility and remain private and secretive if we are to be set free.

Making amends involves more than just saying that I'm sorry and what I did was wrong. Amending something means changing its very structure. Making amends begins with acknowledging the wrongness of my will and way. I follow the words with actions that show my willingness to change the structure of who I am to become safe and nonoffensive to others in the future. I cannot undo the past, but I can determine not to continue to offend and harm others now and in the future.

To me, one of the greatest miracles in recovery takes place when parents who have been emotionally, verbally, and physically abusive come to grips with their pain and make amends to their children by becoming safe, nurturing parents. I have seen abusive parents make amends and restore relationships with estranged children, and the children then feel safe enough to move back home. One father made amends with his daughter for his addiction and abuse and was able to give her away at her wedding when she wasn't even speaking to him two years before his recovery!

Being reconciled does not necessarily mean that the relationship may be fully restored. That depends on the willingness of the other person to receive and accept our amends, and that is not our responsibility. We are not responsible for and cannot control another person. Nor are we to be controlled by the person's unwillingness to forgive.

When one group member attempted to make amends with his family and be reconciled with them, he was rebuffed and even verbally abused each time he attempted to bring up and resolve past issues. Each time he would return hurt, depressed, and bitter with no sense of reconciliation, only more rejection. Then one day he walked in my office to tell me he had finally reconciled and made peace with the family. When I asked what had happened this time, he said that he had finally realized how much he was expecting others to respond to his amends by making amends with him. He had hoped that his amends would restore the family and bring with it the kind of relationship he had desperately sought for so many years: "When I accepted this need, that I was powerless over what my family was willing or able to give me, and let go and turned it over to God, I was able to go in not needing them to accept my forgiveness and offer their amends in return. I only had to offer my own amends for what I had done to finish my business with them and be free to go on with my own life, whether they chose to be a part of it or not."

In Steps Eight and Nine another major theological principle is established, that of reconciliation. And if it is appropriate and possible, restitution is, too. These principles join with conversion, confession, and sanctification to continue discipleship in the lives of those who work the Twelve Steps.

As we work Steps One through Nine, God does the cleansing, freeing, and healing work in our lives that reconciles us to Him, ourselves, and others and transforms us. Steps Ten through Twelve maintain the growth that we have experienced and continue the process of transformation and sanctification.

Step Ten

We continue to take personal inventory and when we are wrong promptly admit it. Here we continue reconciliation with ourselves. We inventory ourselves on a daily basis, or even in the midst of a moment, to determine what we need to turn over to God or what shortcomings or defects of character are operating in our lives that we need to ask Him to remove. We ask God to make everything work together in our lives according to His will for us so that we can be more and more conformed to the image of His Son, Jesus, and be who He created us to be (Rom. 8:28–29). We constantly seek to work Steps Five and Nine to cleanse our lives and maintain a right standing with God and others.

I struggle with this step personally. Everything in me wants to become defensive about my mistakes and protective of my fragile self-esteem, especially in my relationship with my wife. I'll find myself thinking up elaborate excuses rather than simply admitting that I blew it and that I'm sorry for the pain my human imperfections have caused. When I apply Step Ten to my life, I choose to be open and honest with her and with others.

Step Eleven

We seek through prayer and meditation to improve our conscious contact with God as we understand Him, praying only for knowledge of His will for us and the power to carry that out. We continue reconciliation with God by adding to our lives on a daily basis the disciplines of prayer and meditation. When we pray, we talk to God. We humble ourselves before Him and cast all of our cares on Him, knowing that He cares for us (1 Pet. 5:6–7). We are not anxious about anything, but in everything we let God know what we need to experience His peace in our lives (Phil. 4:6–7). We seek, we ask, and we knock to get what we need to live our lives in a manner pleasing to Him (Matt. 7:7–8). Then we meditate and are willing to listen and be still and know His will for our lives. Our prayers do not demand that God work in the way that we think He should work; we ask only to know His will for us and receive His grace to make His way our way.

Step Eleven teaches us to abide. By definition, the word *abide* means "to wait for, to bear patiently, and to accept without objection." To receive God's best for us, we must be able to abide in Christ and His will for us (John 15:1–11). If we wish to know the truth and be set free, we must be willing to abide (John 8:31–32). In Step Eleven we continue to improve our ability to abide so that we can experience our lives fully and completely as God intends them to be.

Step Twelve

We try to carry this message of hope to others who are experiencing what we have experienced, and to practice these Twelve-Step principles now in all of our affairs. We are able and willing to do this now because of the spiritual awakening that we have experienced as a result of following these steps. We have been reconciled with God, ourselves, and others, and that is the message of hope we have to carry to others. Christ has come and is in the world and our lives to bring about that reconciliation.

When I attended one of our Twelve-Step meetings, I met a mother, three daughters, a son, and a daughter-in-law. One daughter had affected the whole family as a result of getting into counseling and then into a support group. The family members were encouraging and supporting one another and healing together. It was a thrilling sight.

Step Twelve establishes this Twelve-Step journey as the way that we will follow the rest of our lives. The Twelve Steps work because they represent all of the major disciplines of the Christian life that Jesus has called those who would be His disciples to follow. They also recognize the power of koinonia fellowship, for the Twelve Steps must be worked with others.

Working the Twelve Steps

Going through the Twelve-Step process is referred to in recovery circles as working the Twelve Steps. They are like any new discipline. The more you work them, the more you learn how to work them. The more you work them, the more you realize the need to continue to work them. I believe a primary task of a Twelve-Step support group is that of getting members involved in working the steps as soon as possible. Each group should constantly present opportunities for members to learn about the Twelve Steps. Our groups encourage this in several ways.

First are the presentations of the white chips. The white chip is an AA tradition that indicates a person's willingness to follow the way of AA to sobriety. It represents desire; it is not a guarantee of success. Only God can provide that. But it does mark the beginning of the Twelve-Step process because it is a public admittance that life is unmanageable and a declaration of powerlessness, which begin the healing of the person.

In the Old Testament, people built altars to mark the spot where God began or did a significant work in their lives. To me, the white chip represents such an altar. As part of the ceremony of the group, we present it as a tangible expression of the desire to take Step One and join in the fellowship of all who are on the same Twelve-Step journey.

Another way that we encourage members to understand and develop the discipline of the Twelve Steps is in the group sharing time. One meeting a month is devoted to a step study; group members discuss the meaning of one step, their need to take it, the difficulties involved in doing that, and the impact on them when they are finally able to do so. Over the course of a year, people will learn about all of the steps.

We also stock excellent resources on the Twelve Steps, both Christian and secular, on the book tables and encourage group members to read the resource that will help them to grow in wisdom and understanding regarding them. Since the Twelve Steps are so spiritually based, group members can take even secular literature and substitute *Jesus* for *higher power* as they read.

It is one thing to encourage understanding of the Twelve Steps. It is quite another to take them. We actively promote the working of the steps in several ways.

The first way involves the relationship with the sponsor. One reason for having a sponsor is having someone to do the hard work of the Twelve Steps with, especially Steps Four and Five. You work through the Twelve Steps with your sponsor, and you continue to do so as part of the accountability of that relationship.

The second way is holding Twelve-Step retreats, which we do regularly. They are intense weekends where a person goes through the entire Twelve-Step process in a forty-eight-hour period with three other persons. The persons may be a part of any of our Twelve-Step groups and do not necessarily belong to the same group. Each group of four is part of a larger group of twelve to twenty people also going through the experience that weekend.

We adapted Lyman Coleman's small group experience, *Twelve Steps: The Path to Wholeness,* to a weekend retreat. By the end of the weekend, people understand the power and the freedom of the Twelve Steps and what is involved in following them as an act of Christian discipleship. Each person also develops a relationship with three other persons who become and remain sources of encouragement and support long after the weekend is over. Just how meaningful these relationships can be became evident to me when I saw several couples for premarital counseling who had met on our first Twelve-Step retreat!

A third way, and the most in-depth way, that we encourage group members to understand and apply the Twelve Steps is through Family of Choice groups, which we will discuss in detail in the next chapter.

I firmly believe that in leading people into the way of the Twelve Steps, we are helping them follow the way of Christ and apply His truth to their lives on a daily basis. I have seen a number of people come to the Lord in our groups as they learned to take these steps, and I feel that group members disciple one another as they work the steps together.

As I worked through my own Twelve Steps, I discovered that at different times and in various ways in my life I had already taken a step here or a part of a step there in my personal and spiritual growth. But I had not established them as a structured, integral part of my life. That is what the steps do. That is why they bring freedom and healing. That is why Bill W. knew and trusted that they would inevitably lead to a spiritual awakening if they were taken with an open and honest heart and mind. Having had that same spiritual awakening and continuing to experience it daily on a deeper and deeper level, I know that my desire is to follow this Twelve-Step way for the rest of my life. I know that it is, indeed, the way of Christ and a gift of God to His church.

Before concluding this book, we need to talk about one last concept that we are beginning to use in our recovery ministry to see our groups and their members continue to grow. We call them Family of Choice groups.

Chapter
18

Family of
Choice

One of our biggest challenges as a recovery ministry has been getting support group members involved in working a Twelve-Step program. In most traditional Twelve-Step programs, people go through the Twelve Steps with an individual sponsor who has experience in working them. In our groups this did not seem to work well. Some people took the initiative to find a sponsor to work the steps with. But most group members seemed content merely to understand the steps without making an effort to apply them to their lives in a disciplined way.

Another problem that we experienced was the inconsistency from group to group in the emphasis placed on working the steps. Some groups strongly encouraged working the steps. Others talked about the principles contained in the Twelve Steps but did not actively involve group members in working through them.

Still another problem was the way group members went about working through the steps. Most groups offered no structured, consistent program to follow. Members were pretty much on their own to figure out what each step meant and what they should do to take the step in their life situation.

With all of these problems, one thing was obvious: the people in the Twelve-Step support groups who managed to find a sponsor or a way to work through the Twelve Steps seemed to grow the most. The people who worked through the Twelve Steps generally remained committed to the group and served the group as trusted servants. And they were the ones who were usually available and willing to help new support group members and to sponsor those who needed help as they recovered and grew.

It became clear to me that the key to the continued growth and ministry of our Twelve-Step groups (which constitute the majority of our support group ministry) lay in developing a strategy to get group members into a consistent, structured Twelve-Step experience. This would not only result in their personal growth and recovery but would help to maintain the health of the recovery ministry by providing persons willing to be trusted servants and sponsors as part of their working Step Twelve.

But how would we involve all of the Twelve-Step groups in this process? And how could we accommodate all of the people who indicated the desire to work the Twelve Steps? We found the answer to both of those questions in the one thing that was the basis of our Christ-centered support group ministry in the first place—koinonia fellowship.

Although the Twelve Steps can certainly be worked in a one-on-one relationship with a sponsor, we believed the experience would be even more effective if it took place in the atmosphere of koinonia fellowship that was so effective in ministering to people in the support group. Rather than work the steps with one other person, why not work them with a group? Only this group would have to be much smaller and more intimate than the support group to be effective. In fact, it would have to be more like a family than a group.

At the time, one of our Twelve-Step groups, the Adult Children of Confusion group, was already working the Twelve Steps in this way. They would take a group member who had worked the Twelve Steps and pair him or her with three to five members who wanted to work the Twelve Steps. They would then split off from the rest of the support group for a period of six to nine months and work through the Twelve Steps together. The idea was for them to become a family, a source of encouragement and accountability, as they worked to apply the truths of the Twelve Steps to their lives. They called this group a Family of Choice because the members chose one another and became part of a new, supportive family, different from their family of origin.

Having gone through this experience myself as part of the group, I knew the profound influence it had. It was a structured journey to healing and recovery that involved taking the steps with others as part of a safe, supportive community—a Family of Choice. As Christians in a Christ-centered support group, what better way to take the risks and face the truths that the Twelve Steps call us to than in a setting of koinonia community?

The concept of Family of Choice was a key to what we needed to do. But there were still the questions of how to consistently encourage members in all of the groups to enter the Twelve-Step process and how to provide them with this opportunity. The answer to both questions was to establish yet another koinonia community.

In a church as large as Mount Paran, it was easy to begin a number of individual groups to deal with specific issues. Six or eight or ten people would get together and begin to meet. Over time the group would grow to fifteen or twenty or more members. At the time, there were more than a dozen groups, each like a little island. The groups knew that the others were there, and occasionally members of one group visited members of other groups on retreats or at covered dish dinners. But they were more disconnected, individual, and isolated groups than a community of recovery. They needed to experience a greater sense of community, to be part of a larger recovery fellowship.

I have struggled to develop this understanding of recovery fellowship and Family of Choice over the past year or so as we have wrestled with our purpose and identity as a Twelve-Step ministry. At the second annual national convention of the National Association of Christians in Recovery, the ideas began to crystallize as I had the opportunity to share with other Twelve-Step recovery ministries from around the country.

As a result, our Twelve-Step support groups have now joined together to form one larger community, which we refer to as the Recovery Fellowship, and the concept of Family of Choice has become the common denominator for all group members who desire to work the Twelve-Step program and apply its truths to their lives. Let me explain how this model of Twelve-Step recovery ministry works.

The Recovery Fellowship

Our Twelve-Step groups used to meet separately at different times and on different days of the week. The groups followed their own formats and were basically independent from the other Twelve-Step groups in the recovery ministry. Now all of the Twelve-Step recovery groups meet on the same night and have joined together to form the Recovery Fellowship.

The Recovery Fellowship is made up of persons who are coming to grips with various substances or experiences that they are dependent on and that have come to control their lives, sabotage their relationships, and distort their ability to view themselves honestly, openly, and appropriately. These persons are members of various groups, including our groups for chemical dependency, eating disorders, codependency (including those dealing with others' chemical dependencies and sexual addictions), sexual addiction (including those in homosexual recovery), adult children of dysfunctional families, and sexual abuse survivors. The Recovery Fellowship does not necessarily include those groups that provide support for persons learning to cope with and overcome present circumstances or conditions such as divorce, death of a loved one, manic-depression, or panic.

The Recovery Fellowship begins by bringing everyone together at the beginning of the meeting to be a part of the larger community of recovery within the church. This group may involve several hundred people representing many different issues, but they all have in common Step One of the Twelve Steps—they need support to deal with those things that they are powerless over and that have made their lives unmanageable.

During the first part of the Recovery Fellowship meeting, we welcome the total community and share the purpose of the fellowship. We present the guidelines and the expectations for group members and affirm Jesus Christ as the center of our fellowship and the highest power who is the source of our healing. There is a brief time of expressing gratitude to God through praise and worship and the sharing of several short testimonies from different group members. We make announcements of interest to the group and relevant to recovery issues and take the group offering.

It is at this point that the Recovery Fellowship breaks into individual groups for the sharing time. Here people are directed into the specific sharing groups (which we refer to as growth groups) to get together with those who are dealing with their problems and their specific issues. Those dealing with chemical dependency go to their growth group meeting in a separate room, as do those dealing with eating disorders, codependency, adult children issues, sexual abuse, and so forth. We even have a general growth group for those who are not quite sure what their issues are or who do not have a specific group to address their particular problems.

We always keep growth groups small enough for people to feel intimately involved with others. It is here that group members introduce themselves and talk openly and honestly about the issues that have brought them to the Recovery Fellowship.

At the same time that the growth groups are meeting, we hold an orientation meeting for those who are new to our fellowship. We introduce the newcomers to the process of recovery, help them understand our guidelines and expectations for group members, and encourage them to begin to apply the Twelve-Step process of recovery to their lives by becoming part of a Family of Choice group at the appropriate time.

Family of Choice Groups

We have already discussed the importance of koinonia fellowship to Christ-centered support groups. We have found that the most effective way for Christians to work the Twelve Steps is in such a fellowship. While we continue to utilize the concept of sponsorship by being mentors, burden bearers, and prayer partners for one another, we find that it is much more effective and practical to work the Twelve Steps in small groups rather than one-on-one. We call these small groups Family of Choice groups.

Family of Choice groups are formed to take recovery group members through the Twelve-Step process. Each group consists of no less than three and no more than five group members, together with a group facilitator who has been through the Twelve Steps and can guide them through sharing their Twelve-Step experience. We divide group members into men's- and women's-only groups to increase the sense of safety and the ability to be honest in the group.

We encourage persons to enter the Twelve-Step discipleship process as soon as they are ready and willing to do so. That expectation is constantly presented in the Recovery Fellowship gathering and encouraged through the testimonies of those who are going through or have been through the Twelve Steps. After persons have been through the newcomers' orientation to the Recovery Fellowship and have participated in a growth group long enough to identify and talk about what is unmanageable in their lives, what they are powerless over, they can join a Family of Choice group to begin to face those issues more directly and intensively. This typically occurs after three to six months in a growth group for their specific issues.

When members feel that they are ready to join a Family of Choice group and work the Twelve Steps to deal with their issues, they indicate that desire to the appropriate leader of the Recovery Fellowship. Once three to five men or women have indicated that desire, a trusted servant is assigned to take them through the Twelve Steps.

Family of Choice groups can be made up of members from any of the various support groups that are dealing with problems by using the discipline of the Twelve Steps. An alcoholic could be in a Family of Choice group with a person with an eating disorder, an adult child of confusion, a person with a sexual addiction, and a sexual abuse survivor. Although some of the issues that brought them into recovery are different, the core issues that must be faced and dealt with are common to them all and provide the basis for identifying and bonding with one another.

The Family of Choice groups meet at the same time as growth groups. Everyone begins the evening together as part of the Recovery Fellowship. (This keeps the group members who are working the Twelve Steps in touch with the group that they will return to later. It also models for other group members the need to eventually become part of a Twelve-Step group themselves.) Then the fellowship breaks into newcomers' orientation, growth groups, and Family of Choice groups. One difference between Family of Choice groups and the other groups is that the Family of Choice group meetings run a little longer to allow for the more intensive sharing that takes place.

Family of Choice members commit to each other for the six months that it takes to work through the Twelve Steps together. While group members are free to come and go from the growth groups as they choose, in Family of Choice groups we expect all members to be there each week, to be accountable to work on their issues as well as provide support to the others in the group.

If Family of Choice members realize that they are unwilling or unable to maintain their commitment for any reason, they simply return to their growth group until they feel prepared to begin the Family of Choice experience again. At times, the group leader may recognize that a group member is not willing or able to take the risks of honesty and vulnerability necessary to work the steps and grow and change. The leader may suggest that the member return to the growth group to continue to develop more awareness and acceptance of his or her personal issues. There is never any sense of failure associated with having to do this, only an understanding that God prepares us all and works in our lives in His own way and according to the timing that is right for us.

We have found it essential to have a structured guide to help group members identify and work through the specific core issues in their lives that they are powerless over and that control their lives and make them unmanageable. Several excellent resources are available. *Recovery Publications* (1201 Knoxville Street, San Diego, CA 92110 (619) 275-1350) puts out a Twelve-Step workbook for Christians who come from dysfunctional family backgrounds, *The Twelve*

Steps: A Spiritual Journey. RAPHA Publishing (8876 Gulf Freeway, Suite 340, Houston, TX 77017 (800) 383-4673) has published several Twelve-Step guides to overcoming chemical dependency, codependency, and eating disorders. We have begun to utilize in our Family of Choice groups a Twelve-Step workbook put out by Mike O'Neill and *PowerLife Resources* (237 Nunley Drive, Nashville, TN 37211 (615) 331-0691), *The Power to Choose: Twelve Steps to Wholeness.* This Twelve-Step workbook has worked well for us because it is not targeted at any specific recovery population but is applicable and helpful to anyone who would benefit from the Twelve-Step recovery process.

Using a structured guide forces group members to systematically identify, face, and work on the things in their lives that have become self-destructive and self-defeating, in order to begin the process of confessing, being cleansed from, and overcoming the effect of all unrighteousness as described in 1 John. Group members must be willing to apply what they learn to their everyday life and to call on one another for support and help outside of the group meeting.

Family of Choice groups can best be understood as a process of group sponsorship. They bond group members into an intimate relationship of encouragement and of accountability to their small group and, ultimately, the larger Recovery Fellowship community.

As group members come out of the Family of Choice experience, they return to the Recovery Fellowship and try to help others who are coming into the fellowship by offering their experience, strength, and hope; by facilitating the newcomers' group or a growth group for their particular issues; or by taking a group through the Family of Choice Twelve-Step journey. As people who work the Twelve Steps come to Step Twelve, they are more ready and willing to be sponsors and trusted servants to others.

In our Twelve-Step recovery ministry, Family of Choice groups provide the ultimate experience in the high degree of honesty, openness, acceptance, responsibility, and accountability that I believe is needed to overcome and change those things that have become such a law of sin and death in ourselves (our flesh). One Family of Choice member told me that it was the greatest experience in her life next to her salvation experience with Jesus. A person who had never been able to feel safe and open up in other group experiences in our church was finally able to admit to the things that he was struggling with in his Family of Choice group. In my own experience, I have turned to the members of my Family of Choice group to help me through a personal crisis that I did not feel safe sharing with just anyone in the church. A member of that group has become one of my closest friends and one of the few people in my life who know me completely and who I can be totally honest with.

The Recovery Fellowship and Family of Choice groups seem to be where all of the experiences of the past five years with recovery ministry and the Twelve Steps have led us. We are constantly learning about and working on all of the things that I have shared with you to continue to develop and maintain the support group ministry that God has called us to. I hope that you will share your experiences with us as part of the larger work that God is doing in this day and age as the recovery ministry continues to grow throughout the church.

In the last section of this book, I will present to you some of the stories of persons who have participated in our recovery ministry. In their own words, they will share with you their experience, strength, and hope and what God has done in their lives through their support group. What better way for you to understand the life-giving nature of this ministry?

Section 5

PERSONAL STORIES

Chapter
19

The Stories of Those
Who Know

The following stories are told by persons who have actively participated in the recovery ministry at Mount Paran Church of God. All of the support groups meeting at the time are represented. The stories are their own, in their own words. They represent the real feelings, struggles, and victories of the people who have experienced them. These people—who are identified only by initial to protect their privacy—hope that by sharing their stories openly with others, more churches will become involved in this life-giving ministry of support. I believe that as you read their stories, you will get a clearer vision of the purpose and power of recovery ministry and Christ-centered support groups in the church.

Families Victorious
Over Sexual Addiction: J's Story

It took every bit of courage that could be mustered to put the key in the car and turn the ignition—heading the car in the direction of I-75 and Mount Paran one Thursday evening in March. Going to my first SAFE (Families Victorious Over Sexual Addiction Through Fellowship and Encouragement) meeting was allowing my denial system to crack, and I didn't like that feeling. Why was I having to be at a Twelve-Step group meeting for families of sex addicts when the rest of the world was at home watching "The Cosby Show" with their families? Where was my ideal Christian family? The family as I knew it came crumbling down when I discovered my husband had been sexually molesting my daughter for the past twelve years.

Although this was my first time at Mount Paran or a Twelve-Step group meeting, I immediately felt the warm, caring spirit of the six women who welcomed me that night. Their openness about their successes and failures in the SAFE group convicted me that I wanted what they had. I was a Christian, but discovered that my codependent behaviors were keeping me from living the life that Christ wanted me to experience. Listening to the stories of where some of the women had been and where they were today in their recovery encouraged me to tackle the Twelve Steps.

I accepted the challenge that March evening to begin "the courageous journey" by making a one-year commitment to the program. Over the weeks ahead my eyes were opened to see that I needed and wanted to experience recovery from my codependent habits. I desired to become an emotionally healthy person based on the serenity that God gives.

With books and workbooks in hand, I was convinced I could go through the program in twelve weeks—one step a week! But something strange would begin to happen whenever I began to get serious with Step One. The Lord would show me that this was an area of my life that needed a good deal of work—admitting I was powerless over the addict and victim in my family and that I *could not* control their actions! Whenever I complained about my frustrations over not moving along at a faster pace, my precious sponsor would always kindly assure me, "You're right where you need to be."

That year has come and gone. I discovered that my journey to recovery has no graduating class. With daily time alone with the Lord in prayer and Bible study, with the support, information, and fellowship from weekly meetings, and with time, I am learning from the Twelve-Step discipleship program to truly live "one day at a time."

Codependents Victorious, Adult Children of Confusion: S's Story

One hot August night, I wandered into a group called Families Victorious at my church. It was not the group I was seeking, and I didn't realize it until the meeting was in progress. As I sat there, I was uncomfortable because I didn't have any "addictions" in my family, but I was too embarrassed to get up and leave. As the sharing got around to me, I admitted wandering into the "wrong" room but enjoyed sitting in on the group. One of the old-timers commented that God works through "mistakes."

At the time, I was suffering a lot of losses; some I couldn't even identify. Actually, I had lost a daughter to suicide who was an alcoholic; and my mother was dying as a result of a combination of addictions. It was a safe place for me to be as I grieved. The people loved me unconditionally, which is something I never had experienced. They convinced me that feelings are real, valid, and my own regardless of what others said to the contrary. This group became the "prep school" I needed before going into the recovery group that would really propel me on my journey.

At our church, all of the Twelve-Step support groups would come together quarterly for a covered dish dinner. At one of these dinners a skit, along with several testimonies, revealed the real reason for that "mistake" ten months earlier. This hosting group was Adult Children of Confusion, a group for adults from dysfunctional families or backgrounds. Within a month, I became involved with this group. Shortly after joining the group, I became aware of a Twelve-Step class that would last forty weeks. It was to be a small closed group on codependency. Since I had already identified this as a major issue for me, I registered for the course.

During the year since I had first wandered into a group, I had lost my mother and my precious little dog, my father had suffered a stroke, I had major surgery, my husband left me, and my daughter broke her leg. ANXIETY? DEPRESSION? You bet! For a while I tried to attend both support groups and the Twelve-Step class. It was too much, so I dropped the original group. It certainly served as a training ground and a catalyst to prepare me for the next part of my journey.

Two months into the Twelve-Step class, I was sinking fast. Dealing with my family of origin issues was too painful. I felt a real need to get into a codependent recovery program, preferably a Christian one. None of the local units were really specializing in a separate codependency unit so I went to a center in the Midwest. Their program was undergoing major changes, and my designated treatment program fell through the cracks. I did gain a great deal of knowledge simply by observation and interaction with the other patients. After the twenty-eight-day program, I returned home hoping to receive the love, compassion, and understanding of my family of origin. That was not to be, so I began the painful process of detachment.

I returned to my group and class where I received the nurturing and encouragement so lacking in my life. My life continued to fall apart, and I was not equipped to handle it. I wanted to die. I felt the only thing keeping me alive was my firsthand experience of surviving a family suicide. I believed that God would forgive me if I just couldn't hang on any longer. God had something else in mind. Part of His plan is what you are reading.

Within a month, I began crisis counseling through the church counseling department; and within an additional month, the counselors recognized the need for inpatient treatment for my major depression. They notified my daughters and with loving direction put us in touch with a local hospital suited to my needs. One thing I simply would not consent to was being in a locked unit. The hospital had an open adult unit, allowing the patients to eat all their meals in the cafeteria. With my doctor's permission, I could walk or sit outside on the hospital grounds. She also allowed me to continue my evening Twelve-Step class and attend church on Sunday mornings. This freedom helped to maintain my dignity. With the combination of in-hospital treatment and therapy, my ongoing attendance in my group and class, and the loving faithfulness of my heavenly Father, I have come through what seemed to be insurmountable problems. Without the compassion, love, and encouragement of my recovery friends at church, I could not have survived in the secular setting of a hospital.

The past two and a half years in recovery have been the most painful of my life; and I've had a life filled with pain. The difference is: "God can't heal what I can't feel," and "You shall know the truth and the truth shall set you free." As a result, I continue to be an active participant in recovery groups and classes. I am currently working my second Twelve-Step program, one for adult children with lots of family of origin work. I helped organize and currently share duties as a facilitator for Codependents Victorious. I am also involved in formulating our first trusted servants training seminar.

All this work has resulted in major changes in my family. One daughter is in a recovery group, and one sister is slowly working a recovery program alone. I have detached in a healthy way from my father and my older sister. The circumstances in my life haven't changed very much. But the freedom that I have gained by working my program along with other committed Christians, who are loving and nonjudgmental, is life worth living.

Sexual Abuse
Survivors Victorious: M's Story

One year ago I was living in a nightmare. Me, the devout Christian wife and mother. I was locked up in an inpatient psychiatric hospital for a month. My worst fears had come true. That came about as a result of my two attempts to end my life. After the first attempt, six months earlier, I pulled myself together, stuffed all the pain, and went directly back to living the same existence. I thought I could take care of myself alone. I shut everyone out of my life. Unknown to me, I was living with a deadly self-hatred, believing that I wasn't meant to be in this world.

My entire life has been a tremendous struggle against myself and depression, and I didn't know why. I kept plugging along in faith that God had everything under control and that all of my pain would be turned into good. I vowed to endure. The tornado of pain grew inside me until I could contain it no more. I took a massive dose of over two hundred prescription pills, drank a full bottle of rum to intensify the drugs, and cut my wrists. It had to work this time. I hid my car where I wouldn't be found for a while, thereby assuring myself that my plan would work. No more would I have to struggle with life, and no more would my family have to endure my pain. As I drove toward my destination, weeping, I called out to God, "Please, if You don't want me to do this, then take away the pain."

I survived for thirty-six hours before being found, and returned to consciousness three days later in intensive care. My doctors marveled that I had lived and that no permanent damage was done to my body. I took that as a sign that God wanted me here and I set out to do whatever it took to recover if He would show me the way. He had heard my prayer, but He chose another direction in bringing me healing. I had to look inside myself and take a long walk back through the journey of my life.

I came to know Jesus at an early age. I promised Him that I would always be a very good girl and I would not be a sinner. I knew the Scriptures and led the life of a born-again Christian. I placed a tremendous burden on myself to be perfect for God and everyone else. It took forty-six years to realize that it was an impossible effort, and I gave up.

God didn't give up on me. He chose to use secular psychiatrists and therapists to show me the destructive childhood I had survived and the secrets I had used all my life to hide behind. I had no other choice. It was either do this or die. The shame I felt from my father's sexual abuse and alcoholism was too painful to face. I vowed to protect my mother from this truth and all the other pain my father caused her. This was more of a task than anyone could fulfill. I never stopped trying. I felt so alone in this truth and could not identify with others. I never seemed to fit in with other people all my life.

The tremendously intense tornado of pain had started four years earlier upon the death of my father. Inside I had confused the love of my earthly father with the love of my heavenly Father. My father let me down, and I thought my heavenly Father had abandoned me, too. Therefore, I pushed God away. I felt like God was very disappointed in me because I couldn't endure the pain. My father must have been disappointed in me, too, or he wouldn't have abused me as he did.

Upon discharge from the hospital I was instructed to find a support group for sexual abuse survivors. This was not an easy task since there were many, many survivors and not enough support groups. Someone told me that there was a group meeting right in my own church. I had not been attending church for over a year and therefore was not fully aware of the new ministry taking place there. After making a phone call to the church, I was instructed to be interviewed by the counseling minister before attending a group. I poured out my heart and story to him with grief. I could tell that he really heard my pain and that he cared. Somehow, he understood.

I started in the Sexual Abuse Survivors Victorious group the next night. I was in the group for about fifteen minutes when I began to experience a feeling of belonging for the first time in my life. These women knew what I felt. They understood me, and I wasn't alone anymore. I discovered that they, too, were having difficulty in their relationships with God and that He loved us even though we were struggling to understand His reality.

Was it possible that the knowledge of psychiatry and therapy could be combined with the love of God to create a complete healing process? Certainly, I needed healing of the mind as well as the soul.

Sharing each week the growth and struggles of fellow Christian abuse survivors has opened a safe and honest atmosphere where I can be who I am in Christ. I have found unconditional and understanding love from these women, and wonderful friendships have evolved. The truth is that there are many more Christians suffering

with pain from dysfunctional childhood experiences. These dysfunctional experiences and their resulting character defects are
keeping us from being who God intended us to be.

There are those who attend these groups out of necessity, and
they don't know the Lord. They come to support groups but not to
church. By meeting their immediate needs of support, we are presenting Christianity to them where they are.

Families Victorious Over Chemical Dependency, Couples Victorious: G's Story

"Families Victorious? But there's nothing wrong with me! The
problems in my marriage are my husband's fault! He's the alcoholic!
He's the one who needs help!" Denial screamed as I slipped deeper
and deeper into depression and anger. . . .

Five years ago I attended my first support group. It was a Christ-
centered group called Alcoholics Victorious (AV), which met at
Mount Paran Church of God in Atlanta, Georgia. I attended with a
man whom I later married. This man was an alcoholic and addict
and had been in recovery for six months. He was also a recently
born-again Christian and had been delivered from his desire to
drink and take drugs. I was a born-again Christian myself and believed that as long as he wasn't actively drinking, everything would
be fine between us. If I had known then what I know now, I would
never have gone out with him, much less married him, recovering
or not.

This AV program was my door into the addictive world. I learned
from that program about alcoholism and the dangers of alcohol
abuse. I myself am guilty of the latter. As the program at Mount
Paran expanded, I was led through more doors. Most of them I went
through kicking, but I went. I thank God that He took me through
those programs and gave me the experience and education that I
received. I now have the knowledge I need to go forward and not
repeat past mistakes.

Less than a year after I attended my first support group, the man and I married. We started having problems almost immediately, and I began going into depression. My anger and bitterness mounted, my illness beginning to consume me.

My husband encouraged me to attend the new Families Victorious (FV) group at Mount Paran. At the time I was in denial and rebellion and refused to go. But as my marriage grew progressively worse, and I became more and more depressed, I knew I had to seek help somewhere. I finally relented and went.

That was the best decision I ever made. I started taking care of myself and looking at myself only. I learned about the disease of codependency and the related issues. I searched my family of origin for clues to my codependency. My family of origin issues are subtle, but they are there. One of my greatest revelations was that I am a relationship addict. Gradually, I began to like myself again. But God wasn't ready to answer my prayers yet about my marriage.

During my time in FV, my husband and I joined a new group at Mount Paran, Couples Victorious. I wasn't very excited about *another* support group. My husband was only in town four nights a week, and we were in support groups *three* out of *four* of those nights! We had some good Christian fellowship during and after those meetings, and there was a great deal of intimate sharing. My husband was slow to share, but he gradually warmed to the group. I was probably more assertive and open than he would have liked. Yet, I believe the time spent in this group helped us to get to know each other better. Much to my chagrin, intimacy for us was and is a process. It takes time and patience.

It took divorce proceedings to finally get my husband's attention of my dissatisfaction with our marriage. Then God sent us a minister willing to go out of his way to counsel us and attempt to teach us how to live a Christian marriage. The healing has finally begun. God has begun to answer my prayers. We are both changing.

In looking back, I can see God's hand. We had to find ourselves before we could find each other. We couldn't have done it without Mount Paran support groups or God's patient handling of our struggle.

Alcoholics and Addicts Victorious, Couples Victorious: N's Story

My victory is in Jesus Christ; my recovery is in the recovery ministry; my new life is in the love of God.

After many detours on my spiritual journey, I am now saved. After twenty years of alcohol and drug abuse, I am now clean and sober. After innumerable failed relationships, I am now happily married. All of this has been possible due to the Lord's amazing grace. None of this would have been possible without fellowship in the body of Christ and in Christ-centered support groups.

I was born in 1949, the first of four sons. We were raised basically happy and healthy in early baby-boom suburbia. With school, sports, church, family, and friends, our "Adventures of Ozzie and Harriet" life-style held great promise. Life was good.

My religious upbringing was in the Episcopal church. This gave me a fundamental belief in Jesus Christ and a rudimentary knowledge of worship that somehow stayed with me throughout many years away from the church. Personal salvation would come much later.

As a fairly typical teenager I couldn't wait to grow up. At the age of fifteen I started drinking alcohol. My parents drank regularly and socially, so naturally I thought it was okay for me. My initiation resulted in my first arrest (for public drunkenness), my first night in jail, and my first hangover. After recovering from this episode I began to go out drinking with my older friends (just for fun, of course). Soon my parents divorced and this, coupled with a driver's license, gave me a newfound freedom that I regularly abused as my drinking progressed.

In 1967 I started college and discovered marijuana. As a true gateway drug, this led to extensive experimentation with other mind-altering chemicals and hallucinogens. In the music business of concert production and promotion, I found sex and drugs and rock 'n' roll to be an accepted part of the countercultural life-style. A young marriage and an attempt at the "straight" life proved to be futile and short-lived. Soon cocaine became a drug of choice. Although I was not a dealer, per se, it was not uncommon in my position for large quantities to cross my desk. As I witnessed the loss of several friends to prison, overdose, and death, I knew I had to change my self-destructive course, but I didn't know how.

A close personal friend with patience and love led me to the Lord. I accepted his invitation to a Full Gospel Businessmen's Fellowship banquet, and on that night in 1984 I accepted Jesus Christ as Lord and Savior of my life. At this time I was in abstinence. I was also in denial. Since I had given up alcohol and drugs for the season of Lent, I thought I could maintain sobriety on my own. Wrong. Well then, as a born-again Christian I could practice moderation. Wrong again. I was powerless, and my life was unmanageable. This same friend told me about a small group called Alcoholics Victorious at Mount Paran Church of God where I was a regular visitor in worship.

At my first AV meeting I was greeted by a lady who said, "God loves you and so do we!" I knew I was in the right place, with other Christians who were struggling with life's problems. I immediately found love, acceptance, honesty, and victory. Unfamiliar with other recovery groups or programs, I was guided step-by-step through the Twelve-Step process. Through this ministry I was anointed with oil and prayer, delivered from bondage, and blessed with a fellowship of love and support. Although our meeting was just once a week, the power of the Holy Spirit working through the strength of the group became a central part of my life. True friendships developed; good times were shared; special opportunities arose; a new life evolved. At this writing, I have been free of alcohol and drugs for over six years.

Couples Victorious was one of several groups to evolve from the AV group, which was originally one ministry with a wide range of recovery representation. Originated to strengthen marriages in recovery, this couples group became a timely blessing to my wife and me. Here we could share ourselves openly and honestly with ourselves and with other couples who were working through relationship issues and marital difficulties. This shared love added a new dimension to our marriage. At this writing, we have overcome a near divorce and have been married five years.

I thank God for the recovery ministry at Mount Paran Church of God. As a trusted servant, I was given a new understanding of commitment, cooperation, and compassion. As a sinner, I have learned that with Jesus Christ all things are possible, and that a spirit-filled, Christ-centered support group can work in ways heretofore unimagined. In fellowship and in love I can now proclaim, "Victory in Jesus." ALLELUIA!

Sexual Abuse
Survivors Victorious: P's Story

My story is similar to an incident recorded in the book *The Pilgrim's Progress*. John Bunyan symbolically portrays through Christian, the main character, the religious struggles and experiences of a person on his way to the Celestial City. When Christian comes to the Wicket Gate and goes through it, it is a picture of salvation. As he continues this journey, he is carrying a burden on his back. This burden stays with him until he reaches the cross, where it is loosed from his shoulders.

I had accepted Christ as my personal Savior when I was in the fifth grade, but I, too, had been carrying a heavy sack of burdens on my shoulders for twenty-two years. My burden bag was filled with the sudden death of my father when I was ten years old. This left me with feelings of abandonment and of disappointment with God that He did not answer my prayers and heal my dad. I was hurt that I never was able to go to the hospital to see him. Dad never told me good-bye or said anything, and in just ten days he was gone.

About a year and half later, my mom remarried, and my stepfather sexually abused me. This abuse continued through my junior-high-school years. Added to my burden bag were the stripping away of my dignity, trust, and self-esteem; the robbing of my sexuality so that I would struggle with relationships and intimacy; the crushing of my spirit so severely that I could no longer feel and no longer wanted to live; the creating of a deep sense of insecurity and an overwhelming feeling of helplessness, hopelessness, and guilt.

My mother also added to my burden bag. She did not come from a loving family; and therefore, she transferred her dysfunctions to her children. I longed for a mom who would express love to me—one who would hold me in her arms, one who would kiss me and say, "I love you." My soul yearned for that type of mother-daughter relationship, yet it would never be. My mom started going out to bars, which eventually led to her sleeping with men and not coming home until the next morning. She lived with a married man for approximately three years and then married him after he divorced his first wife. That tore me up inside. I was ashamed of my mother and was embarrassed to have friends come over to my house. Since I was the oldest of five children, I'd worry that something would happen to her when she would stay out all night and that I'd be left all alone, not knowing what to do. My second stepfather beat my mother. I can remember being awakened late at night by the yelling, fighting, and screaming, "Call the cops; he's killing me!" I was so scared. All I could do was lie in my bed and cry. Added to my burden bag was a load of weights. I'll just mention a few: losing my childhood, never to regain it; taking on the role of the responsible child; falling into the performance trap; and having a tremendous fear of rejection.

Hiding my true self and wearing a mask became an everyday ritual. On the outside, everything seemed to be great. People thought I was "up" all the time and on top of the world, but inside, my spirit was crying out for help. The fires of hate, bitterness, revenge, and anger were blazing in the core of my soul. Not only was this anger directed against the people who had hurt me, but it was also directed toward God. I was angry with God because if He had not taken my father, none of these other things would have happened. I felt as if God really didn't love me. Here I was—a graduate of a Christian high school, a graduate of a Christian college, and a teacher in a Christian school—and had it not been for the reality of hell, I would not have wanted to be a Christian. I wanted to get even; and I vowed that no matter how long it took, I was going to get even.

Needless to say, my Christian life was a mess. Because of growing up in such a dysfunctional home, I easily fell prey to churches, schools, relationships, etc., that were controlling, authoritarian, legalistic, perfectionist. I learned to be a human doing rather than a human being. My worth to people, the church, and God was based upon my performance—keeping a list of do's and don'ts. Guilt was my motivator rather than love. I tried getting my life right with God. I'd give up this and do that. I'd try to keep the law. I'd read my Bible, memorize Scripture (KJV of course), go out witnessing, etc. The harder I tried, the emptier I felt. I was on a spiritual roller coaster—up and down, up and down—but most of the time down. The abundant life was the proverbial carrot on a stick always just out of my reach. Life was not living; it was existing, tolerating, and enduring.

Bunyan's Christian had his burden loosed from his shoulders when he reached the cross, which was a picture of his receiving the assurance of his salvation. My cross experience was an inner healing that took place in April of 1987. After Dr. Tony Dale spoke in our Sunday morning service, his wife, Felicity, got up and said, "The Lord has revealed to me that there is someone here that was sexually abused when she was ten or eleven, and the Lord wants to heal you of that." I made an appointment to talk with Felicity. As she prayed for me, I could visualize myself back during the times of hurt. And for the first time in my life, I could see that Christ was there all the time. He didn't abandon me or reject me. He was there loving me and holding me as a little child, and I fell in love with my Lord and Savior, Jesus Christ. At that moment He took my burden bag from my shoulders, opened it up, reached inside, and touched all the hurts and pains of the past with His healing nail-pierced hands.

I thought that my inner healing experience emptied my burden bag and that my past was instantly healed. Later the realization hit me that healing is a process, and my inner healing was the beginning of my recovery journey. It is like coming out of a coma, and then there is all the therapy.

God graciously opened the door for me to attend a therapy group for incest survivors and later a support group, Sexual Abuse Survivors Victorious (SASV), at the Mount Paran Church of God. My group provided a shelter for me, a wounded child of God, to be nurtured in love. They gave me space and time to heal. They provided a safe place where it's okay to be me, it's okay to be human, it's okay to fail. This has given me the courage and strength to remove my mask slowly inch by inch. SASV has demonstrated freedom in Christ, which is setting me free from the bondage of legalism. Their living in the spirit of the law rather than the letter of the law is bringing me life instead of death. God is using Mount Paran to paint on the canvas of my mind the true picture of Himself, a loving, caring, compassionate Father, so that I would have something to compare and replace the false portrait of God that life has painted.

God used SASV to ignite within my breast a spark of encouragement and the hope of change. I'm learning to step out of denial and into reality, out of the lies and into the truth, which is setting me free. The dignity, trust, and self-esteem that were stripped away are gradually being rebuilt. Having a place to let my "secrets" out is causing them to lose their power and hold over me. The emphasis is one of acceptance, love, and honesty. Through sharing our pain, by being transparent, by exposing our wounds, through our stripes, healing is taking place. God has used Mount Paran to build a door through my thick walls, so that He and others could reach in and touch my life, and I'm eternally grateful.

Codependents Victorious, Adult Children of Confusion: L's Story

My external appearance has always been deceptive. Behind the masks of intellect (which got me attention), looks, antidependence (which turned to codependency in intimate relationships), and a status-symbol career in the airlines lived the real me—the ugly, "different," isolated, fearful, shy, addicted, and lost little girl still enmeshed and controlled by the violent verbal abuse of an angry, emotionally frozen father and an emotionally frozen, "peace at all costs," codependent mother. At the age of thirty-three, I had no intimate friends, no purpose in life, and a history of unhealthy sexual relationships with men, which I almost unconsciously sabotaged. A freak accident interrupted my life for four years and twelve surgeries, but Jesus reached me during that time and I was reborn.

The next ten years were filled with some growth, and I developed one intimate friendship with a girlfriend, but feelings of worthlessness, ugliness, and uselessness would overwhelm me, and I judged myself mercilessly for my failure to be a "real" Christian. I exhausted myself trying to meet the needs and expectations of my family, friends, and neighbors and do it all perfectly. Addictions to food, alcohol, and nicotine surrounded me like prison walls. Depression incapacitated me for weeks and months, and still, I could not say no to those I loved. My whole life seemed to be wrapped up in being "needed" or useful to others.

In desperation, I started attending church at Mount Paran, and through insightful and faithful teaching, I began to realize that the life I was living was not what Jesus or God intended for me. A small insert in the church bulletin about an Adult Children of Confusion (ACOC) group caught my eye one morning. I had "assembled together" in the church sanctuary, but I had never "assembled" with other Christians who were like me—overloaded with guilt, shame, fear, inadequacy, pain, and anger—and able to be open and honest about it. God used the openness and honesty of this support group to really show Himself to me. The remote, distanced, indifferent God of my childhood whose attention was always on my sins, faults, and failures showed me Himself in the unconditional love and acceptance I experienced in that group. The message of God's love started moving from my head to my heart . . . and I started the painful but exhilarating process of "feeling my feelings." God became real, and I know He touched me and began a healing in my life.

The ACOC group really shook the foundation of my "prison of

self" as I came to understand my childhood abuse and childhood molestation, without blaming or shaming my parents, but the walls came crashing down during a subsequent Twelve-Step codependency recovery group. That got me into the "here and now" and "what do I do now?" God used the unconditional love and acceptance of this group to finally penetrate the invisible wall of fear that had prevented me from experiencing intimacy with others and honesty with myself. (I had to do Step Five *twice* under the guidance of the Holy Spirit. I omitted the "most" shameful incidents the first time.)

I now feel like God's child and not an orphan who has to "perform" perfectly in order to be accepted. I don't know how or when that change happened. My past life seems to belong to some other person. All I know is that God has used these support groups to help me become real and to understand, accept, and even feel His reality. I still sometimes struggle with the "old" feelings and my recovery is not perfect, but God has been using even my imperfect recovery to reach out to others. I do volunteer work at Mount Paran and am still thrilled and excited and scared and happy at "belonging" to Him now and being used. My recovery has been a miracle to me, and I know that it will continue for the rest of my life.

Families Victorious Over Sexual Addiction, Kids Victorious: I's Story

Coming from a moderately dysfunctional family, I found Christ in my early twenties. I also found a church that became a "family," complete with all of the rules I grew up with . . . "Don't admit problems, keep up a good front, performance means acceptance . . ."

After ten years of single life, I met a wonderful guy who had a remarkable testimony of finding Christ and of leaving the "gay" lifestyle. He was a very easy person to be with, and we became close friends. In 1981 we were married. Another comfortable, familiar relationship that seemed terrific on the surface. We were active in church and in a ministry to "ex-gays." We began a business together and had two children. In the next few years I lost both parents to cancer, and we lost our house to a fire. It seemed that one crisis followed another.

In the midst of all the chaos, my husband admitted that he still struggled with his sexual identity, and that he had been active outside our marriage. He expressed a desire to seek professional help, and chose to enter a Christian treatment center to deal with his issues of compulsive sexual "acting out." As long as he was seeking help, I was more than willing to work to save the family.

I had learned to be a good codependent in the church I was so long connected with. That church had really tried to change my husband, but the pastor's counseling sessions consisted of lectures and no opportunity for authentic dialogue. He seemed intent in "winning" my husband by persuading him to do what was right. I also believed this would work. My focus was to get him "straightened out" so that our family could be a successful example of the power of God. The only problem was that I was the "god"!

Then we found the recovery ministry at Mount Paran Church. From attending the Families Victorious meetings, I learned that I also needed help and recovery! What a shock! As I listened to people share about the issues of codependency and the pain of living with an "addict," I found myself identifying with the stories. Many of the same patterns of enabling and caretaking had strong roots in our relationship. I became bolder as I attended meetings. I chose to leave the unhealthy church. God became so real to me.

At first I felt so guilty for "abandoning the family," but the Lord assured me that He was my Shepherd. The Holy Spirit has been a force of mercy and grace to me. I found in group a safe place to feel my "unacceptable" feelings. One by one the Lord showed me people in "program" with whom I could share the specific issues that I faced as a "sexual coaddict." The shame that kept me silent kept me in my sickness. When I found others who were also hiding in shame, the Lord opened another of His famous doors!

In the fall of 1989, I began a breakaway meeting for other family members who were living with sexual dependency. Six months later, with the support of the counseling department, we officially began the Families Victorious Over Sexual Addiction (Through Fellowship and Encouragement). We call our group SAFE. I have been so encouraged to have the support of the courageous women who take that first step to come to our fellowship and to begin dealing with their confusion and pain.

The "old me" would like to end the story here. However, I no longer can hide and pretend as I could before I began my journey of recovery. My "perfect family" was not to become the "perfect recovery family" (according to my expectations). I felt that if I just worked the "program" hard enough, my husband would "straighten out," and of course the kids would never have to deal with the same problems we had. Sound familiar? Yes, I was still in my performance trap. After all, I had been the one to start the group. I had to show everyone "how it works"! God has such wisdom . . . the SAFE group needed birthing and I was a surrogate. God doesn't let us forget that it's His group as we all serve and are served.

The time for me to be served came when my husband, on the advice of a secular counselor, decided that he should accept his sexual "orientation" and give up trying to make a "doomed" marriage work. I was devastated! After all I had given to preserve the family and to "help" him! Now to be left with the children! My new family was there when I relapsed into self-pity and resentment. Christ in His gentle way taught me to let go of the outcome. My sponsors were there for me. The pain I had feared to face was not so awesome, for the comfort was so real. Not the pity and advice I had received from well-meaning "friends" in the past, but acceptance from my God and my group enabled me to accept myself and to face my radical self-reliance for the sin that it is.

I've come to learn that there is no resurrection without a grave. My old relationships are dying. But that no longer is a thing to fear for me. A new me is emerging. Not a hardened bitter woman, but a human, feminine, loving, forgiving, honest, and vulnerable woman. At least now that is my goal. My family and marriage are in God's hands. My son is working on his issues in the Kids Victorious program. He knows that our problems are not his fault, and he is learning to acknowledge his feelings and needs.

God is not finished with us yet! We are a family with many problems, but now we can deal with them, one day at a time, by His grace!

Families Victorious
Over Chemical Dependency: C's Story

"Oh, God! I can't believe this is happening. Please, God, don't let this happen. Why, God, why?" These thoughts screeched across my brain as I watched my daughter furiously throwing piles of clothes, a stereo, and other teenage essentials into the back seat of her car. Angry words hurled across the yard. "I'm leaving and I'm not coming back. I don't want to see you again—EVER! I hate you, Mom! I HATE YOU!" Her words crushed my heart as I staggered back inside.

Head clasped in hands, I sat at the breakfast table. "Dear God, I just can't handle anymore. Oh, God, please help me." Tears streamed down my cheeks. My daughter had gone from being a straight A student, cheerleader, and political science enthusiast to a withdrawn, unrecognizable creature. No amount of talking helped. There were constant fights, slammed doors, nights when she did not come home at all.

Years of dealing with an alcoholic husband had taken a toll on us all. Husband-wife, father-daughter, mother-daughter relationships had broken under the strain. He was verbally abusive to both of us when we did something wrong, which seemingly was all the time. No matter what we did, we never pleased him. I had tried to relieve some of the pressure on him by taking on more and more of his responsibilities. Surely that would help. It didn't. I thought that if I did everything just right, took good care of everyone, kept a spotless house, had his favorite meals, surely he would stop drinking. I tried everything I knew. I had threatened, cried, yelled, and begged. I had gotten tough and allowed him to stay in jail after a DUI. I had tried gentleness and forgiveness. I had even tried acting like he had not done the inappropriate things that he had done. Nothing worked.

And now this. Tears overflowed as I sobbed, "God, if You really love me, please show me what to do. Please, could we just be a family again?"

The following Sunday the assistant pastor announced the start of a Families Victorious support group. It would be made up of the friends and loved ones of persons addicted to alcohol, drugs, food, work, sex, money, and religion. Right away I knew I should go, for here was my answer. I would find out exactly what to do, write it all down, take it home, and "fix" all our problems.

On the way to the first meeting, I prayed, "God, I have been told that this is a twelve-week program. I will commit to twelve weeks. If at the end of that twelve weeks, nothing has changed, I will totally give up. I am walking away from it all. You included."

At the door I was met by a lovely lady who had such a peace about her. Soon the room was filled with people; some wore looks of quiet desperation, others, calmness and serenity. The woman who greeted me quietly shared her story.

She then explained Step One: *We admitted that we were powerless over alcohol; that our lives had become unmanageable.* This step is by no means a statement of despair and hopelessness. It merely reminds us of our human limitations.

In Step Two, *we came to believe that a power greater than ourselves could restore us to sanity.* There is a power greater than we are. Comfort and a peaceful heart are the rewards of those who rely on His help.

As *we make a decision to turn our will and our lives over to the care of God as we understand Him,* we find through Step Three that our burdens are lightened. Our Higher Power provides the guidance and the strength to take the right action.

During the following weeks, we discussed each of the Twelve Steps. Stories of broken promises, broken lives, and broken dreams were shared. Faith, hope, and trust in Jesus Christ became our reality. Love and acceptance were found within the group. I was able to share my deepest hurts, my anger, bitterness, resentments, and frustrations.

On the twelfth Monday night, a friend was sharing Luke 4:18: "He has sent Me to heal the brokenhearted. . . ." Suddenly, the realization that that was exactly what He had done hit me. God had known all the deep wounded places in my life. He had seen all those tears I had cried. With His gentle touch, He had healed my heart and my life.

By continuing in the support group, by spending time in prayer and meditation, by giving and receiving love from my new friends, I have come to know the fullest meaning of the Serenity Prayer.

Heartmending Grief Group: H's Story

For me, healing has come in stages. Not necessarily distinctively, sometimes overlapping and sometimes relapsing, but usually at a different level. Ten years ago, I was diagnosed with systemic lupus, a disease without a cure. I prayed for healing, but the answer I got was, "If I healed you, My child, you would not learn what I have for you to learn." I believe now that had God healed me at that time, I would have developed something else because I had a hole in my soul. And until there was emotional healing, the physical healing could not occur.

The first thing God taught me about was praise. I couldn't. I didn't seem to have it in me, so I bought a stereo and some praise tapes, which I played over and over until I could begin to praise. It was then that I began the arduous task of recovery. I learned about grieving, forgiveness, dysfunctional families, and codependent relationships.

My father had committed suicide when I was a child. Following this, my mother went into a deep depression and withdrew from us. After his death, it was as though he had never lived. It was a shameful thing he did, and therefore, we avoided it, his memory, and our grief. I integrated all of this into my soul and carried his shame.

While I did some work on grief and forgiveness, it was not until the death of my son's girlfriend in a fiery crash five years ago that I truly began to work through my grief. We formed the Heartmending support group. This proved to be a safe, supportive place to grieve as we ministered to each other. I found that not only was I grieving for this girl, but I was also going through the grief process for my father, for whom I had never grieved. What a blessing it was to share with others who were going through the same thing!

Once I had worked through much of my grief, I realized there were much deeper issues that needed to be dealt with. I had begun to learn about Adult Children of Confusion and recognized that I needed to now concentrate on these issues. The group experience was very powerful in validating feelings and thoughts from child-hood. It took a lot of work and was very painful, but the healing continued.

Of course, with that history, it was almost to be expected that I would have developed some very poor relationship patterns. It be-came painfully obvious to me that not only had I come from a dys-functional family, but I had married a man from a dysfunctional family and we had established—what else?—a dysfunctional family! Current issues of codependency would have to be dealt with; old patterns needed to be recognized and changed. Again the interac-tion of a Twelve-Step codependency group became part of a power-ful healing process. It was such a liberating experience. Not only am I being healed, but I am seeing my child sharing in this. Not only does my future have hope, but the patterns are being changed in this life, also.

Sex Addicts Victorious:
R's Story

I was a Christian for ten years before God moved me to step out from behind my sin and admit my failure. I was in bondage to sex-ual lust for fifteen years, and my first step to wholeness was confess-ing my sin to others. That was a very big (and costly) step because I was a member of a fundamental denomination that allowed little room for the admission of sin in anyone's life, much less sexual sin. My experience with this legalism and condemnation from the church served as a catalyst to drive me deeper into denial and deeper into my addiction.

I didn't understand myself, I hated myself (not just my behavior, but my very self), but I sincerely wanted to please and obey Christ. I realized that I couldn't stop the addiction on my own. Countless times I resolved that this was the last time, and I would never fail again, only to have the same old cycle resurface in a short time.

I tried all kinds of standard Christian remedies to cure sin: memorize Scripture, pray more, just trust God more, have more faith, go to church more, more, more, more, all to no avail. For me, these standard remedies were futility and only created more despair and discouragement.

Finally, God moved in my life, and I began to seek professional Christian counseling and a support group that dealt with my specific addiction. I learned that there is hope for one who humbly acknowledges his failure before the Creator of the universe. I learned that this one can then find forgiveness and, in that forgiveness, hope for a new life.

Slowly, fearfully, we come to the realization in the group that we are not alone; we have come to a place of acceptance. I am not the only Christian to struggle with sexual lust. There are other Christians who have the same relentless battle with their sexual urges. Strength comes in numbers, and as we open up to one another, pray with and for one another, and understand one another, we gain strength.

The deep, dark secrets are no longer hidden from sight. They are out in the open before God and man. The power is broken! The truth of James 5:16 is evidenced before our very eyes. How wonderfully true! To see Scripture in action is a remarkable experience. Within the group, we find Christians who can understand and encourage rather than judge and condemn us when we make unhealthy choices. We feel compassion and empathy rather than shame and fear. We experience the true ministry of the body of Christ.

As we persist in this safe environment of the group, we learn to bear one another's burdens, and to comfort one another with the comfort we have received from Christ. As a group, we travel along this continuum of recovery from sickness to wholeness, and in the process we begin to function for one another as the body of Christ.

This element of real ministry seems to be lacking in much of the organized church in America today. I thank God for the church that recognizes the need for a recovery ministry that enables its participants to become the body of Christ to one another, and that sets about putting this ministry into action. In the safety of such a ministry, we find that the power of sin and the bondage that enslaves can be broken in our lives.

Sex Addicts Victorious:
O's Story

My secret was finally out in the open. I had just been advised by a Christian organization that it was not set up to deal with my particular sin. I was advised to go to this prominent doctor's clinic that specialized in such behavior.

I felt like an alien from the very first visit at this clinic, which was secular oriented and not based on Christian values. I prayed to the Lord and felt I was going to the wrong place. After a few more visits to the clinic, I felt the Lord leading me to a Christian counseling center.

I contacted them and asked if they had someone who would counsel me in my particular sin. After a couple of weeks, I received a call from a man I will call Larry. I was confident from my first visit that I was with the Christian clinic and counselor the Lord desired me to be with, and I felt very thankful to the Lord for His forgiving grace.

Larry and I prayed during every one of my visits. I learned new terms like *dysfunctional families*. Larry desired that I go to a weekly Twelve-Step program in addition to the counseling.

My wife had learned from the Christian counselor she was going to that Mount Paran Church of God had a ministry specializing in support groups based on the Twelve-Step program. She began going to weekly meetings where she gained insight into my problem as well as how to deal with her fears, feelings, and frustrations my problem had caused in our lives. After she had been going a few weeks, she heard that a new support group for my problem was beginning. I shared this with Larry, and he suggested I call Mount Paran. I am sure I bothered Paula, the secretary for Bill Morris, with many phone calls stating my desire for the new group to begin. One Sunday afternoon I finally met with Bill and a few other men to start the new support group. The men in the group were nothing like I envisioned they would be. I liked them from the start. After a few more meetings, Bill Morris announced that there would be a weekend retreat for all support groups. My wife and I decided to go.

The first night of the retreat, Bill separated us into groups of three or four persons—all strangers. He gave us questions to share our lives with one another and limited each series of questions to a specific time. During a break, I shared with Bill that I could not tell my group what I did. Bill said to pray and let the Lord lead me. By Saturday night I knew the intimate details of each group member's life, and they knew my secret—and did not hate me for the sin. The last morning all the groups met together singing and praising the Lord. Then Bill stated he felt the Lord was leading people to give their personal testimonies. The Lord spoke to me, and I knew I had to share my secret. There were two miracles performed that day. First, I have a great fear of public speaking, and second, the Lord had me share my secret with this large group.

I said, "I was raised in a Christian family, and my father was chairman of the board of deacons, my mother a Sunday school teacher, and both sang in the choir. After being single for a number of years, I met my wife in a singles Sunday school class. She was a widow with a young daughter. My wife and I built a new home and traveled to Europe as well as the Holy Land. I had served in our local church in several capacities, one being assistant Sunday school director. Then one day my wife discovered my secret—I was a child molester and had molested our daughter. My wife told me to leave the house. My world and secret world were crushed. I shared my secret with my dad, brother, sister, and their families. I prayed to my Lord for two miracles. First, He would save my marriage, and second, my Christian testimony would not be destroyed."

After giving this testimony to the group, I felt the love of my wife, Bill Morris, and the other Christian brothers and sisters there that day. But most of all, I felt the love of Jesus Christ and His forgiving grace, and I felt like that was a turning point in my life as well as in my marriage and family.

The support group I belong to is Sex Addicts Victorious. On a week-to-week basis, I have learned through hearing others' stories some common problems we share. I have learned to love the men in this group, to study God's Word, and to pray daily, striving each day to look to Jesus for my strength, my hope, and my future.

I thank the Lord for Bill Morris, whose insight and establishment of the Twelve-Step support groups have touched so many lives and turned them toward Christ.

My wife and I are back together, as a family, looking daily to Christ to show His will for our lives.

I feel that in every church there is a need for a recovery ministry, whether from food, alcohol, or sex addictions. I pray that the Lord can use my story to help others and turn them to Christ—our only hope.

Children of Divorce, Divorce Recovery: T's Story

I divorced on January 28, 1986. I had a two-year-old child, and I was an alcoholic/addict "bottoming out" into a surrendered state where God could work in my life.

I grew up in a southern home where alcohol was consumed on a daily basis. I thought it was part of everyday life. I attended the First Baptist Church, sang in the choir, and began to learn about God. In 1969, I left my hometown of Louisville, Georgia, to go to school at the University of Georgia in Athens. I continued to smoke pot while attending journalism school and working at Channel 8, Georgia Public Television. I also did an internship in the press department for Governor Jimmy Carter. When Carter went to Washington, I traveled in Europe a few months where I began to drink on a daily basis—part of the European way of life. I returned to the U.S. and started skydiving. I met my husband and was hired by Delta Airlines as a flight attendant. My husband and I traveled all over the

U.S. to compete in world record skydiving attempts and operated a skydiving center in LaGrange, Georgia, on the weekends. My alcohol and drug use escalated in this environment.

I drifted away from my Christian upbringing and walk with the Lord. Through the years before my divorce, my husband and I would visit Mount Paran Church. A sweet spirit was present during the services. I'm grateful God kept my foot in the door.

After getting sober in Alcoholics Anonymous in December 1985, and working the Twelve-Step recovery program, I became open to support groups, spiritual healing, and developing a personal relationship with Christ. I have been sober since then; drinking was only a symptom of my problems. I had to clean house—an internal cleansing of spirit, mind, and body. I attended the Fresh Start seminar in November 1986 to begin to deal with the pain of my divorce. Mount Paran, the church my son and I had been attending, offered a support group for children of divorce—Rainbows for All God's Children.

My son had been having disciplinary problems at school. He was acting out lots of anger and insecurity. The school counselor even mentioned that I may need to put him on a drug for hyperactivity. The divorce and my alcoholism had manifested itself into some dysfunction. I had my son professionally tested. He was not attention deficit or hyperactive. We turned to God to heal our hurts, and Mount Paran support groups helped us on our journey of recovery and healing. We discovered we were not alone, and the support of others was vital to our healing.

We joined the Children of Divorce group in September 1987. I helped as a facilitator in another age group. My son joined children four years old whose parents were also going through a divorce. The children learned how to talk about their feelings. They played a game called Stuff-it, where they put little sponge characters into a little box. Each sponge was a negative feeling. When the box got too full of negative feelings, it exploded. This helped the children see what would happen to them if they kept all their negative feelings inside. The children became familiar with the terminology. What does divorce mean? Daddy may not live here anymore, but he's still your daddy.

We attended Children of Divorce again in September of the next year for another twelve weeks. I attended the parents' group that met while the children were in their group. Much hurt and pain was shared. I began to understand much of my son's anger was being acted out in disciplinary problems. Healing began in these groups for him and me. It has continued through the years. We discovered that our pain was normal for what we had experienced. We moved through the pain into healing. My son accepted Jesus as his Savior during the 1988 session. He was five years old. Only the beginning of many miracles, he began to understand God's love. God will always love him no matter what pain he experiences. The groups helped us both regain our self-worth and trust of ourselves and others. My son's father joined us for the Celebrate Me Day, December 10. It was a special day when we asked each other's forgiveness. We wrote our hurts down on pieces of paper, put them in a balloon, filled the balloon with helium, and released it into the clear blue sky.

My relationship with God has become much stronger and more bonded. God revealed my woundedness to me, and I have to stay surrendered to His healing power.

I also attended the Divorce Recovery group, Adult Children of Confusion group, and a codependency group. Each group was a link in the chain of recovery.

Adult Children of Confusion: Y's Story

My background is probably very similar to that of many men my age. I grew up in a time when men were told, "Don't cry," and the goal was always to work hard and survive in life. I came from an upper-middle-class home with a mother whose job was to raise the children and a dad who worked all the time. I had always considered my family as average and very normal. I remember being sad and I guess angry that my dad never came and saw me play a ball game or went camping with me. He was always working. I remember that he was always angry at me for not doing things right: "You will never make anything of yourself." I grew up, and just as I had been trained, I formed the same work habits and worked all the time. I also expected my children to do everything right, just as my dad had expected me to do.

In my early forties I began to notice that I was getting tired at unusual times: after lunch and right after work. I was so tired that I had to lie down and sleep. My doctor said that it was just stress, and all his tests confirmed that he was right. My body was in great shape. Just lose a few pounds and I'd be fine. A year later my blood pressure began to elevate, and I had trouble remembering things. Again, my doctor, said "You are just feeling your age. Take these pills, and you'll be okay."

About this time a close friend suggested that I listen to a tape that dealt with burnout. Well, I listened, and it sounded like maybe I had reached a burnout point. I called a friend at church who headed the counseling department, and he suggested that I see a friend of his, a doctor of psychology.

Well, I took his advice, and several weeks and many tests later, he confirmed that I was a "classic" burnout victim. Weeks and several doctors later, I was diagnosed with CFS (chronic fatigue syndrome). I had most of the symptoms of the disease by then and had gone into a deep depression.

To complicate things, I was losing my business, and my income was rapidly dropping. I was simply unable to do anything about it. I was living with a deep feeling of hopelessness, despair, and failure. We still had three preteens living at home at the time, and it all came crashing down on my family when I was unable to cope. I finally ended up in an outpatient program that RAPHA had just set up. During my weeks at RAPHA with the help of loving therapists, I came to know what brokenness really meant, and God was able to get through to me even though I had been born again and Spirit-filled for almost ten years.

After getting out of the RAPHA program, I went to my church for my aftercare, as my therapist had suggested. Because the meetings took place at my church and the program was run by a member of the church staff, it gave me a sense of well-being and safety at a time when I was hopeful but confused. I believe that God used my church as my way of escape and a place to stay focused on God, my healer.

I saw people at the meetings I had seen in church and people I had known for years. I can't tell you how it made me feel. I was not the only one with problems. There was such a feeling of camaraderie in the Lord as we shared in one another's burdens. We were taking our first steps to healing. Another important fact for me was that my pastor understood what I and my family were going through and helped me by supporting this wonderful program in the church.

The structure of the program helped support the idea that recovery is a process and not an event or a quick fix. I knew for me that this was going to be a big commitment. Maybe several years! I had six weeks of being faithful to Step One, the introduction, and now had to decide whether or not to continue. Was I really serious about my recovery? It wasn't until much later that I really found out what a life-changing commitment I had made.

As the months went by and I continued to go to group each Tuesday night, I began to realize that the problems I was having were not the result of anything my wife, children, or anyone else around had done to me, but that they were connected to my childhood and the emotional abuse I had received while growing up.

Every week God very gently would use the kind and loving group leaders to open the doors to my past and allow me to see what had really happened to me and how it had affected every part of my life and relationships.

As time went on, I was chosen to enter the next step of the program to be a part of the Family of Choice group. There I began to actively work the Twelve-Step program that I had heard so much about. Each week five others and I along with two trusted servants would meet for two to three hours. I learned that I indeed had some very deep and significant issues with which to deal. The make-up of our group was so special to me. We all knew that God was at work just because of the unique personalities He put together.

There were several people whose issues were similar to mine and people who reminded me so much of my family of origin and even members of my immediate family. What awareness and understanding this gave me. There was a person who acted exactly the way my sister had always acted toward me. It gave me a safe place to understand and heal from so many hurts. The group continued to grow in these new relationships, and God brought us all new and clearer insight into our inappropriate behavior.

I learned that anger and control had been so much a part of my life. They were the only way I knew to meet the need I felt to be wanted and cared for. The guilt I carried never allowed me to care for myself or to be intimate in any of my relationships. I always felt so much fear around angry people, and the only way I would respond was by being overresponsible and caretaking all those around me. No wonder I finally burned out. The miracle was that it didn't happen earlier. All these dysfunctions had hung around my neck as a millstone for so many years. My group was so supportive as our trusted servants took us through layers of awareness and God's leading.

The hardest thing for me was learning how to trust God so I could take the next step in recovery. At times I did not know who I was anymore or where I was going, only that God was always there ready to take the next step with me. The way out was risky. It always involved acting on my behavior, which I learned was unhealthy. This is where members of my group came in with daily exhortations and many times gently and lovingly confronting me and my feelings. I began to see that even though I had a long road in front of me, there was a way out. A new and better way to live without constant pain of being driven by some unknown force while denying all the feelings of pain. Praise God for truth that set us free!

As I trusted God to show me the changes I needed to make, the "dance steps" began to change in all my relationships. First, my relationship with God was no longer based on me trying to manipulate Him but to submit and love Him.

My changing family relationships were the most difficult for me. Years and years of bad habits were little by little exposed, and I had to deal with them. It was much harder for me to trust God when it involved others who were close to me and not just Him and me.

The choices were always with me. To be comfortable with the old and familiar habits, not to rock the boat, or to press on, trusting God in recovery. As I pressed on, the fruit of all my years of dysfunctions hit me. It was a terrible time for me, but I always believed that God was with me and this was exactly what He wanted me to do. I was learning to forgive others. But more important for me, I was learning to forgive myself.

It was a recurring cycle for me. First awareness, then the risk of asking for what I needed, exposing my feelings, and finally allowing God's love in me to change my unhealthy behavior. Sadly, some relationships were lost. My family had no choice but to respond to the changes I was making, but I always knew somehow God would see us all through.

All the while the members of my support group were getting closer and closer, and we were coming together to lift and support one another as God directed. Watching the trust build between us was so wonderful. In the end God's love never failed or came to an end. His gentle hand guided us to our health. His faithfulness was always present to answer our prayer for healing the pain and shame that bound us.

At this point I don't know what the future holds, and that is scary for me. But I do know that His grace is sufficient for me. I'm looking forward to serving others and being used by God to help, just as others have helped me. There is no way for me to express my gratitude to my heavenly Father for using so many wonderful and loving people to help. Thank You, Father. I love You.

Living Stones (Homosexual Recovery), Kids Victorious: E's Story

"I'll never do this again; I'll stop before I get this far next time." I said those things to myself so many times, and yet so many times the whole process repeated itself over and over. . . .

I grew up in a middle-class normal-enough-looking family. I was always a quiet boy, feeling more comfortable playing alone or with imaginary friends than with other boys. My mom always said that she'd quit her full-time job when school was out for summer, so she could stay home like the other moms, but today she still works at the same job that she has had forty years now. My dad has never been emotionally present. It seems that he was always working late, doing "projects" around the house, or otherwise "checked out" for most of my childhood. One brother was born when I was six; the other when I was ten. Because of the age differences, there was never much bonding with them during childhood either.

I always knew that my mother wanted a daughter. It was communicated very strongly, though not always directly. As long as I can remember, I seemed to feel as though it was my place to be that daughter for her. I know it doesn't make sense, but my earliest memories are of playing with toys that were gender inappropriate. Along with the trains and toy cars I got for Christmas, I also got dolls, ironing boards, and tea sets. I really don't know whether I was treated differently because I played with the inappropriate toys or I played with those toys because I was treated differently. But regardless of which came first, I grew to realize that I was different, and I didn't "fit in" with my peers.

I was the object of ridicule and jokes during my school years and had only a few friends. My self-esteem was wrapped up in my grades and internal pride rather than my relationships with God and others. I spent adolescence with a small group of friends and found my acceptance through drugs and the fact that I had a car. I comforted myself alone with pornography, drugs, and compulsive masturbation. I told myself that other boys probably did the same things, though I knew deep down that it was not the truth. I knew that my fantasies about other boys and men were not normal, but I resolved to keep them buried deep down inside. "Besides," I told myself, "I'm also attracted to girls and would love to have a girlfriend if only one would show some interest."

I met someone when I was barely eighteen. We met at a pot party held at a mutual friend's apartment. She was like no one I'd ever been around before. We both seemed to feel a magnetic attraction and ended up spending the whole evening talking and kissing. The next day, I asked her to marry me, and six months later we were husband and wife. I have to admit that the "glue" that held us together those first years was the sex. I was also convinced that finally, now that I had a wife and regular heterosexual sex, those "secret" feelings would dissipate. That, of course, was not the case.

Another part of the attraction to her was the fact that she seemed to need me. She had always had a weight problem, and the dysfunction of her own family of origin had left her with her own issues of low self-esteem and depression. We literally spent the first eleven years of our marriage focusing on her problems and depression. Our daughter's birth after five years of marriage also gave me something else to focus my attention on, diverting my awareness away from my own pain and compulsive behavior.

Through all this, I continued to act out sexually, rationalizing that as long as I didn't physically involve anyone else, I wasn't really being unfaithful. My pornography, voyeurism, and masturbation seemed to comfort me through the pain but only served to keep the cycle of shame going in my life. It tortured me that I would have to keep this terrible secret hidden deep within my soul for the rest of my life. I wanted to share it with my wife but feared that she would either leave me or go completely mad, and neither option seemed worth the risk.

God really seemed to reveal His grace during the twelfth year of our marriage. My wife had started attending the Eating Disorders Victorious (EDV) group at Mount Paran, and my daughter was attending the Kids Victorious group. Probably more out of obligation than anything, I began to attend the Families Victorious group. There God really began to cause me to look at my own shame and codependency. I was forced to quit focusing on my wife's behavior and start to focus on my own. While the support and healing I received in that group helped me to be victorious in my codependency issues, I continued to heap shame upon myself as I acted out sexually and with recreational drugs and alcohol.

While I was helping my wife with an EDV summer advance, the Lord told me that my life would change radically and that He could use me in ministry if I would only trust Him completely. He told me that I would be able to tell my wife about the homosexual secret in my life, and that I only had to trust. Within two weeks that's exactly what had happened. The initial sense of relief that I experienced as a result of breaking the thirty-year silence was exhilarating. The Lord had indeed been faithful, but now came the "trusting Him completely" part.

I soon began attending a group for homosexual recovery being held at another church in another part of town. The Lord again was faithful in allowing me to form a very healing and lasting relationship with the leader of the group. As our relationship grew deeper, he began to affirm in me the call on my life that God had already been whispering to me for some time. I had for several months been hearing the Lord urge me to approach Bill Morris about beginning a ministry for homosexual recovery at Mount Paran. I had tried to bargain with God, "Please, not at Mount Paran. People know me there. It's easy to be in a group at another church, but Mount Paran?"

God showed me through my friend who led the other group that He would go before me and prepare the way. So a year and a half ago, I obediently went to Bill, and we, along with several others God had also been working with, began the Living Stones fellowship. In the months that have followed, I have been continually encouraged by the way God works so perfectly. The struggles that I and other group members have encountered have been met with support, acceptance, and the love of Christ. Words cannot express how much God shows me at each meeting that He can use every part of our lives—the struggles, hurts, ugly parts, and especially those dark secrets—every part that we submit to Him completely can be used for healing.

So many of us felt rejected most of our lives, but we call our group the Living Stones because

[as you come to Him] as to a living stone, rejected indeed by men, but chosen by God and precious, you also, as living stones, are being built up a spiritual house, a holy priesthood, to offer up spiritual sacrifices acceptable to God through Jesus Christ (1 Pet. 2:4–5).

Families Victorious
Over Chemical Dependency: A's Story

When I hit the bottom of pain and despair, the church I called had a counseling department. An appointment was given in response to my sobbing. The next morning, sitting in Bill Morris's office, I can remember the peace I felt in his soothing voice. I could not tell you anything specific that was said. I suppose I was dumping out my story in a full gush to my first willing ear. At the close of the session he recommended a Christian counselor for me to see and suggested I read the book *Women Who Love Too Much*. That was six years ago.

It was determined that I was a codependent married to an alcoholic. These words are nothing new now, but six years ago strange sounding to me. The process of understanding started back then with one-on-one professional counseling. When the healing and discovery process was well on its way, my counselor suggested a Twelve-Step support group. There was a choice of Al-Anon and a new group forming at Mount Paran Church called Families Victorious. This is a Christ-centered Twelve-Step support group. I joined, participated as a trusted servant at the Central Church location, then opened a new group with several others at the North Church location. I remained with the North group almost four years.

My life has been totally renewed through opening many of the locked doors that hid the pain of grief, shame, and confusion. After our divorce five years ago, I have "let go and let God." Going along the stream of His grace and guidance, I have completed a degree in individual and group communications and am ministering in the counseling field as I receive further accreditation. I will continue to support Bill and the Twelve-Step process in any way that I can. I have witnessed those who stay in a support group recover and maintain a walk of strength and courage. I have also witnessed those who relapse when they don't participate wholeheartedly in a support program.

The Twelve-Step process is never ending . . . the group gives a safe supportive place to be real, to uncover who you are, praise God for His unconditional love, and give and receive the love of brothers and sisters in Christ. The group becomes whatever the people who are in it create it to be. It is the perfect example of "what you give is what you get." There are no professionals and it's free . . . and you are free . . . to choose.

From a life that was saved, thank You, God, for support groups!

Eating Disorders Victorious, Families Victorious Over Sexual Addiction, Kids Victorious, Couples Victorious: W's Story

When I try to remember who I used to be, it is difficult to recall that person of five years ago who came to Eating Disorders Victorious (EDV) for help. I know that I truly am a new creation in Christ. I walked through those doors the first time a belligerent, angry, self-centered, confused, sin-sick child-woman. My goal in life was to be happy by achieving and maintaining a "perfect" (or at least normal) body weight. *If only I could hang on to weight loss, I knew I'd be happy, my husband would be happy, and we would have the perfect little family.*

Not that I knew what a family was; mine I knew had been pretty weird. I had three brothers and one sister, all older, an alcoholic father who left us all when I was about five, and a mother who acted more like a child than an adult with her manic highs and depressive lows. My sister, who was the oldest, married at age sixteen, leaving the two brothers just older than me to be my primary caregivers.

Teenage boys aren't very good at nurturing and parenting a little girl, and the years that followed were filled with confusion, doubt, fears, and stolen boundaries that could never be reclaimed. Sexually inappropriate behavior had scarred my relationships with others for the rest of my life by affecting my ability to trust and my view of myself. I learned in those early, lonely, pain-filled years that the world isn't a safe place, people can't be trusted, and nobody really cares. I needed a friend I could trust. I found that friend in food. I began relying on it to escape; it quickly became a reliable friend that calmed and soothed and was always there for me.

I lost a lot of weight after my senior year in high school due to major surgery. During this "thin" period, I met and married my husband. I immediately began regaining the weight. I dieted and turned to the local doctor for help. I began using appetite suppressants. When the regular dose didn't seem to curb my hunger, I just doubled or tripled it. I lived in a world of drug-induced highs and near suicidal depressive lows. I lived this way—dieting, losing weight, starving myself to stay thin, exercising to burn off calories.

I found myself seeing doctor after doctor, functioning day after day only with antidepressants and periodic hospital stays. My goal continued to be to achieve and maintain that one elusive goal—"normal."

When I came to EDV, group members helped me realize that I was capable of being loved no matter what I looked like. What a shocking revelation that was to me! *Could it be that I was acceptable just as I was . . . that I didn't have to earn approval or acceptance . . . that what I looked like on the outside had very little to do with who I was on the inside?* I began a journey, with Jesus Christ as my tour guide. He patiently and lovingly introduced me to who I am in *Him*. It hasn't all been pleasant. Along the way He's shown me that I can be painstakingly honest, as long as He's holding me. Unless I totally surrender and give control of my life to Him on a daily basis, I will pilot my own life right down the road to self-destruction.

As I began to live with food in a proper perspective, God opened doors to work in other areas of my life. As my husband saw the changes in my life, God began to show him the ways that our family was dysfunctional. My husband then began to admit his own addictions, and I turned to the SAFE and Couples Victorious groups for support. There I learned to stay focused on myself, my attitudes, and there I received the constant encouragement that the only person I can ever make changes in is myself.

The story continues, however. During the years of craziness, my daughter learned some of the same rules that I did about trusting, feeling, etc. Again I turned to the support groups at Mount Paran. Kids Victorious has helped my twelve-year-old daughter to learn to acknowledge things openly and honestly. I think the most important thing she's learned, though, is that she can turn to Jesus Christ for strength and support.

Through the recovery process, God has taught me that change doesn't happen from the outside in but instead from the *inside out*.

Adult Children of Confusion, Sexual Abuse Survivors Victorious, Kids Victorious: D's Story

I came into the Adult Children of Confusion group because I had nowhere else to go. I was suicidal, confused, desperate, and depressed. I was very angry and felt hopeless and helpless. Completely out of touch with a majority of my feelings, I knew that I needed to make some major changes in my life but had no idea where to begin or what was wrong. I felt out of control and didn't know what "normal" was. Therapy wasn't helping, and I had no friends or family that I could trust. I was parenting my children like I was parented. They were rebelling, angry and hostile, and deep down I felt they were being abused. I experienced many of the characteristics of being raised in an alcoholic family, but neither of my parents drank.

Because of the enforcement of safe guidelines during group, I experienced the first real safe place I had known in my life. Through my safe place, I found unconditional acceptance, respect, and love. I cried every meeting for three months and did not know why until just recently. Experiencing love, acceptance and, above all, a true sense of safety after all those years of fear, pain, and terror was unfamiliar, welcome but foreign. Bittersweet. There were weeks I felt I had crawled into Jesus' lap, and He was cradling me while He wiped my tears. "He restored my soul. My cup began to run over."

Because I felt safe and was learning when and who to trust, I began to allow God to reveal some of my long-forgotten childhood experiences and put others in proper perspective. Feelings began to connect with memories, and pieces fell into place. I became aware that I had been sexually abused for fifteen years by a cousin and a neighbor. I grew up with a deep sense of shame, thinking that there was something wrong with me and that it was up to me to protect myself. No wonder I learned to be vigilant, controlling and experiencing feelings of being responsible for situations and people beyond my control.

Because of the codependent relationship of my parents, I experienced emotional abandonment as a child. Physically, my parents were there, but emotionally, I feel, they were not there on a consistent basis. My parents were unable to provide the safety and nurturing I needed growing up because they weren't given those things themselves. My paternal grandfather was physically handicapped and an alcoholic. My maternal grandfather was an incest survivor and himself a perpetrator. The results of addiction, abuse, dependency, and codependency are generational, affecting children, grandchildren, and great-grandchildren.

Besides the Adult Children group, two other groups are being most helpful to me. My incest survivor group is helping me deal with the ramifications of the sexual abuse and those core issues. The Kids Victorious group gives me and my children the skills to resolve conflict, identify and express feelings in appropriate ways. I learn how to be more emotionally available and am developing more well-rounded parenting skills. I am learning that I do like myself. I am human, trustworthy, valuable, and wounded. I can trust God. He is capable and is restoring what the locusts have eaten.

Through the groups, I am supported and am able to be supportive while I struggle to make some necessary changes in my life. We are generally loving people; many of us are Christians, and I feel empowered by the Holy Spirit, gaining wisdom, understanding, and new skills so that I do not continue to live my life in a self-destructive manner, making unhealthy choices. Experiencing increased self-esteem, liking who I am, and feeling safe enable me to be vulnerable and intimate with others.

God is revealing to me that precious part of me He created wonderfully and fearfully. I am growing into more of the person I feel that God wants me to be. The Holy Spirit is able to fill in the gaps where my parents could not. I am experiencing Jesus as my older brother and healer of the deep wounds of my childhood. The Lord is closer to me than my breath, and I know Him as my protector, counselor, and Father. Praise His holy name!

Adult Children of Confusion: F's Story

I heard about the Adult Children of Confusion (ACOC) class when my wife started going. I was not interested in going, but I was interested in what my wife was learning and what she was up to. I would read the books she brought home to be knowledgeable in current psychology because I felt threatened by some of her new noncodependent behavior. I thought I could use some of this information to my advantage in advancing my views in various disagreements with my wife. The information I gleaned from the books and Twelve-Step group handouts I had not learned when I was in college.

I first came in contact with the groups at Mount Paran when my seventeen-year-old nephew came to live with us. He had been dropped off at a mental health facility by his parents for treatment of drug, alcohol, and runaway problems. He stayed there for one and a half years before running away from his parents again. We entered him in the Teens Victorious group, and I started going to the families support group. I came to realize that there was a lot of dysfunction in my family and my family of origin. I went to the family support group for the wrong reasons—I went for my nephew, not for myself.

About a year later—many books later and many family problems later—I began to realize my marriage was not going to survive and I needed help. I went to the ACOC group. I began to see the issues that were affecting my life. I had a problem with intimacy, which I associated with the childhood message "you are what you do" that I received while growing up. My "working" or "doing" would take preference over taking the time out to maintaining relationships in my life. I also had a hard time playing and having fun. I had to grow up at an early age, and it was hard for me to let my kids act like kids. Also, there was generational emotional and physical abandonment in my family. My mother and her side of the family were alcoholics. Although they were very hardworking people, they were seldom there for me emotionally. My mother sent me to stay with my uncle for one summer. At the end of the summer my father called one night wanting to know where my mother was. This is how I found out they were getting a divorce. It was my understanding that I was going to stay at my uncle's indefinitely. I stayed there one year. I've had many stumbling blocks in my relationships because of fear of rejection and abandonment. I came to realize I had many weak boundaries and I was codependent where my family was concerned.

I learned a lot from attending ACOC meetings. I felt accepted and I didn't feel judged. I received affirmations, and I came to realize my situation was not so unique. This helped me to come out of isolation. I saw God in action in the group. Now my kids are going to Kids Victorious, and my whole family is learning what "normal" is. God bless Bill Morris and the trusted servants of ACOC.

Alcoholics and Addicts Victorious: Q's Story

"Welcome in the name of our Lord Jesus Christ." Hearing this for the first time in a Twelve-Step meeting, even though I knew beforehand that it was a Christian group, caused a reaction I can scarcely describe. With my introduction to Alcoholics and Addicts Victorious (AAV), I finally felt truly a part of the group, not just another alcoholic struggling to stay sober, but a victorious saint, staying on God's grace.

I had spent over twenty years of my life as an untreated alcoholic/addict. From one bad relationship or jail cell to another until, in 1981, God met me in an astounding way and saved my soul. After marrying an addict a year later and going into the ministry, I had been struggling for four years until 1985 when my wife left me and went back to the streets. Having no real recovery to fall back on and knowing nowhere to find support in the Christian community, I got drunk for the next eighteen months. During this time, I gave up my ministry, fell away from the Lord, and almost died more than once from an overdose. Finally, in desperation I sought help in a secular program, which introduced me to AA.

Working the steps and staying sober one day at a time worked awhile, but after three years of being sober and still feeling as if I might drink any day, I was led to an AAV meeting by an announcement in a church bulletin. My walk with the Lord since then has become consistent and is growing all the time. By His grace, I'm now in a group where Christ is honored, and I no longer feel separated from Him.

Another plus I've found in AAV is the chance to minister Christ to hurting brothers and sisters without violating the boundaries of others. Christ, not my alcoholism, is the focal point of my recovery. The early church must have been much like the groups I'm involved with now. We have identification with other believers and the support that brings shared unconditional love and accountability. The Twelve-Step model is effective in many areas in my home church, such as other substance abuse, divorce recovery, eating disorders, codependence, sexual disorders, etc. God grant that this movement will grow and bring healing to many of my brothers and sisters as well as salvation to many who are lost.

Phobics Victorious:
B's Story

On August 18, 1986, at the age of thirty-eight, I started having frightening physical symptoms, which were identified as panic attacks. Despite prompt treatment with a tranquilizer, the attacks continued at a rate of three or four a day, and I began to avoid the place where they happened. Within six months I had quit my job and was housebound because the panic attacks happened everywhere! I couldn't even walk out to my mailbox, eat dinner at my parents' house, or make a telephone call without being overwhelmed by the dizziness, shaking, rapid heartbeat, and sense of being trapped and in danger. I had become an agoraphobic, with a special problem with social phobias.

I sought counseling at Mount Paran, thinking that my problem could be straightened out in a few months. Actually, it was two or three long years of forcing myself to face the situations I was avoiding before I was about to go places with any degree of comfort at all. During the second year, Mount Paran started a support group called Phobics Victorious for people with phobias and anxiety problems. I was asked to help plan it, to tell the leaders what would be helpful for me. Even the planning meetings caused my panic symptoms to flare, but I felt that I was wanted, needed, and included.

After attending perhaps six meetings, I found that, for me, there were both advantages and disadvantages to the group. My many social phobias prevented me from relaxing and enjoying even one minute of close fellowship. Any discussion of symptoms was sure to bring mine on. Often, I left the group early and cried all the way home in frustration. I wanted so much to be a part of this group, and that was the one thing I could not do. This failure emphasized to me my isolation and the feelings of hopelessness and helplessness.

On the other hand, some good things happened. Once I was asked to lead a meeting when the leaders were out of town. Although it seemed impossible, I did it and regained some of my lost confidence. Another time, I shared that I had been feeling suicidal. That was difficult to say, but immediately several other group members shared that they, too, had felt suicidally depressed because of their phobias.

On the first night that the group met, the leaders announced that it was perfectly all right to leave the room if we needed to. That was helpful, even though it was hard to actually stand up with everyone watching and walk out. Phobics tend to panic if they feel at all trapped, so our leaders made sure the room had two doors and was near an outside exit.

Sometimes I felt really good (not anxious) and decided to do something *fun* instead of attending group (and talking about anxiety). Other times I felt really bad (anxious) and dreaded trying to sit still for an hour when I was already exhausted from fighting the anxiety before the meeting began. I had to battle with myself every time I went to a meeting.

Still, I felt loved because my church cared enough to *try* to provide a place where I could meet with people with similar problems. And the group members *did* love one another and prayed for one another. It was so good to be able to describe something that had happened and see everyone nod in understanding. We encouraged one another to hold on to God when it seemed as if the rest of our lives was slipping away. One of my favorite Scriptures was Jeremiah 29:11: "For I know the thoughts that I think toward you, says the LORD, thoughts of peace and not of evil, to give you a future, and a hope." There were so many times when I lost all hope of ever getting better.

Another very encouraging part of meetings was hearing from those who had recovered. However, once in a while someone would tell us of an instant and miraculous recovery through prayer, and while I felt happy for that person, I also wondered why God hadn't answered *my* prayers in the same way. It was easy to wonder if I was a "bad Christian" because I felt so much fear and was not healed.

Gradually, with time, counseling, concerted effort, and better medications, my panic attacks lessened. I enjoyed going to the group when I could help others by sharing a coping technique, a Scripture, a success. Although we did not follow a strict "Twelve-Step" format, we found the steps to be a useful guide to recovery. Our lives were certainly out of control! I knew it was worth being there when a new member attended and expressed relief that she wasn't the only person in the world with this problem. It was important to be there for one another, even though we were imperfect.

Grief Group:
K's Story

I always believed in God but never felt that one-to-one relationship. Over the next three and one-half years He would reveal Himself many times to me.

The Lord has challenged my faith from time to time in the past, but what was to come in the next few years would encompass the entire family. My husband had just accepted a new job, which would mean we would have to move 225 miles away from the town we'd lived in over twenty years. It was not fair, I thought, to pull the children out of school in mid-term. My daughter was in the first grade and would adapt easily, but my son, a high-school senior, wanted to graduate with his class. My husband and I both agreed that I would stay behind with the kids until after graduation, and he began his monthly commute. The children and I would have to adjust without dad on a daily basis. My son took over most of the manly duties, and the household ran smoothly.

When graduation came in June, it was time to move. We were happy and sad at the same time. We had planned to enjoy the summer in our new location but hated to leave so many dear friends and family behind.

My husband had already found our son a job, and he began work immediately. After three weeks of working the three-to-eleven shift, he was ready to go home. He was torn between the love of his family and the homesickness that he felt. He said that his grandparents were back home all alone, and he realized that they wouldn't be around forever. He wanted to go back and begin his young adult life. This being his first major decision, I felt he needed my support. He left the next day with high expectations of what was yet to come. His first love was the outdoors, and he was lucky to be hired right away as grounds keeper for a local country club. He worked hard and took pride in his accomplishments. We saw him several times that summer and could see that he was very happy, but he also missed being a part of the immediate family unit. I never regretted giving him the time to be himself.

When school started, I began to seek temporary employment. I registered with several temporary agencies and went to work in mid-September.

October 3, 1988, started out to be just another rainy Monday until my husband appeared around 8:30 at the office where I was working. He said he had received a call that our son had been in an automobile accident and that we were to come right away. No one could tell us about the extent of the injuries or the circumstances concerning the accident. The road that day seemed unending. By the time we arrived at the hospital, it was midafternoon. All sorts of thoughts kept running through my mind. *Was he all right? Were there others hurt?* If we only knew.

We were escorted into a private waiting area where they told us that the accident occurred before 7:00 A.M. and that our son died instantly. I could not believe what I was hearing. I never for one minute thought *fatal*. The doctors assured us that he felt no pain. The patrol officer's report stated that the rear axle had snapped, the car lost a wheel, and our son had no control of the car. He then crossed the grassy median and hit an eighteen-wheeler head-on. The driver of the truck was not injured. I often wonder what went through his mind those final seconds.

God had shielded our family on that long trip to the hospital. For some unknown reason we couldn't pick up our favorite local station on the radio. Since our son was eighteen, the authorities did not notify all family. As soon as he was identified, the bulletin came across the wire about the eighteen-year-old young man who had lost his life that morning. You see, if we had been listening, we would have found out before we arrived at the hospital. The Lord covered us with His mercy that dreadful day and so many days to follow.

The entire family was devastated. Why? He had his whole life ahead of him. The emergency room physician prescribed a sedative to help me through the painful task to come. I felt numb, but I had to find strength to console all the many friends and classmates that I knew would be coming to pay their last respects. Over four hundred students filed through the funeral home doors. What a tribute to this fine young man! He was buried in his letterman's jacket that he so richly deserved. They retired his football number. What a painful realization—a parent *never* expects to outlive her children.

Trying to make some sense out of what happened, I began my quest, reading all I could about death, but it left me empty. The answers just were not there. My daughter and I began to visit different churches, thinking surely the answers would be there. It became an obsession to know where my son was. And was he safe? Religion at that time made me very emotional. I cried all the time. There were so many unanswered questions, and I felt totally alone in this world. Being in a new place, I didn't know anyone to discuss my feelings with, and my husband buried himself in his work, so I repressed my pain. My obsession only grew until one day a lady at church told me that I needed to take control of myself and go on with my life. For the grieving person, there is no going forward until you make peace with the present. Being convinced that I would never know about my son's salvation, I drifted into a deep depression.

I finally sought medical advice and was given an antidepressant to help me "cope." That went on for over a year. My husband sensed my despair and became both mother and father to our daughter. Along with working long hours at his job, he cooked, cleaned, and did laundry. I just couldn't seem to handle the simplest tasks. Some mornings it was all I could do to get out of bed.

Before I could begin to work through the depression, the company where my husband worked shut down and sold out. To support the family, I was forced back into the work force. God moved me ever so gently. I telephoned the temporary agency just before Christmas of 1989. They were sorry, but orders were down with the holidays approaching. I asked them to please consider me for any upcoming placements and told them that I would be returning home just before New Year's. It was not their policy, but they held a job open for me to begin the day after New Year's. I believe with all my heart that the job was heavensent. I continue to work at the same place today.

Life seemed to pass by—one day at a time. I continued to be depressed, lonely and still searching for those answers to all my unanswered questions.

In the summer of 1991, God revealed Himself through my daughter in a dream. My son came to the door and rang the bell, and my daughter invited him in. She was so elated to see him. They snacked in her room and talked for what seemed to be forever. She doesn't remember the conversation, but what she does remember is far more important. She said that her dream was so beautiful, flowers blowing in the breeze and sunshine peering through the clouds. Then the heavens opened up. Jesus extended His almighty hands and told my son that it was time for him to return *home*. What a comfort I felt for the first time in so many months! A peace over- whelmed me that I cannot explain. The Lord *had* answered my ques- tion. I believed I could begin to live again. That was over two and one-half years after the accident. God has His own timetable. Praise You, Jesus!

A coworker who had lost her mother in early 1991 invited me to join her in a grief support group she had heard about. It was heavy on my heart until I accepted. September 18, 1991, was to be our first meeting. I didn't know what to expect. In fact, if the truth be known, if I had been driving that night, we would have never made it because I would have probably turned around and headed for home. *I was so scared!* We traveled about seventy-five miles, and every mile I could think of a good reason not to participate in the group. I realized I may have to talk or, even worse, share my "story." It was so painful to even fathom that I would have to dredge up feelings I'd buried long ago. My way of dealing or coping was to not dwell on the past and it would go away. How wrong could I be? Why put yourself through all the pain and heartache? What was I doing here?

We were greeted by two facilitators and eight other ladies were part of the group. Before we began, we prayed that the Holy Spirit would come into our midst and be with each one of us as we took turns telling our stories.

Grief work is hard work. Taking it one step at a time, we explored many areas in which to begin making our comeback to the human race. You see, we felt all alone. We had no one who understood our frustrations. The group enabled each one of us to open up to be ourselves, finally having a haven where we could feel safe and know that people really cared. And we do care for one another. We are friends for life. We have felt one another's pain and have bonded with one another. I feel that only the grace of God and the Holy Spirit could render such peace. I believe there could be no other group to match this one. I am so blessed to have been a part of this.

I can honestly say that it probably saved my sanity. My pain and grief were so embedded that only through an anointed group could I have been healed. The group has given me the confidence I needed to open up to people again.

After almost two and one-half years of unemployment and menial jobs to supplement our family's income, my husband has now returned to the work force. With so many people out of work, we feel that through our prayer and perseverance, God opened the door for my husband. Only by the grace of God does he have this position. We have been prayerful and patient for God to work in His time frame, and He does! But you have to be open to what *He* has in store for you and be ready to accept the challenge.

Through the support of the group I have another obsession. And that is to help people with the knowledge that I have learned. *It is okay to grieve*. Society has been conditioned to "replace" everything—NOW! There has to be that time to work through your thoughts.

I thank the Lord every day for His gracious mercy on each of us. Without support groups such as these, there is no hope for recovery. Christian ministry like this one, in my opinion, is so very important for the recovery of grieving persons. It allows them to work in their own way at their own pace with guidelines that will aid them and bring them a new awareness of themselves.

I have the utmost respect for the ministries of Mount Paran Church of God. They are giving the community an opportunity to gain through the different ministries. We would be wise to learn all we can and then share with others so that one day they might feel the love, peace, and contentment that only the Holy Spirit can bring.

Divorce Recovery:
U's Story

When I came to the Divorce Recovery support group, it was a cold and windy night. My body, mind, and spirit had been ripped apart to the point of suicide.

It was at this point in my life that the Lord sent His grace to rescue me from what seemed like a bottomless pit of hell. He provided a messenger to share with me that it was not time for me to leave this world, that He was not finished with me yet. He ministered to me while I lay sobbing with grief for the loss of my loved one. I did not want to surrender my wounded heart; I just wanted to cry, and had for days, weeks, and months. Yet the Lord seemed to call out my name. He understood the great pain and suffering I was going through and gave me an assurance that He would only allow what I could bear.

Yes, it was only the beginning of my walk with Jesus. That very night I walked into the church and into that room where the healing process was about to begin for me. It was only a baby step. In fact, it wasn't even a step; I felt like I was crawling on my hands and knees, crying out to Jesus to pick me up and reassure me that this was not happening to me.

But as I entered that room, I felt like I had entered a hospital full of "wounded souls." Everyone in the group that night was hurting and had either been down the same road I was on or was in the process of going down it with me. The people were able to share and comfort one another, and those folks really knew how to comfort!

I learned that it was okay to bear one another's burdens and that it was safe to trust the other group members because they were hurting, too, and even cried out for help just like me. As I started the healing process by opening up, sharing with the group, and developing a bond with the other group members, it became less painful each and every time I walked through that door. The comfort and love I received made it seem as if Jesus were right there in the room, holding my hand and saying, "I will not leave or forsake you, my child. I have great plans for you. Plans to prosper you, not to hurt you. I love you in spite of yourself and will restore these broken pieces."

I attended the support group regularly for over a year and a half. There were times when I couldn't discuss the pain it was so great, and yet I was reassured over and over by the group that it was all right and that I didn't have to share unless I wanted to. Many other hurting souls came through the door during that time, some with a heart willing to deal with the situation and to heal, others who were not yet ready to let go and let Jesus be Lord of their situation. I learned so much about myself and what I needed to help me. I regained my self-esteem. Through the stumbling, the wavering, and the falling flat on my face with self-pity and self-inflicted pain, I learned to grow and receive help from the group.

Now, after two years, I still attend the group as often as I can, with a softened and willing heart to help support others who are going through the process of a divorce. I just want to assure them that it does get easier and that time will heal their broken heart as it did mine. I want them to learn, as I learned, that honesty with, trust in, faith in, and obedience to the Father and oneself are the keys to recovery. The Father will restore the broken pieces as we are willing to accept and depend upon His grace.

I encourage people to give themselves another chance and join the group. The Lord chose me, and He calls out to you, "Come, come, My door is open." I write this as one who is in love with Christ and the body of Christ who saved me and brought peace, love, and joy back into my heart.

As we move on to the conclusion, I would like to share some thoughts about the partnership of God and His people to bring about the healing of the body of Christ and what ultimately makes a support group and a recovery ministry successful.

CONCLUSION
Lazarus, Come Forth!

Several years ago at our annual support group retreat, we asked groups to prepare and present a skit on any aspect of recovery that they wanted to illustrate. All of the skits were entertaining as well as enlightening, but one skit made a deep impression on me.

One group reenacted the story of Christ raising Lazarus from the dead (John 11). The skit built up to the scene where Jesus stood before the tomb containing the dead body of Lazarus and cried out in a loud voice, "Lazarus, come forth!" And Lazarus came forth from his tomb, bound from head to toe with wrappings. He was vividly portrayed by a support group member wrapped in a great deal of toilet paper!

The story of Lazarus has always been a powerful and inspiring one to me, but at that point it took on a new and fresh meaning. That was merely the beginning of the skit, not the ending. As Lazarus came forth from his tomb, the group member playing Jesus turned to the crowd, played by the rest of the support group, and instructed them, "Loose him, and let him go!"

The skit concluded as the crowd removed the graveclothes from Lazarus and set him free to rejoin his family and friends and once again enjoy the fullness of life.

I immediately saw and understood the meaning of recovery as illustrated by that skit. We are not capable of raising ourselves or others from the dead, no matter how much we care for them or how much we desire for them to live again. In recovery, we realize that we are unable to raise ourselves through our own effort or willpower from the death-style that imprisons us. Only Christ can speak those words that call us forth from a death-style to a new lifestyle. His words are truth, and only His truth can ultimately set us free. Jesus Christ must be the center of recovery if there is to be any healing, deliverance, and freedom from whatever wraps itself around our lives, binds us, and entombs us.

But Christ recognized the need for the support of others and the power of people helping one another to unwrap those things that bind us and blind us. He is the source of life and the One who calls us forth to life, but we are the ones who are now to minister to one another on His behalf so that we can partake of that life. Christ has given us the job of unbinding one another and letting one another go to experience the life and freedom that He has called us to.

That is the process of recovery in Christ-centered support groups. That is the power of Christ-centered support groups. The new wine has been poured into a new wineskin, and it is bringing healing and deliverance to those within the church as well as reaching out and offering hope to those who need a safe place, a refuge in the shadow of almighty God.

No special expertise is needed to remove graveclothes (especially when they're made of toilet paper!). It does not take trained leaders or require any supervision. There is no need to structure the experience. But a great deal of time and a desire to see those who were dead live again are needed. People can do it if they have love, joy, peace, longsuffering, gentleness, kindness, goodness, faithfulness, and self-control—the fruit of God's Holy Spirit working in their lives and freely offered to others (Gal. 5:22–23). Especially love.

The Role of Love

If I speak eloquently about recovery and safety and healing, but do not have love, I am only a noisy gong or a clanging cymbal. And if I know all there is to know about addiction and dependencies and codependencies, and passionately believe in what I am doing, so as to move mountains, but do not have love, I am nothing. And if I spend all of my time formatting, structuring, training, and supervising trusted servants, but do not have love, it profits me nothing. Paul wrote,

Love suffers long and is kind; love does not envy; love does not parade itself, is not puffed up; does not behave rudely, does not seek its own, is not provoked, thinks no evil; does not rejoice in iniquity, but rejoices in the truth; bears all things, believes all things, hopes all things, endures all things. Love never fails. . . . And now abide faith, hope, love, these three; but the greatest of these is love (1 Cor. 13: 4–8, 13).

The secret to success in recovery ministry is not contained in this book. It is not accomplished through formats, guidelines, traditions, principles, and training, as necessary and helpful as those things may be. According to 1 Corinthians 13, it is ultimately about love. When people feel loved, accepted, and valued, they recover. When groups are loving and accepting and value one another, they succeed. If churches and recovery ministries love, accept, and value people, they become cities set on a hill and a light to a lost and dying world (Matt. 5:14–16). Love heals. Love casts out fear. Love covers a multitude of sins. Love never fails. Love is the ultimate secret to successful support groups.

I have shared with you everything that we have learned about recovery ministry and recovery from our experiences over the past few years. There is a great need for this ministry, the church has a great calling, and we have a great resource to offer to a world increasingly caught up in addictions, compulsions, dependencies, and codependencies—Jesus Christ, the highest power.

Last year I was attending one of our group's last meetings before Christmas. I was facilitating the meeting that evening so I chose as our topic for discussion the gift of recovery that we have received from God during the past year. I listened while group members talked about the difference between where they were last Christmas and where they were today. Many talked about how alienated they had been from God and how meaningless past Christmases had been before the process of recovery and the Twelve Steps had brought them out of their isolation, secrecy, and shame and had begun to restore their relationship with God, themselves, and others. At least a half-dozen people gratefully expressed the feeling that this time last year they had not cared whether they lived to see another Christmas and credited God for saving their lives through the support of the group.

I became grateful for the gift that God gave me and others who started our support groups. God always gives His people a gift of vision, for without it we would surely perish. Often that vision is not understood by others. Sometimes we do not even understand it ourselves initially. There are times when it is lonely having a vision and finding no one to share it with. But we follow the vision in the same way that we follow Christ—in faith, believing.

Today, that vision is becoming clearer and more focused. And I am finding others who have shared that vision. We are beginning to build on the vision that God has given us together. This book is about that vision. My prayer is that God will use it to open the eyes of His church to the incredible need and opportunity that it has to reclaim what rightfully belongs to it. There is no higher power than that of Jesus Christ present in the midst of koinonia fellowship. That is His legacy He expressly left to the church.

I believe God tried to give His church the gift of the Twelve Steps and recovery process through Bill W.'s association with the Oxford Group and Sam Shoemaker's church more than fifty years ago. It was a message the church was given by Jesus Christ to deliver to a world lost and dying in its dependencies and codependencies. The church refused to accept what became the AA movement because of denial, fear, and judgment of those addicted to alcohol. I believe that today He is giving us another chance. The world has discovered the need for recovery and the Twelve-Step process. The church is waking up to its need to offer support to its own who are being conformed to the pressures and stresses of this age. There is a new opportunity. Do we accept the challenge this time, or do we refuse, once again, to face life as it really is?

I believe that Jesus calls us to do whatever accomplishes His will and purpose. In the fourth chapter of the book of Luke, Jesus clearly stated that purpose when He declared that He had come to fulfill Isaiah 61:1-4:

The Spirit of the Lord GOD is upon me,
Because the LORD has anointed Me
To preach good tidings to the poor;
He has sent Me to heal the brokenhearted,
To proclaim liberty to the captives,
And the opening of the prison to those who are bound;
To proclaim the acceptable year of the LORD,
And the day of vengeance of our God;
To comfort all who mourn,
To console those who mourn in Zion,
To give them beauty for ashes,
The oil of joy for mourning,
The garment of praise for the spirit of heaviness;
That they may be called trees of righteousness,
The planting of the LORD,
    that He may be glorified.

   This is our calling, and this is the message communicated and brought to remembrance whenever a Christ-centered support group meets. I join with Paul in declaring to you, "Blessed be the God and Father of our Lord Jesus Christ, the Father of mercies and God of all comfort, who comforts us in all our tribulation, that we may be able to comfort those who are in any trouble, with the comfort with which we ourselves are comforted by God" (2 Cor. 1:3–4).

God is rich in mercy and comfort. Christ offers us grace and calls us forth from death into life. We are to help one another in removing those things that have bound up our lives and blinded us to the truth that was meant to set us free. I hope that you will join those of us who have united in offering this fellowship of support to one another and to those the Lord brings to us to find refuge and healing.

I look forward to the journey and the labor together, for the way no longer seems empty and lonely. My sight and my vision are clearer now, and I look out and see that there are many streaming onto this new way—the way of Christ, the way of recovery. May He lead and guide all of our steps into His way, His truth, and His life.

RESOURCES

The following resources have been especially helpful in developing our recovery ministry and addressing the needs of our group members. This is a representative list. More and more quality Christ-centered materials are becoming available as the interest in recovery ministry grows, and you may want to add to this list.

Some resources are secular in nature. They are useful to Christians who are able to exercise discernment in separating the thoughts and ways of God from those of human beings. Resources written from a Christian point of view are noted with an asterisk (*).

Abortion Recovery

*Conquerors Post Abortion Support Group Manual
*Helping Women Recover from Abortion—Nancy Michels
*The Mourning After—Terry Selby and Marc Bockmon
*Post-Abortion Counseling—Dr. Anne Speckhard
*Post Abortion Counseling and Education (PACE) Support Group Program
*Will I Cry Tomorrow—Dr. Susan Stanford-Rue

Addictive-Compulsive Behavior

The Addictive Personality—Craig Nakken
*Before Burnout—Dr. Don Hawkins, Dr. Frank Minirth, Dr. Paul Meier, and Dr. Chris Thurman
*The Compulsive Woman—Sandra Simpson LeSourd
*Healing Grace—David Seamands
*Imperative People—Dr. Les Carter

The Man Within—Serenity Meditation Series
Pace Yourself—Serenity Meditation Series
Sin—J. Keith Miller
Time Out—Serenity Meditation Series
Tired of Trying to Measure Up—Jeff VanVonderen
Toxic Faith—Stephen Arterburn and Jack Felton
A Walk with the Serenity Prayer—Serenity Meditation Series
We Are Driven—Dr. Robert Hemfelt, Dr. Frank Minirth, and Dr. Paul Meier
The Woman Within—Serenity Meditation Series
The Workaholic and His Family—Dr. Frank Minirth, Dr. Paul Meier, Frank Wichern, Bill Brewer, and States Skipper

Adult Children

The Adult Child of Divorce—Bob Burns and Michael Brissett
Adult Children and the Almighty—Melinda Fish
Adult Children of Abusive Parents—Steven Farmer
Adult Children of Alcoholics—Janet Woititz
Adult Children of Legal and Emotional Divorce—Jim Conway
Creating a Safe Place—Curt Grayson and Jan Johnson
Days of Healing, Days of Joy—Earnie Larsen and Carol Larsen Hegarty
The Family—John Bradshaw
Finding Your Way Home—Kenneth Schmidt
Forgiving Our Parents, Forgiving Ourselves—Dr. David Stoop and Dr. James Masteller
Free to Forgive—Serenity Meditation Series
God, I'm Still Hurting—Claire W.
Growing Up Holy and Wholly—Donald Sloat
Healing Adult Children of Alcoholics—Sarah Hines Martin
If My Dad's a Sexaholic, What Does That Make Me?—Barbara and Rick Lair Robinson
It Will Never Happen to Me—Claudia Black
Let Go and Grow—Robert Ackerman
Old Patterns, New Truths—Earnie Larsen
Pain and Pretending—Rich Buhler

Repeat After Me—Claudia Black

*Secrets of Your Family Tree—Dave Carder, Dr. Earl Henslin, Dr. John Townsend, Dr. Henry Cloud, and Alice Brawand

*Shame on You—Sarah Hines Martin

*The Twelve Steps: A Spiritual Journey—Recovery Publications

The Twelve Steps: A Way Out—Recovery Publications

*The Twelve Steps for Christians—Recovery Publications

*Unfinished Business—Charles Sell

*When I Grow Up I Want to Be an Adult—Ron Ross

Anxiety/Phobias

Anxiety, Phobias, and Panic—Reneau Peurifoy

Breaking the Panic Cycle—Dr. Reid Wilson

The Complete Agoraphobic Sourcebook—Joan Orrico and Teresa Salas

*The Good News About Worry—William Backus

Overcoming Panic Attacks—Shirley Babior and Carol Goldman

*A Spiritual Guide Through Anxiety—Marjorie Working

*Uncovering Your Hidden Fears—H. Norman Wright

*Worry-Free Living—Dr. Frank Minirth, Dr. Paul Meier, and Dr. Don Hawkins

Chemical Dependency

*Addiction and Grace—Gerald May

Alcoholics Anonymous: The Big Book—AA World Services

The Dilemma of the Alcoholic Marriage—Al-Anon Family Group Headquarters

*Dying for a Drink—Anderson Spickard, M.D., and Barbara Thompson

Getting Them Sober, vols. 1, 2, and 3—Toby Rice Drews

*God Grant—Paul Keller

*Good News for the Chemically Dependent and Those Who Love Them—Jeff VanVonderen

How to Stop the One You Love from Drinking—Mary Ellen Pinkham

*Letting God—Philip Parham

Marriage on the Rocks—Janet Woititz
One Day at a Time—Al-Anon Family Group Headquarters
*RAPHA's 12 Step Program for Overcoming Chemical Dependency—
Robert McGhee, Pat Springle, and Susan Joiner
Twenty-Four Hours a Day—AA World Services
When Someone You Love Drinks Too Much—Christina Parker

Children's Issues

*Children and Divorce—Archibald Hart
*Confident Kids (Children of Dysfunctional Families Support
Group Program)
Double Duty—Daniel Mason
Healing the Hurt—Dr. Rosalie Cruise Jesse
Helping Children Cope with Separation and Loss—Claudia Jewett
*Kids Who Carry Our Pain—Dr. Robert Hemfelt and Dr. Paul Warren
*Rainbows for All God's Children (Divorce Recovery Support
Group Program for Children)
The Seasons of Grief—Dr. Donna Gaffney

Codependency

Beyond Codependency—Melody Beattie
Breaking Free—Pia Mellody and Andrea Wells Miller
Broken Toys, Broken Dreams—Terry Kellogg
*Can Christians Love Too Much?—Dr. Margaret Rinck
*Close Enough to Care—Pat Springle
*Codependency—Pat Springle
Codependent No More—Melody Beattie
Codependent's Guide to the Twelve Steps—Melody Beattie
*Day by Day, Love Is a Choice—Serenity Meditation Series
Facing Codependency—Pia Mellody, Andrea Wells Miller, and J. Keith
Miller
*God, Where Is Love?—Claire W.
The Language of Letting Go—Melody Beattie

Love Is a Choice—Dr. Robert Hemfelt, Dr. Frank Minirth, and Dr. Paul Meier

Love Is a Choice Workbook—Dr. Robert Hemfelt, Dr. Frank Minirth, Dr. Paul Meier, Dr. Deborah Newman, and Dr. Brian Newman

Loving Yourself as Your Neighbor—Mark Lloyd Taylor and Carmen Renee Berry

New Choices, New Boundaries—Rich Buhler

One Way Relationships—Alfred Ells

Please Don't Say You Love Me—Jan Silvious

The Pleasers—Kevin Leman

RAPHA's 12 Step Program for Overcoming Codependency—Pat Springle

Setting New Boundaries—Serenity Meditation Series

The Truth Will Set You Free—Father Jack McGinnis and Barbara Shlemon

Couples

The Act of Marriage—Tim LaHaye

Building Up Your Mate's Self-Esteem—Dennis and Barbara Rainey

The First Years of Forever—Ed Wheat, M.D.

For Better or For Best—Gary Smalley

Free to Soar—Dr. David and Jan Congo

Getting the Love You Want—Harville Hendrix

Heirs Together—Patricia Gundry

His Needs, Her Needs—William Harley

If Only He Knew—Gary Smalley

Intended for Pleasure—Ed Wheat, M.D., and Gaye Wheat

The Joy of Committed Love—Gary Smalley

Love Life—Ed Wheat, M.D.

Love Must Be Tough—James Dobson

Making Peace with Your Partner—H. Norman Wright

The Marriage Builder—Larry Crabb

Married Without Masks—Nancy Groom

Relationships in Recovery—Emily Martin

Telling Each Other the Truth—William Backus

When Victims Marry—Don and Jan Frank

Depression

*Beating the Blues—H. Norman Wright
*Blow Away the Black Clouds—Florence Littauer
*Depression—Don Baker and Emery Nester
Feeling Good—David Burns
*Happiness Is a Choice—Dr. Frank Minirth and Dr. Paul Meier
Here Comes the Sun—Gayle Rosellini and Mark Worden
Hidden Victims—Julie Tallard Johnson
*How to Win Over Depression—Tim LaHaye
*The Masks of Melancholy—John White
Overcoming Depression—Paul Hauck
A Reason to Live—Melody Beattie, ed.
*A Season of Suffering—John Timmerman

Divorce Recovery

*Beginning Again—Terry Hershey
*Finding Your Place After Divorce—Carole Sanderson Streeter
*Growing Through Divorce—Jim Smoke
*Living Beyond Divorce—Jim Smoke
*Marriage and Divorce—M. G. McLuhan
Rebuilding—Dr. Bruce Fisher
*Through the Whirlwind—Bob Burns

Eating Disorders

Abstinence in Action—Barbara McFarland and Anne Marie Erb
Compulsive Overeater—Bill B.
Fat Is a Family Affair—Judi Hollis
Feeding the Empty Heart—Barbara McFarland and Tyeis Baker-Baumann
*Food for the Hungry Heart—Serenity Meditation Series
Food for Thought—Hazelden Meditation Series
*Free to Be Thin—Neva Coyle and Marie Chapian

*Getting Your Family on Your Side—Neva Coyle and David Dixon

The L.E.A.R.N. Program for Weight Control—Dr. Kelly Brownell

*Love Hunger—Dr. Frank Minirth, Dr. Paul Meier, Dr. Robert Hemfelt, and Dr. Sharon Sneed

*Love Hunger Weight Loss Workbook—Dr. Frank Minirth, Dr. Paul Meier, Dr. Robert Hemfelt, and Dr. Sharon Sneed

*The Monster Within—Cynthia Joye Rowland

*RAPHA's 12 Step Program for Overcoming Eating Disorders—Robert McGhee and William Drew Mountcastle

*There's More to Being Thin Than Being Thin—Neva Coyle and Marie Chapian

Grief Recovery

*After Suicide—John Hewett

*Because You Care—Barbara Russell Chesser

*December's Song—Marilyn Willett Heavilin

*Don't Take My Grief Away—Doug Manning

*Empty Arms—Pam Vredevelt

The Fierce Goodbye—Lloyd and Gwendolyn Carr

*Good Grief—Granger Westberg

*Grief for a Season—Mildred Tengbom

The Grief Recovery Handbook—John James and Frank Cherry

*Helping People Through Grief—Delores Kuenning

*Life After Loss—Bob Deits

*On Wings of Mourning—Carol and William Rowley

*Roses in December—Marilyn Willett Heavilin

Silent Grief—Christopher Lukas and Dr. Henry Seiden

Suicide Survivors—Adina Wrobleski

*To Live Again—Catherine Marshall

Homosexuality

*Beyond Rejection—Don Baker

*Counseling the Homosexual—Michael Saia

The Healing of the Homosexual—Leanne Payne
How Will I Tell My Mother?—Jerry and Steve Arterburn
Leadership—Frank Worthen
Overcoming Homosexuality—Ed Hurst and Dave and Neta Jackson
Pursuing Sexual Wholeness—Andrew Comiskey
Pursuing Sexual Wholeness: The Workbook—Andrew Comiskey
Steps Out of Homosexuality—Frank Worthen
Strangers in a Christian Land—Darlene Bogle
Where Does a Mother Go to Resign?—Barbara Johnson

Leadership/Sponsorship

Conducting Support Groups for Elementary Children—Jerry Moe and
  Peter Ways
The Fine Art of Mentoring—Ted Engstrom and Norman Rohrer
RAPHA's Handbook for Group Leaders—Richard Price, Pat Springle,
  and Dr. Joe Kloba
Right Step Facilitator Training Manual—RAPHA

Men's Issues

Catching Fire—Merle Fossum
Crisis in Masculinity—Leanne Payne
The Flying Boy—John Lee
The Friendless American Male—David Smith
Healing the Masculine Soul—Gordon Dalbey
Maximized Manhood—Edwin Cole
Men Have Feelings, Too!—Brian Jones and Linda Phillips-Jones
Men without Friends—David Smith
The Secrets Men Keep—Dr. Ken Druck and James Simmons
Strong Men, Weak Men—Len LeSourd
Uneasy Manhood—Robert Hicks
Unfinished Business—Donald Joy

Rape/Sexual Assault

If She Is Raped—Alan McEvoy and Jeff Brookings
If You Are Raped—Kathryn Johnson
*Invisible Wounds—Candace Walters
Recovering from Rape—Linda Ledray
Surviving Sexual Assault—Joan Sutherland and Rochel Grossman

Relationship Addiction

Addictive Relationships—Joy Miller
How to Break Your Addiction to a Person—Howard Halpern
Is It Love or Is It Addiction?—Brenda Schaeffer
Leaving the Enchanted Forest—Stephanie Covington and Liana Beckett
Smart Love—Jody Hayes
Women Who Love Too Much—Robin Norwood

Sex Addiction

Back from Betrayal—Dr. Jennifer Schneider
Contrary to Love—Patrick Carnes
Don't Call It Love—Patrick Carnes
*Eros Defiled—John White
The First Step for People in Relationships with Sex Addicts—Mic Hunter and Jem
Hope and Recovery—CompCare Publishers
Hope and Recovery: The Workbook—CompCare Publishers
Lonely All the Time—Dr. Ralph Earle and Dr. Gregory Crow
*The Myth of the Greener Grass—J. Allan Petersen
Out of the Shadows—Patrick Carnes
*The Prodigal Spouse—Dr. Les Carter
*Restoring Innocence—Alfred Ells
The S.A. White Book—Sexaholics Anonymous
Sex, Lies, and Forgiveness—Dr. Jennifer Schneider and Burt Schneider
*Tearing Down the High Places of Sexual Idolatry—Steve Gallagher

What Everyone Needs to Know About Sex Addiction—CompCare Publishers

Sexual Abuse

Abused Boys—Mic Hunter
Adults Anonymous Molested as Children—Bob U. (CompCare Publishers)
Allies in Healing—Laura Davis
The Courage to Heal—Ellen Bass and Laura Davis
*A Door of Hope—Jan Frank
Ghosts in the Bedroom—Ken Graber
*Healing Victims of Sexual Abuse—Paula Sanford
*Helping Victims of Sexual Abuse—Lynn Heitritter and Jeanette Vought
How Can I Help Her?—Joan Spear
Incest and Sexuality—Wendy Maltz and Beverly Holman
*My Father's Child—Lynda Elliott and Dr. Vicki Tanner
Outgrowing the Pain—Eliana Gil
*Renew: Hope for Victims of Sexual Abuse—Robert McGhee and Harry Schaumburg
*Restoring Innocence—Alfred Ells
*A Silence to Be Broken—Earl Wilson
Victims No Longer—Mike Lew
*We Weep for Ourselves and Our Children—Joanne Ross Feldmeth and Midge Wallace Finley
*When Victims Marry—Don and Jan Frank
*The Wounded Heart—Dr. Dan Allender

Spouse Abuse

*Battered into Submission—James and Phyllis Alsdurf
*Christian Men Who Hate Women—Dr. Margaret Rinck
*In the Name of Submission—Kay Marshall Strom
*Keeping the Faith—Marie Fortune
*No Place to Hide—Esther Lee Olson and Kenneth Peterson

Turning Fear to Hope—Holly Wagner Green
Violent Voices—Kay Porterfield

The Twelve Steps

A Gentle Path Through the Twelve Steps—Patrick Carnes
*A Hunger for Healing—J. Keith Miller
*The Serenity Bible—Dr. Robert Hemfelt and Dr. Richard Fowler
*The Twelve Step Life Recovery Devotional—Stephen Arterburn and David Stoop
*Twelve Steps: The Path to Wholeness—Serendipity Support Group Series
Understanding the Twelve Steps—Terence Gorski

Two organizational resources on the cutting edge of recovery ministry and support groups are:

- Serendipity House, P.O. Box 1012, Littleton, Colorado 80160, 1-800-525-9563. The Serendipity Support Group Series is an excellent resource for beginning support groups on a variety of issues.

- The National Association of Christians in Recovery, P.O. Box 11095, Whittier, California 90603, 1-213-697-6201, publishes a "STEPS" newsletter on recovery issues and resources as well as sponsors conferences on Christian recovery issues.